IN DEFENSE OF
Advertising

IN DEFENSE OF
Advertising

Arguments from Reason, Ethical Egoism, and Laissez-Faire Capitalism

JERRY KIRKPATRICK

QUORUM BOOKS
Westport, Connecticut • London

Library of Congress Cataloging-in-Publication Data

Kirkpatrick, Jerry.
   In defense of advertising : arguments from reason, ethical egoism,
and laissez-faire capitalism / Jerry Kirkpatrick.
     p.   cm.
   Includes index.
   ISBN 0–89930–855–4 (alk. paper)
   1. Advertising—Philosophy. I. Title.
HF5821.K49   1994
659.1—dc20   93–32880

British Library Cataloguing in Publication Data is available.

Library of Congress Catalog Card Number: 93–32880
ISBN: 0–89930–855–4

First published in 1994

Quorum Books, 88 Post Road West, Westport, CT 06881
An imprint of Greenwood Publishing Group, Inc.

Printed in the United States of America

The paper used in this book complies with the
Permanent Paper Standard issued by the National
Information Standards Organization (Z39.48–1984).

10 9 8 7 6 5 4 3 2 1

Copyright Acknowledgments

The author and publisher gratefully acknowledge permission to reprint material from the following copyrighted sources.

From "A Philosophic Defense of Advertising," by Jerry Kirkpatrick, in *Journal of Advertising* 15:2 (June 1986), 42–48, 64.

From "Platonic Compensation," by George Reisman, in *The Objectivist* (August–September, 1968), Aug: 9 11, 16, Sept: 7, 8–9, 10.

From "Advertising," by Israel Kirzner, in *The Freeman* (September 1972), 5–6.

From *Human Action*, by Ludwig von Mises, © 1949. Used with permission of Contemporary Books, Inc.

From *Socialism: An Economic and Sociological Analysis*, by Ludwig von Mises, translated by J. Kahane (London: Jonathan Cape Ltd., 1936; reprint, Indianapolis: Liberty Fund, Inc., 1981).

From *Capitalism: The Unknown Ideal* by Ayn Rand. Copyright © 1962, 1963, 1964, 1965, 1966 by Ayn Rand. Used by permission of New American Library, a division of Penguin Books USA Inc.

From *Introduction to Objectivist Epistemology*, by Ayn Rand, edited by Harry Binswanger and Leonard Peikoff. Copyright © 1966, 1967 by The Objectivist, Inc. Used by permission of New American Library, a division of Penguin Books USA Inc.

From *The Virtue of Selfishness*, by Ayn Rand. Copyright © 1961, 1964 by Ayn Rand. Used by permission of New American Library, a division of Penguin Books USA Inc.

To Linda

CONTENTS

PREFACE

Do you remember the television commercials for Noxzema shaving cream—the ones with the stripper music and Swedish model Gunilla Knutson whispering: "Men, take it off. Take it *all* off"? Do you remember Mr. Whipple, chiding his shoppers, "Please don't squeeze the Charmin"? And, of course, who can forget the Wisk "ring around the collar" commercials? Or, from more recent times, the John Hancock "real life, real answers" advertisements?

What do you think of these advertisements? Are they entertaining? Boring? Distasteful, obnoxious, and irritating? Or worse? Well, I like all of them. However, I have not always liked them (Noxzema excepted). Sometimes I wanted to throw my shoe at the television set when Mr. Whipple appeared, and sometimes I felt like shooting the people who wrote the "ring around the collar" ads. Even my first reactions to the "real life, real answers" ads were negative. But over time my evaluations of the ads—and the corresponding emotional reactions to them—changed.

My attitudes changed because my knowledge of advertising expanded beyond the popular misconceptions I had acquired in my youth—misconceptions that most people still hold today. Because emotions are not causeless, I identified and changed the premises that underlay the negative reactions I felt toward the four television commercials mentioned above. As a result, my emotions changed and I now feel positive emotions toward all four commercials—not the same emotion toward each, to be sure, but a positive emotion, nonetheless. I like them because they all meet the standards of both good advertising and good taste. Part of my purpose in writing this book is to convince readers of this point.

A more significant part of my purpose, however, is to address the "or worse" response you might have had to the above ads and to address the negative evaluation you might have of advertising in general. Advertising today is under attack from many quarters. The most serious charges question its very existence. Other criticisms hold that advertising is a powerful force that must be regulated by the government. These issues cannot be taken lightly. A major purpose of this book is to demonstrate that advertising is, at once, a rational, moral, productive, and above all, *benevolent* institution of lassiez-faire capitalism.

The source of the "social" and economic criticisms of advertising is much more basic and fundamental than most people realize. In fact, a complete philosophic world view, or weltanschauung, underlies them. This means that not only do ethics and economics play a key role in the criticisms, but also metaphyics, epistemology, politics, and esthetics. Bringing to light and refuting the philosophic and economic premises of the critics of advertising is the primary goal of this work.

Finally, appeasement and apology are rampant today among business and advertising practitioners who attempt to defend advertising. (This includes business school professors who choose to defend advertising—many, however, are vocal critics.) Paraphrasing Frederic Bastiat in his introduction to *Economic Sophisms*, I am not engaging here in controversy with the Marxists, the socialists, or anyone else openly hostile to capitalism or to advertising. "Rather, I am trying to instill a principle into the minds of sincere men who hesitate to take a stand on the issue because they are in doubt."[1] What I hope to provide practitioners, academics, and intelligent laymen is the intellectual ammunition with which to take a hard-hitting moral stand against the critics. My goal is to dispel any doubt you may have about the legitimacy of advertising and to give you the the confidence to speak with conviction when fending off the onslaught.

Throughout this book I use the word "man," in the tradition of Western-civilization scholars, to designate the concept of an animal possessing the capacity to reason. This is the meaning Aristotle (and other Greeks) gave the word *anthropos*, from which "man" is a translation. Indeed, the *Oxford English Dictionary* reports that the original meaning of the term "man" is the "thinking" or "intelligent being," not a male person. Substituting such terms as "men and women," "people," "persons," "humankind," or "human being" for the word "man" excises from the English language the concept of "rational animal." Such excision surrenders the intellectual foundation of Western civilization and its life-giving achievements. Consequently, I use the word "man" to refer equally to females and males. (Even the word "human" is not an exact synonym of "man," for according to the *O.E.D.*, it often means "mundane," "secular," "opposed to the divine," implying limitation or inferiority.)

My foremost acknowledgments are to the philosophy of Ayn Rand and the economics of Ludwig von Mises. My understanding of the two authors, and of philosophy and economics generally, is due in no small part to the teaching and writing of Leonard Peikoff and George Reisman, respectively. My understanding of psychology, which, in addition to philosophy and economics, provides a theoretical foundation for the applied sciences of marketing and advertising, is due to the invaluable teaching and writing of Edith Packer. Any errors, of course, in the application of philosophy, economics, and psychology to advertising are entirely mine.

Portions of this manuscript were read by Gary Hull and Diane and Don LeMont; I thank them for their helpful comments, as well as for the many hours of discussion—sometimes focused on advertising—we have shared over the years. Finally, I cannot thank enough the person without whom this book would not have been written, my intellectual soul mate and partner in life, Linda Reardan.

NOTE

1. Frederic Bastiat, *Economic Sophisms*, trans. and ed. Arthur Goddard (Van Nostrand, 1964; reprint, Irvington-on-Hudson, N.Y.: Foundation for Economic Education, 1975), 3. Bastiat's controversy was with the protectionists.

IN DEFENSE OF
Advertising

Chapter 1

THE ORIGINAL SIN OF CAPITALISM

Advertising today does not have a good press.

Arnold Toynbee, for example, reportedly said, "[I] cannot think of any circumstances in which advertising would not be an evil."[1] Not to be outdone, a professor at the New School for Social Research in New York said: "Advertising is a profoundly subversive force in American life. It is intellectual and moral pollution. It trivializes, manipulates, is insincere and vulgarizes. It is undermining our faith in our nation and in ourselves."[2] By comparison, John Kenneth Galbraith seems tame. He only accuses advertising of creating desires that otherwise would not exist and of manipulating consumers into buying unneeded new brands of breakfast cereal and laundry detergent.[3]

The list of alleged sins committed by advertising is limited only by the creativity of its critics. Advertising has been accused of everything from the cheapening of newspapers and television to media rape. Advertising, the critics say, increases prices without adding value to the product; it encourages monopoly; it corrupts editors; it foists inferior products on the unwitting and helpless consumer; it makes people buy products they do not need; it promotes dangerous products and encourages harmful behavior; it is deceptive and manipulative; it is intrusive, irritating, offensive, tasteless, insulting, degrading, sexist, racist; it is loud, obnoxious, strident, and repetitive to the point of torture; it is a pack of lies; it is a vulgar bore.

Refutation of the criticisms of advertising—from surface level to economic and philosophic fundamentals—is the purpose of this book.

THE ASSAULT ON CONSCIOUSNESS

The critics who denigrate advertising attack not only advertising but also—by logical necessity—capitalism, ethical egoism, and reason.

As an insitution in the division of labor and an instrument of capitalistic production, advertising communicates to many people at one time the availability and nature of need- and want-satisfying products. In essence, advertising is salesmanship via the mass media; as such, it is the capitalist's largest sales force and most effective means of delivering information to the market. In addition, advertising by its essential nature blatantly and unapologetically appeals to the self-interest of consumers for the blatant and selfish gain of capitalists. To criticize advertising is to criticize capitalism and ethical egoism.

At the most fundamental level, the attacks on advertising are an assault on reason—on man's ability to form concepts and to think in principles—because advertising is a *conceptual* communication to many people at one time about the *conceptual* achievements of others. It is attacked for precisely this aspect of its nature. The goal of advertising is to sell products to consumers, and the means by which this goal is achieved is to communicate what advertisers call the "product concept." An advertisement is itself an abstraction, a concept of what the capitalist has produced. Thus, advertising is a conceptual communication—in a market economy—to self-interested buyers about the self-interested, conceptual achievements of capitalists. To criticize advertising—at the most fundamental level—is to assault man's consciousness.

From its earliest days, critics attacked capitalism for its dependence on the profit motive and the pursuit of self-interest. As the most visible manifestation, or "point man," of capitalism, advertising can be called the capitalist's "tool of selfishness." In a world culture based on altruism and self-sacrifice, it is amazing that advertising has lasted as long as it has. Indeed, its growth was stunted in Great Britain and Ireland for 141 years by a tax on newspapers and newspaper advertising.[4]

As a result of the deregulation of professional advertising (by doctors, dentists, and lawyers), some professionals have expressed hositility toward their associates who advertise. For example, a psychiatrist who doubled the number of patients treated by his psychiatry-neurology group by advertising on television tried at a party to shake hands with a medical doctor; the doctor replied, "Take your dirty, filthy, advertising hands off me."[5] And, of course, the chief justice of the Supreme Court, William Rehnquist, is on record as saying that the First Amendment of the United States Constitution, the free speech amendment, is demeaned by its association with advertising.[6]

A history of the last one hundred years of American advertising captures the essence of the critics' hostility toward egoism. The book is *The Mirror Makers*, by Stephen Fox. On the last two pages of this otherwise well-written, well-researched book, the author states:

> Thus the favorite metaphor of the industry: advertising as a mirror that reflects society back on itself. Granted that this mirror too often shows our

least lovely qualities of materialism, sexual insecurity, jealousy, and greed. The image in the advertising mirror has seldom revealed the best aspects of American life. But advertising must take human nature as it is found. We all would like to think we act from admirable motives. The obdurate, damning fact is that most of us, most of the time, are moved by more selfish, practical considerations. Advertising inevitably tries to tap these stronger, darker strains.[7]

If selfishness is the original sin of man, according to Judeo-Christian ethics, then surely advertising is the original sin of capitalism. More accurately, advertising is the serpent that encourages man to pursue selfish gain and, in subtler form, to disobey authority. In contemporary economics, pure and perfect competition is the Garden of Eden in which the lion lies down beside the lamb and this "dirty, filthy" advertising is entirely absent—because consumers allegedly have perfect information. Small wonder that advertising does not have a good press.

At the level of fundamental ideas, three attacks on advertising constitute the assault on consciousness. One attack attributes to advertising the coercive power to force consumers to buy products they do not need or want. At the level of metaphysics, this attack denies the volitional nature of reason, that is, free will; consequently, it denies, either explicitly or implicitly, the validity of human consciousness as such. A second attack derides advertising for how offensive it allegedly is; ultimately, critics advocate regulation to control the allegedly offensive advertising. At root—that is, at the level of ethics—this attack denies that values are objective, that values are a product of the relation between material objects and a volitional consciousness that evalutes them. Consequently, it denies the existence of rational options.

A third attack, which derives from contemporary economics, views advertising as a tool of monopoly power. At the level of epistemology, however, this attack denies the possibility of truth and certainty, because reason allegedly is impotent to know reality; all man can do is emulate the methods of physics, by conducting statistically controlled experiments, and attempt to establish an uncertain, probabilistic knowledge.

These three assaults on consciousness form the philosophic foundations of what are commonly known as the "social" and economic criticisms of advertising, the first two forming the foundation of the "social" criticisms, the third the foundation of economic criticisms.

THE "SOCIAL" AND ECONOMIC CRITICISMS OF ADVERTISING

The quantity of literature that attacks advertising approaches the infinite. The list of complaints is long, and each one has many variations.

Explicitly or implicitly, all attacks attribute to advertising the power to initiate physical force against both consumers and competitors. The "social" criticisms assert that advertising adds no value to the products it promotes; therefore, it is superfluous, inherently dishonest, immoral, and fraudulent. The economic criticisms assert that advertising increases prices and wastes society's valuable resources; therefore, advertising contributes to the establishment of monopoly power.[8]

The "Social" Criticisms

In essence, there are two "social" criticisms. The first explicitly charges advertising with the power to force consumers to buy products they do not need or want; the second implicitly charges advertising with this power. According to the first, advertising changes the tastes and preferences of consumers by coercing them to conform to the desires of producers. For example, consumers may want safer automobiles, but what they get, according to the critics, are racing stripes and aluminum hubcaps. Forcing consumers to conform to the desires of producers, the critics point out, is the opposite of what advocates of capitalism claim about a free-market economy—namely, that producers conform to the tastes and preferences of consumers. Within the first criticism there are two forms.

The more serious claims that advertising, by its very nature, is inherently deceptive, because it manipulates consumers into buying products they do not need or want. The most specific example of this criticism is the charge of subliminal advertising. Thus, when looking at a place mat in front of you at a Howard Johnson's restaurant, with its picture of the fried clam special, you might be deceived and manipulated into changing your taste—from a hamburger to clams. How? By the sexual orgy subliminally embedded in the photograph of the clam special.[9] Freudian psychology has strongly influenced the advocates of this first form of the first "social" criticism.

The other form claims that advertising is "merely" coercive, by creating needs and wants that otherwise would not exist without it. That is, highly emotional, persuasive, combative advertising—as opposed to rational, informative, and constructive advertising—is claimed to be a kind of physical force that destroys consumer sovereignty over the free market.[10] This is Galbraith's "dependence effect," so called because our wants, he claims, are dependent on or created by the process by which they are satisfied—the process of production, especially advertising and salesmanship. Our wants for breakfast cereal and laundry detergent, says Galbraith, are contrived and artificial.[11] The psychology of behaviorism has strongly influenced this second form of the first "social" criticism.

Both forms of the "coercive power" charge refer repeatedly to the advertising of cigarettes, liquor, drugs, sports cars, deodorant, Gucci shoes, and color television sets as evidence of advertising's alleged power to force unneeded and unwanted products on the poor, helpless consumer. The charge of manipulation and deception is more serious than "mere" coercion because manipulation is more devious; a manipulator can make consumers buy products they think are good for them when, in fact, that is not the case. The charge of manipulation, in effect, views advertising as a pack of lies. The charge of "mere" coercion, on the other hand, claims that advertising is just brute force; advertising in this view, in effect, is excessively pushy.

According to the second "social" criticism, advertising offends the consumer's sense of good taste by insulting and degrading his intelligence, by promoting morally offensive products, and by encouraging harmful and immoral behavior. Prime targets of this "offensiveness" criticism are Mr. Whipple and his Charmin bathroom tissue commercials, as well as the "ring around the collar" commercials of Wisk liquid detergent and the Noxzema "take it all off" shaving cream ads. But worse, the critics allege, advertising promotes products that have no redeeming moral value, such as cigarettes, beer, and pornographic literature. Advertising encourages harmful and immoral behavior and therefore is itself immoral. Although this criticism does not begin by attributing coercive power to advertising, it usually ends by supporting one or both forms of the first "social" criticism, thus calling for the regulation or banishment of a certain type of offensive— meaning coercive—advertising.

In the textbooks, these are called "social" criticisms. At their roots, however, they are philosophic. It is by reference to philosophic principles that answers to the charges against advertising will be made.[12]

The Economic Criticisms

The economic criticism—it is really only one charge with several variations—claims that advertising is a means by which businesses establish monopoly power over the market. In essence, there are only two forms to this charge. In both, the Garden of Eden—that is, the doctrine of pure and perfect competition—is the standard by which the monopoly charge is made.

The first form claims that advertising is a barrier to entry that prevents competitors from challenging the market position of a large firm. The barrier is erected by a firm's large advertising expenditures. The alleged process of establishing monopoly power runs as follows. Heavy advertising differentiates the advertiser's product, whether or not there are real differences between it and the competition's. The differentiation created by techniques of persuasive advertising makes consumers loyal to the advertiser's brand. Brand loyalty of consumers, then, is the actual barrier that prevents other firms from entering the market. It is a barrier because the competitor would have to advertise at least as heavily to overcome it. Thus, advertising causes product differentiation, product differentiation causes brand loyalty, and brand loyalty is the barrier.

Economists frequently cite Bayer aspirin to illustrate this form of the criticism. Aspirin is aspirin, the critics say, but Bayer's heavy advertising differentiates the product in consumers' minds and makes them loyal. Competitors cannot obtain the resources necessary to compete with Bayer; hence, Bayer has restricted their freedom of competition and is therefore anticompetitive.

The other form of the monopoly argument claims that advertising increases prices. In the imperfect world in which we live, this charge says, informative advertising is used to reduce consumer ignorance, but persuasive advertising differentiates what essentially are homogeneous products. The differentiation causes consumers to prefer the advertiser's brand and to become loyal to it, thus reducing consumer sensitivity to changes in price. The reduction in sensitivity to price changes enables the advertiser to charge more than what would otherwise occur under perfect competition or through the use of informative advertising. The price premium, according to the law of demand and supply, reduces total output. Consequently, advertising is wasteful. Or: advertising causes product differentiation, product differentiation causes abnormally high prices, high prices reduce output and waste society's valuable resources.

To see this more clearly, say the critics, just observe the aspirin market. Nationally advertised brands, such as Bayer, are priced substantially higher—20 percent or more—than privately produced store brands, such as Safeway, Kroger, or A & P. These store brands, however, are seldom advertised. Hence, advertising must necessarily raise the price of the product.

THE NATURE OF MARKETING AND ADVERTISING

Marketing is the parent discipline of advertising; both are products of capitalism and the Industrial Revolution.

To be sure, elements of both marketing and advertising have existed since antiquity: the first trade between primitive people was a market transaction, and traces of media advertising (signs) have been found as long ago as Babylonian times. But it is the extensive division of labor and mass production brought about by the Industrial Revolution that gave rise to the institutions of marketing and advertising. It was not an accident that both were made predominantly illegal in socialist countries of the twentieth century—as a theory, socialism loathes such egoistic, capitalistic activities.

Marketing Is Entrepreneurship

Marketing is the function of business that identifies and anticipates the needs and wants of consumers, creates products to meet those needs and wants, and then delivers the products through various techniques of promotion and distribution. At its strategic or top management level, marketing is an expression of entrepreneurship, because it unites innovation with execution; that is, marketing unites discovering an idea with putting the idea into action. Marketing creates need- and want-satisfying products and then delivers them to consumers.[13] Advertising is a vital part of the delivery process.

The genus of marketing is entrepreneurship; its differentia is the creation and delivery of need- and want-satisfying products. An entrepreneur is the person who perceives ahead of anyone else profit-making opportunities in the marketplace then more importantly, acts to take advantage of those opportunities.[14] Many people throughout history have come up with brilliant ideas, but what distinguishes them from entrepreneurs is that entrepreneurs not only conceive new ideas but also act on them. Inventors, as history has shown repeatedly, are not often also entrepreneurs; Thomas Edison was an exception.

An entrepreneur, as the word's French etymology indicates, is an "undertaker," the person who initiates action or takes the first step. There are two types of entrepreneurship: financial and marketing. The financial entrepreneur is the capitalist in the traditional sense of the term: one who raises equity and debt capital, then allocates it to the most profitable opportunities; metaphorically, the financial entrepreneur provides the financial superstructure of a profit-making skyscraper. The marketing entrepreneur uses the capital to identify markets and develop new products, then to deliver the products to the markets; the marketing entrepreneur, metaphorically, provides the floors, windows, office (the product), and the elevator and stairs (the means of distribution). The marketing entrepreneur is the producer in the traditional sense of the term.[15]

Advertising Is "Just Salesmanship"

Advertising is mass-media selling. It is the communication of product information by means of the mass media, the purpose of which is to sell products to consumers.[16] At the turn of the twentieth century, when newspapers and magazines were the primary media available to advertisers, advertising was referred to as "salesmanship in print."[17] One writer referred to advertising as "multiplied salesmanship."[18] Advertising is a method of communicating to consumers that is less expensive than other methods. That is, it is cheaper to communicate to many consumers at one time through the mass media than to one person at a time, as through one-on-one personal selling, and it is more effective than relying solely on the process of word-of-mouth communication.

This means that there are only two major differences between advertising and personal selling: (1) advertising's selling message is delivered to *many* people at one time, whereas the salesperson's message is delivered to *one* (or at most, a few) at a time, and (2) advertising's message is delivered through a communication medium, such as television or newspapers, whereas the salesperson's message is delivered without the intervention of a medium, that is, it is delivered *personally*. The genus of advertising is salesmanship; its differentia is the means by which the selling is done, namely, via mass media.[19] To understand advertising, therefore—what it is, how it works, and the nature of its alleged power—we must always relate advertising back to its genus.

Advertising is mass-media selling. Its purpose is to sell products. This does not mean, however, that with advertising "you can sell anything to anyone." The first principle of good advertising is what the textbooks call "the primacy of the product." That is, without a good product—a product that meets the needs and wants of consumers—you have nothing; good advertising cannot sell a bad product. In fact, many an advertiser has said that the surest way to kill a bad product is to advertise it.[20]

The purpose of advertising is to sell products, but this does not mean that good advertisements must be funny or entertaining or sexy—any more than a good salesperson in order to be successful must be funny or entertaining or sexy. Humorously entertaining and sexy ads tend to win awards, but they seldom sell products. It is notorious in the advertising industry that consumers respond to such ads by remembering the joke, the music, or the sexy model, but forget the product—or worse, they attribute the ad to the competition. Advertising is salesmanship, not entertainment.[21]

There is nothing mysterious or incomprehensible about the way advertising works. In content, an advertisement says only one of three things (sometimes two or three of these in combination). In introductory campaigns, the ad says, "New product for sale." In competitive campaigns, the ad says, "Our product is better than the competition's." In reminder campaigns, it says, "We're still here, don't forget us." That is all.

In method, the persuasive structure of advertising copy is based on principles first set down by Aristotle over 2,000 years ago in the *Rhetoric*.[22] They are the appeal to emotion, the offer of proof, and the appeal to the credibility of the communicator. The appeal to emotion (which is *not* the fallacy of the same name) is a statement of the benefits consumers will get out of the product by buying and using it; it can be either a positive appeal to the desire to achieve pleasure, such as the appeal to physical attractiveness issued by some brands of toothpaste, or it can be a negative appeal to the desire to avoid pain, such as the appeal to cavity prevention issued by other brands of toothpaste. The appeal to emotion, in truth, is an appeal to values, what consumers value and are therefore looking for in products.

The offer of proof is a statement of reasons or evidence why the product will deliver the claimed benefits; in advertising, this is often referred to as "reason why" copy. Often, although not always, this reason why copy is a statement of the product's features. There is a cause and effect relationship between features and benefits: namely, features cause benefits. Consequently, for example, the reason why one brand of toothpaste will increase your physical attractiveness is because of its whitener and mouthwash ingredients; the reason why the other brand will help prevent cavities is because of its fluoride ingredient.

Appealing to the credibility of the communicator is an appeal to the honesty and integrity of the advertiser. After all, why should anyone believe what the advertiser has said in the first two steps of the peruasion process? This includes references to the longevity of the advertiser and the use of testimonials and endorsements, expert or otherwise.

The use of these three steps of Aristotle's *Rhetoric* constitutes rational persuasion. There are, of course, other less rational forms of communication practiced, not just by advertisers, but—to keep a clear perspective on advertising—by politicians, teachers, journalists, and even by parents. These other forms of communication or irrational persuasion—puffery, sophistry, and deception and fraud—will be discussed in chapter 3.

The Industrial Revolution

Marketing and advertising both came into existence as products of capitalism and the Industrial Revolution. Modern industry evolved during the eighteenth century in several stages. Initially, traders bought the goods of household producers and sold them in distant markets. Some traders, however, began to provide the household producers with additional money, equipment, and materials with which to produce goods. Eventually, in order to maintain better control and because of the sheer size of the operation, some traders brought together numerous household producers, along with their equipment and materials, under one roof, the building of which became known as a "manufactory." The trader became known as a manufacturer; the selling and delivering of products was taken over by local merchants and salesmen called "commercial travelers" in Britain and "Yankee peddlers" in the United States, forerunners of the modern salesman and advertiser.[23]

What is interesting to note about these traders who became manufacturers is that they were performing both functions of entrepreneurship, finance and marketing. They are the ones who identified market opportunities for the goods of the household producers; provided capital and, often, guidance and know-how to producers who seemed promising; and took the goods to market. Insofar as they became manufacturers, and then relied on other parties to take their manufactured goods to market, the division of labor simply separated the creation function of marketing entrepreneurship from the delivery function. The two functions did not unite under one roof in any significant way until the twentieth century development of modern marketing, especially through the functions of market research and product development.[24]

Throughout the nineteenth century, as production expanded and transportation improved, manufacturers started distributing their goods hundreds and thousands of miles away from their factories. To assist their commercial travelers and Yankee peddlers, "announcements" (as early advertisements were called) were placed in newspapers to reach many more people at one time. The result was a reduction in the cost of communication over what it had been using travelers and peddlers exclusively. Thus, mass communication through advertising made it possible for manufacturers to sell their goods at a faster rate, enabling them to recover their investments more quickly. The faster recovery of investments, in turn, provided a strong incentive for the manufacturers either to reach out to still more distant markets or to develop new products.

Thus, advertising came into existence as a form of specialization in the division of labor. Advertising is a form of promotion that the marketer uses to produce economies of scale in the distribution of his products. The distribution economies, however, also create production economies by making it possible for the producer to sell an even larger quantity of goods, thus reducing the cost per unit of production. The economies created make it possible for the producer to earn greater and greater sales and profits at a faster and faster rate. One writer has referred to this phenomenon as the "multiplier effect" of advertising, giving Keynes's term a new twist.[25] Advertising is an acclerator—it speeds up the acceptance of new products, thus encouraging the development of still more new products.

The Nature of Applied Science

As disciplines of study, marketing and advertising are applied sciences.

Some sciences are more fundamental than others. Philosophy, for example, is the most fundamental of all sciences—fundamental in the sense of being more basic and universal in applicability than the others. The special sciences depend on, are derivatives of, or are applications of the fundamental sciences. Physics, biology, psychology, and economics, for example, are fundamental special sciences, all of which in turn depend on philosophy. But engineering, medicine, and marketing are several steps removed from (that is, are more concrete than) the fundamental sciences and therefore are applied sciences. The applied sciences draw their most fundamental principles from their parent disciplines—engineering from physics and chemistry, medicine from biology, marketing from psychology and economics; new principles defined in the applied area, arising from new facts discovered, must be consistent with the more fundamental sciences.

The applied sciences, as concepts, are concepts of method. "Concepts of method," states Ayn Rand, "designate systematic courses of action devised by men for the purpose of achieving certain goals. . . . All the applied sciences (that is, technology) are sciences devoted to the discovery of methods."[26] Marketing and advertising are normative, or "how to," disciplines that define principles to guide man in the achievement of specific goals. The goal of marketing is the creation of need- and want-satisfying products and the delivery of them to consumers. The goal of advertising is communication to make a sale. Marketing and advertising rest most directly on, and derive their most basic principles from, psychology and economics. But psychology and economics, in turn, rest on philosophy.

By examining the fundamental sciences on which advertising rests, it will be possible to discover the roots of the criticisms of advertising.

THE POWER OF IDEAS

Accordingly, an underlying premise of this work is that ideas cause action.

As Ludwig von Mises puts it: "The history of mankind is the history of ideas. For it is ideas, theories, and doctrines that guide human action, determine the ultimate ends men aim at and the choice of the means employed for the attainment of these ends."[27] The attacks on advertising are a form of action—intellectual action that is all too frequently followed by political action to regulate and control advertising. And "ideas, theories, and doctrines"—through the critics' acceptance and internalization of false philosophic and economic ideas—are what have caused today's exceptional hostility toward advertising. Only better ideas—refutation of the false and demonstration of the true—can combat the attackers.

More specifically, it is *philosophic* ideas, theories, and doctrines that guide human action, for it is philosophy that determines the ultimate ends men aim at and the means men employ to attain those ends.[28] To be sure, philosophy does not determine every detail of one's life—only the broadest goals and broadest methods of achieving those goals.[29] (The special sciences guide men in the choice of details.) Ultimately, it is only by reference to philosophic ideas that the criticisms of advertising can be challenged. Only by identifying and refuting the false premises of the critics' philosophic world view can the ground be cleared for a proper defense of advertising. And only by presenting and understanding the alternative—and true—

philosophic world view can the rationality, morality, productiveness, and benevolence of advertising be appreciated.

It is to these two competing world views that we now turn.

NOTES

1. Quoted in David Ogilvy, *Confessions of an Advertising Man* (1963; reprint, New York: Atheneum, 1980), 149.

2. Quoted in David Ogilvy, *Ogilvy on Advertising* (New York: Crown Publishers, Inc., 1983), 206.

3. John Kenneth Galbraith, *The Affluent Society*, 3d ed. (New York: New American Library, 1976), 124–26.

4. Frank Presbrey, *The History and Development of Advertising* (Garden City, NY: Doubleday, 1929; reprint, New York: Greenwood Press, 1968), 74–84. See chapter 4 for more details about this historical experiment in government interference in the freedom of speech and press.

5. "Doctors Are Entering a Brave New World of Competition," *Business Week,* July 16, 1984, 57.

6. *John R. Bates and Van O'Steen* v. *State Bar of Arizona*, 433 U.S. 404 (1977). Not an advocate of turning the other cheek, I am tempted to say to Mr. Rehnquist: It is advertising that is demeaned by its association with lawyers like you.

7. Stephen Fox, *The Mirror Makers: A History of American Advertising and Its Creators* (New York: William Morrow, 1984), 329–30.

8. See John S. Wright, Willis L. Winter, Jr., and Sherilyn K. Zeigler, *Advertising*, 5th ed. (New York: McGraw-Hill, 1982), 31–50, for a standard textbook presentation of the "social" and economic criticisms of advertising. My presentation is an essentialized classification of the criticisms that populate the literature.

9. Wilson Bryan Key, *The Clam-Plate Orgy: And Other Subliminal Techniques for Manipulating Your Behavior* (New York: New American Library, 1980), 2–8.

10. The dichotomy between persuasive, combative advertising, on the one hand, and informative, constructive advertising, on the other, dates at least as far back as Alfred Marshall, *Industry and Trade* (London: Macmillan, 1919), 304–7.

11. Galbraith, *Affluent Society*, 121–28.

12. Indeed, it is a misnomer to refer to these charges as "social" criticisms, for the term "social" implies that morality is essentially a social concept. It is not. Morality defines a code of values to guide *each individual* in his choices and actions. Hence, the quotation marks around "social."

13. Marketing must not be confused with consumerism. Under the guise of wanting to satisfy the needs and wants of consumers, consumerists are pressure groups that lobby government legislators to persuade them to pass laws favoring their groups' particular needs and wants, not the needs and wants of consumers in general. The result is an increase in government control over the economy and a decrease in actual marketing, which means a decrease in overall consumer satisfaction. Consumerism is a product of socialism, and over the years the leaders of consumer movements have been either socialists or socialist sympathizers. Marketing is a product of capitalism. Cf. Robert O. Hermann, "The Consumer Move-

ment in Historical Perspective," in Conrad Berenson and Henry Eilbirt, eds., *The Social Dynamics of Marketing* (New York: Random House, 1973), 73–81.

14. Ludwig von Mises, *Human Action: A Treatise on Economics*, 3d rev. ed. (Chicago: Henry Regnery, 1966), 327–29. See also Israel M. Kirzner, *Competition and Entrepreneurship* (Chicago: University of Chicago Press, 1973), 30–87.

15. In this distinction between financial and marketing entrepreneurs, I am rejecting the more traditional, three-way classification of the operating functions of business: finance, production (or operations), and marketing. This distinction, I submit, restricts marketing primarily to its selling and distributive functions. I am saying that, in essence, there are only two functions of business: finance and marketing, with production (or operations) being a function of marketing. I am using the term "production" in its broadest sense, which includes both the manufacture of tangible goods and the provision of intangible services; this last includes wholesaling, retailing, personal selling, and advertising as forms of production.

Cf. Peter F. Drucker, *Management: Tasks, Responsibilities, Practices* (New York: Harper and Row, 1974), 61–64; W. Duncan Reekie and Ronald Savitt, "Marketing Behaviour and Entrepreneurship: A Synthesis of Alderson and Austrian Economics," *European Journal of Marketing* 16 (1982): 55–65; Jerry Kirkpatrick, "Theory and History in Marketing," in Ronald F. Bush and Shelby D. Hunt, eds., *Marketing Theory: Philosophy of Science Perspectives* (Chicago: American Marketing Association, 1982), 47–51; and Kenneth Simmonds, "Marketing as Innovation: The Eighth Paradigm," *Journal of Management Studies* 23 (September 1986): 479–500.

16. A formal definition of advertising, in order to distinguish it from publicity, would specify that the communiction is made through a *paid* medium and that the sponsor of the message is known or identified in the communication. Publicity does neither.

17. Fox, *Mirror Makers*, 50.

18. "To properly understand advertising or to learn even its rudiments one must start with the right conception. Advertising is salesmanship. Its principles are the principles of salesmanship. Successes and failures in both lines are due to like causes. Thus every advertising question should be answered by the salesman's standards.

"Let us emphasize that point. The only purpose of advertising is to make sales. It is profitable according to its actual sales. . . .

"Advertising is multiplied salesmanship. It may appeal to thousands while the salesman talks to one. It involves a corresponding cost. Some people spend $10 per word on an average advertisement. Therefore every ad should be a supersalesman." Claude Hopkins, *Scientific Advertising* (1923; reprint, Chicago: Crain Books, 1966), 220–21.

19. General or image advertising cannot close a sale, which gives us a third difference between the two methods of promotion. But direct response advertising—which includes direct mail, as well as other types of advertising that provide consumers with a means by which to order the product—can and does do everything that a salesperson can do.

20. Implication? If you have a bad product, do not advertise it! Ah, but you say, you see all kinds of terrible products being advertised; why? My reply at this point is: check your premises, and see chapter 4 for a detailed discussion of the nature of product quality.

21. This is a point to keep in mind when I discuss the Mr. Whipple commercials in chapter 4.

22. Aristotle, *Rhetoric*, trans. W. Rhys Roberts, in Richard W. McKeon, ed., *Basic Works of Aristotle* (New York: Random House, 1941), 1329.

23. Marshall, *Industry and Trade*, 48–51, 715–18. Cf. T. S. Ashton, *The Industrial Revolution 1760–1830* (London: Oxford University Press, 1948).

24. "In considering the whole field of selling, I developed the idea that personal salesmanship and advertising had to do simply with the final expression of the selling idea. My experience with the Procter and Gamble Company [1907–10] had convinced me that a manufacturer seeking to market a product had to consider and solve a large number of problems before he ever gave expression to the selling idea by sending a salesman on the road or inserting an advertisement in a publication." Ralph Starr Butler, commenting on the influences that shaped his outlook on marketing.

In 1910, Butler prepared a correspondence course for the University of Wisconsin. "The subject matter that I intended to treat," states Butler, "was to include a study of everything that the promoter of a product has to do prior to his actual use of salesmen and of advertising. A name was needed for this field of buisiness activity. I remember the difficulties I had in finding a suitable name, but I finally decided on the phrase 'Marketing Methods.' " Quoted in Robert Bartels, *The History of Marketing Thought,* 3d ed. (Columbus, OH: Publishing Horizons, 1988), 24, 295. Butler's course was one of the first uses of the term "marketing" and one of the first treatments of the field as a conceptual discipline more fundamental than selling, advertising, or distribution.

25. Robert L. Steiner, "Does Advertising Lower Consumer Prices?," *Journal of Marketing* 37 (October 1973): 26.

26. Ayn Rand, *Introduction to Objectivist Epistemology,* expanded 2d ed., ed. Harry Binswanger and Leonard Peikoff (New York: New American Library, 1990), 35–36.

27. Ludwig von Mises, *Planned Chaos* (Irvington-on-Hudson, NY: Foundation for Economic Education, 1947), 62.

28. In essence, philosophy as the cause of history is the theme of the title essay in Ayn Rand, *For the New Intellectual* (New York: New American Library, 1961), 10–57. Cf. Leonard Peikoff, *The Ominous Parallels: The End of Freedom in America* (New York: New American Library, 1982).

29. At the cultural level, philosophy determines whether mankind enjoys a golden age or suffers a dark age, whether the members of a culture enjoy a century of freedom and peace, material progress, and great art and literature, or a century of concentration camps, world wars, and declining standards of living. Cf. Leonard Peikoff, *Objectivism: The Philosophy of Ayn Rand* (New York: Penguin Books, 1991), 451–460.

Chapter 2

TWO PHILOSOPHIC WORLD VIEWS

To understand the attacks on advertising—and to understand what is wrong with them—we must examine the ideas that make the criticisms possible. To defend advertising properly, alternative ideas must be presented.

The world view of the critics of advertising is a collection of ideas that pictures man as a blind and helpless pawn who requires guidance from an authoritative elite. The alternative world view pictures man as a self-determined and self-responsible individual who requires political freedom as precondition to the pursuit of his own values and happiness. At the deepest level, the attacks on advertising derive from the modern philosophical assault on man's ability to think conceptually. The proper defense of advertising, therefore, must extend to and penetrate the foundations of human knowledge. This clash of world views is not just idle, academic debate, for its outcome ultimately determines the direction and survival of civilization.

THE AUTHORITARIANISM OF THE CRITICS' WORLD VIEW

The following doctrines constitute the critics' world view.

In philosophy, specifically metaphysics, the branch of philosophy that studies the nature of the universe as a whole, two doctrines provide the foundation of the critics' beliefs: determinism and the mind/body dichotomy. In epistemology, the branch of philosophy that studies the nature of human knowledge and the process by which man acquires knowledge, the doctrine of intrinsicism underlies the critics' ideas. In ethics, a moral version of intrinsicism, along with the morality of altruism, permeates the attacks on advertising. In political philosophy, the unadmitted doctrine that motivates the critics is political elitism. And in esthetics, or the philosophy of art, the doctrine of the equivalence of art and advertising enables critics mistakenly to judge advertising on esthetic grounds. Finally, in economics, the doctrine of pure and perfect competition underlies the economic criticism of advertising; this doctrine itself, however, rests on the philosophic doctrines of logical positivism, the epistemology of the eighteenth-century German philosopher Immanuel Kant, the mind/body dichotomy, and the theory of concepts (or universals) known as nominalism.

Not every critic of advertising, of course, espouses all of these doctrines—they should be so consistent—but the ideas run through all the various attacks made. To demonstrate the moral and benevolent nature of advertising, it will be necessary eventually to answer each of the doctrines.

The Philosophic Doctrines

The doctrine of determinism asserts that man does not possess free will—that any freedom of choice we seem to possess is illusory, and that all of our actions are ultimately determined or caused by forces beyond our conscious control. The external environment and our inner instincts (or heredity) are the most frequently cited deterministic factors. The logical conclusion is that advertising causes ill effects on consumers—directly as a powerful force in our environment or indirectly as a devious means of tapping our inner instincts.

The mind/body dichotomy assumes that our minds (that is, consciousness and reason) are eternally at war with our bodies (and the material world in general). The doctrine stems from the notion that the inner contents of consciousness do not and cannot ever match the outer facts of reality. This notion permeates the history of philosophy. Consequently, man must choose—and, historically, men have chosen—one world or the other: either the sacred, moral world of mind or the profane, practical world of matter. This doctrine is the source of many derivative dichotomies, such as reason vs. emotion, theory vs. practice, the moral vs. the practical, the spiritual vs. the material—and in marketing and economics, respectively, informative advertising vs. persuasive advertising and production costs vs. selling costs. Since advertising—and all business enterprise—operates in the profane world of matter, according to this doctrine, it deserves no moral glory. The material world of practicality, indeed, is often denigrated as immoral.[1]

Intrinsicism—a term coined by Ayn Rand and a doctrine identified by her as false—is essentially a theory of concepts.[2] It holds that man's mind is passive and, consequently, contributes nothing to the process of concept formation, that is, to the process of acquiring knowledge of reality. The mind, according to this doctrine, is like a mirror: it simply reflects the essences of the things we observe. We expose ourselves to the objects of reality and automatically receive illumination. Conceptual knowledge is acquired without effort by looking out at the world, just as perceptual knowledge is acquired without effort by looking out at the world. The concepts we hold in our minds are reflections of these essences. The doctrine is called "intrinsicism" because the essences are held to be intrinsic to the objects of reality; for example, in each individual man, as it were, there exists embedded a nugget of the essence "manness," analogous to a nugget of ore embedded in sedimentary rock. (The opposite side of the intrinsicist coin, as Rand identifies it, is "subjectivism."[3])

The mind has no specific nature, holds intrinsicism, and therefore is a passive responder to the objects of reality that operate upon the mind. This means that concepts are not formed through a rational process; rather, they are revealed to us through nonsensory or extrasensory means. Knowledge is acquired automatically through what has variously been called mystic insight, intuition, or revelation. The intrinsicist "just sees" the truth lying before him. Those who do not see the truth are often told to keep looking or, after a period of trial, are said not to possess the superior insight or intuitive faculty that "the ones who know" happen to possess. In short, the intrinsicist "just knows" what is true because he has a strong *feeling* that it is so. Thus, emotions, not reason, are man's means of gaining knowledge. The doctrine of intrinsic essences ultimately reduces to mysticism and, as such, is a rejection of reason and the conceptual level of consciousness.[4]

Now determinism, the mind/body dichotomy, and intrinsicism all form an integral part of the same world view. Determinism is consistent with intrinsicism because the passive mind is acted upon by an external reality. We are determined by environmental and hereditary factors to "just see" the truth; there is no room in the theory of intrinsic essences for choice or options. The mind/body dichotomy is consistent with intrinsicism because, as in Plato's philosophy, knowledge of "true" reality—the reality of permanence and truth—requires a special insight or intuitive sense that clashes with the concrete, material reality in which we live—the reality of change and error. Reason has been reduced to a form of mystical insight; hence, there is no method of resolving the clash that occurs between the two worlds: the inner world of "true" reality and the outer world of material reality.

The doctrine of intrinsicism enters the criticisms of advertising in the notion that repetitive advertising is unnecessary and wasteful. After all, say the critics, if the product has been advertised once and the consumer clearly received the message, there is no need to advertise again. Why? The consumer now knows that the product exists; the consumer has been informed. Any additional advertising, say the critics, would be "persuasive" advertising, which in their minds is bad.[5] The point here is that the impression has been made; the assumption is that physical reality directly operates upon the human mind, writing its messages, as it were, on the soul. So also, advertising directly stamps its messages on the consumer's mind, indelibly fixing the impression in the consumer's memory.

Intrinsicism in ethics is the doctrine of intrinsic value, the moral version of intrinsic essences. If all knowledge comes to us through direct observation of essences in physical objects, then so too does moral knowledge. Values, according to this doctrine, are intrinsic to the objects and actions of reality, embedded, again, like the nugget of ore in rock. Values are self-evident and value judgments are automatic. According to intrinsicism, the good

> is inherent in certain things or actions as such, regardless of their context and consequences, regardless of any benefit or injury they may cause to the actors and subjects involved. It is a theory that divorces the concept of "good" from beneficiaries, and the concept of "value" from valuer and purpose— claiming that the good is good in, by, and of itself. . . . The intrinsic theory holds that the good resides in some sort of reality, independent of man's consciousness.[6]

In the marketplace, this means certain products, regardless of context or consequences of use, possess less moral value than others. For example, cigarettes and laundry detergent are said to have less intrinsic value than Eugene O'Neill plays and the recycling of paper and plastic. (As in epistemology, subjectivism in ethics is the counterpart of the doctrine of intrinsic value.[7])

Continuing to unravel the critics' world view: altruism is the theory of ethics that motivates the hostility toward capitalism and egoism. According to altruism, a morally good action is one that places others above self; as such, altruism commands self-sacrifice. It does not mean kindness or gentleness, but the act of giving up a higher value for the sake of a lower value or non-value. Considering that advertising appeals to consumers to give up a lower value—namely, money—for the sake of a higher value—goods and services, and that producers use advertising to help them give up a lower value—the goods and services—for the sake of a higher value—the money, altruism can never grant moral value to advertising.

Now, altruism is consistent with the mind/body dichotomy because man, according to altruism, must sacrifice his profane, material body to the sacred, spiritual other world. And altruism is consistent with the doctrine of intrinsic value, because personal gain cannot be achieved if man's duty is to seek values that are good "in, by, and of themselves"; man, according to altruism, is supposed to pursue these intrinsic values "for their own sake," not for personal gain or consequence. Thus, when one writer, commenting on the McDonald's "We do it all for you" slogan, says, "That, of course, is a lie. McDonald's does it all for McDonald's,"[8] it is the writer's altruistic hostility toward egoism that is speaking.

The doctrine of the equivalence of art and advertising is rampant among the critics of advertising. Such critics—as well as many laymen and practitioners—judge advertising using the standards of the fine arts. A major premise, however, supporting this defense of advertising is that, in essence, advertising is "just salesmanship," not entertainment or art. The mind/body dichotomy is the philosophic doctrine that motivates critics to evaluate advertising as art. That is, ads that are more spiritual and artlike—which usually means more humorous and entertaining, or cute and clever—are more likely to be judged favorably, whereas ads that are materialistic, earthy, and, above all, hard-selling are judged negatively.

At this point, the doctrines of determinism, the mind/body dichotomy, intrinsicism, altruism, and the equivalence of art and advertising come together to form the central doctrine that motivates the critics of advertising: political elitism, the twentieth-century version of noblesse oblige.

The mere assertion by critics that there are products consumers do not (read: should not) need or want is a claim by the critics that they are members of the "noble class" of intellectuals—the elite class—who know what is best for the lower classes of unwashed mobs. When these modern aristocrats complain that the Charmin bathroom tissue commercials are stupid, offensive, and cater to the lowest common denominator, it is their alleged moral and cultural superiority that gives them a prissy self-righteousness when discussing bad taste and advertising in the same breath. The authoritarian implications are obvious. What the elitists mean is that there are products *they* think consumers should not need or want. Why?

The reason is their intrinsicism. If certain products possess value "in, by, and of themselves," regardless of context or consequences of product use, and if certain people know which products are intrinsically valuable, then these people, the elite, will insist that there are certain products consumers should not need or want. The mind/body dichotomy determines which products are valuable, and the doctrine of the equivalence of art and advertising determines which advertisements are valuable.

What underlies the critics' elitism and intrinsicism, in turn, is the doctrine of determinism—the doctrine that man does not have free will, that man is just a passive responder to internal and external stimuli. Elitists, of course, are just as determined as anyone else to believe what they do, and to prefer the products they do, through no choice of their own, but they supposedly have acquired their cultural and moral superiority by virtue of their noble birth, special education (especially the possession of a Ph.D. degree), or other privileged status that has revealed to them which are the intrinsically valuable products.

The Economic Doctrine

In economics, the doctrine of pure and perfect competition dispenses with the layman's conception of competition—namely, that it is a rivalry among producers for the same source of revenue. Dominant economic theory today—mainstream "Neoclassical" theory—holds that "pure and perfect" competition is a passive and spontaneous adaptation by participants to changes occurring in the market. It holds that no one participant has the ability to control or influence any aspect of the market, especially prices. Anyone who does exercise such control or influence is said to have introduced "impure" or "imperfect" elements into the competitive state. Hence, such a competitor becomes monopolistic and anticompetitive. Since advertising—and marketing in general—explicitly attempts to control and influence the advertiser's segment of the market, advertising, the doctrine concludes, is inherently monopolistic.

To evaluate this doctrine, however, we must resort to philosophic analysis. Indeed, the doctrine's existence is made possible by the philosophy of logical positivism, which holds that all theory is inherently probabilistic (not universal) and must be tested and verified "empirically," often through the collection of statistical data, before generalizations about a theory's supposed truth or falsity can be concluded.[9] (*Actual* truth or falsity, according to logical positivism, can never be concluded.) Since prediction, according to this doctrine, is the essential purpose of science, the theory to be tested does not even have to be realistic.[10] Hence, Milton Friedman declares, the main criticism of economic theory—that its assumptions are unrealistic, especially the assumptions of pure and perfect competition— "is largely irrelevant."[11]

Logical positivism, in turn, rests on the philosophy of the eighteenth-century philosopher Immanuel Kant, which states that reason is incapable of knowing reality. Any knowledge that we acquire of reality, says Kant, is necessarily tainted by the innate structure of man's consciousness. Hence, he concludes, reason is limited and objective knowledge impossible.[12]

This conclusion makes Kant a subjectivist in epistemology, and a skeptic. But he is a "complacent" skeptic, because every human being's perception of reality is tainted by the same innate structures. The universality of this tainting property of the mind supposedly gives us a means to "intersubjectively verify" our knowledge, which means it gives us a semblance of workable truth or knowledge when a consensus among experts is achieved. (In ethics, Kant is an intrinsicist, which gives him the dubious distinction of being a "subjective intrinsicist.")

As followers of Kant, the logical positivists accepted Kant's premises that reason is limited and universal principles cannot be discovered, but in addition they sought to reclaim the reputation of science as the pursuit of what they considered to be "objective" knowledge. Their "solution" was to adopt what they "took to be the essential feature of scientific method," namely, the verifiability principle, which holds that a proposition is meaningful only if it ultimately can be verified through direct, perceptual observation.[13] According to the later positivists, this meant emulating the methods of the physical sciences, notably physics; thus, scientific theory was to consist solely of quantitative hypotheses, subsequently subjected to empirical testing through the experimental methods of the physical sciences and "intersubjectively verified" through a procedure of replication and peer review. Any conclusion drawn from such studies, once again, would be probablistic, because the tainting properties of our minds precludes drawing universal conclusions. Science, for the positivists, therefore, has become an endless series of hypothesis testing—rejecting some hypotheses and supporting others, but never asserting the achievement of truth or falsity.[14]

Logical positivism and Kant, it should be apparent, both subscribe to the mind/body dichotomy because theory, the inner contents of man's mind, cannot ever exactly match reality, the outer material facts of the external world. Concomitant to and often underlying the mind/body dichotomy is the doctrine of nominalism, a theory of concepts (or universals) holding that concepts are entirely the subjective products of our minds and, therefore, are mere "names" that we assign to groups of perceptual concretes based on the concretes' vague and shifting "family resemblances."

From such philosophical theory, the economic doctrine of pure and perfect competition arose. From logical positivism, and ultimately from Kant, the mind/body dichotomy, and nominalism, today's economists—and marketing professors—derive their conviction that theoretical research must consist of an eternal stream of statistical studies. From this epistemological foundation, economic critics derive their arguments against advertising as a tool of monopoly power. This book will show to be false both the doctrine of pure and perfect competition and the philosophic foundation upon which it rests.

The Role of Marxism

Marxism, another offshoot of Kant's philosophy, by itself is a complete world view that incorporates nearly all the doctrines described above: determinism, the mind/body dichotomy, intrinsicism, elitism, and, in economics, the doctrine of pure and perfect competition (which last to this day is espoused by Marxian economists). The one difference between Marxian and non-Marxian critics of advertising is that Marx opted for the "body" side of the mind/body dichotomy.

Physical, manual labor was the only thing of real—intrinsic—value to Marx. Such professions as agriculture, mining, and manufacturing are valuable and productive because they produce intrinsically valuable physical goods, such as food, shelter, and clothing. But intangible services, such as wholesaling, retailing, and, especially, advertising do not even produce goods; they simply add to the price of the product without adding corresponding value. This view, however, is not original to Marx; its origin is ancient. Marx simply formalized the view into his exploitation and concentration doctrines.

The exploitation theory states that capitalists charge higher prices than the intrinsic physical labor value of the product; by retaining this "surplus value," or profit, the capitalists, according to Marx, exploit labor.[15] By extension, the huckstering agents of the capitalist, the advertisers, exploit labor (and consumers who are the capitalists' laborers) by adding no value to the products; the advertising is superfluous at best, inherently fraudulent at worst. The concentration theory states that capitalism, as a result of its exploitation of the worker, inherently tends to move toward the concentration or centralization of capital, that is, toward the establishment of one giant monopoly.[16] By extension, advertising is a crucial element helping to establish this one giant firm. Thus, the exploitation theory provides a basis for the "social" criticisms of advertising, and the concentration doctrine provides a basis for the economic criticisms.

Again, I must emphasize that not everyone who criticizes advertising on "social" or economic grounds is a Marxist—at least, not explicitly. Volitional consciousnesses are fallible; to maintain consistent and accurate mental contents requires effort. Whoever fails to maintain this effort 100 percent of the time is capable of holding contradictory ideas. Indeed, many people today hold a mixture of "spiritualist" ideas—ideas that originate on the mind side of the mind/body dichotomy—and "materialist" ideas—those that originate on the Marxist, or body, side of the dichotomy, And many critics are capable of asserting both in the same sentence.

The Role of Kant

Kant's influence on the critics of advertising cannot be underestimated, although most probably have never heard of Kant or, at least, do not know his philosophy. To be sure, the historical roots of the "social" criticisms of advertising predate Kant: due to the mind/body dichotomy, trade and money-making activity have been denigrated for thousands of years. And advertising, when it began to develop in the seventeenth and eighteenth centuries, was viewed by critics as a variant of usury.

Nevertheless, Kant's philosophy over the past two hundred years has entrenched altruism in our culture in a way the Judeo-Christian religions by themselves could never have achieved. Loving your neighbor was not enough for Kant. Loving your neighbor when you do not desire to, or when you do not receive any pleasure from loving him, or, better yet, when your neighbor deserves your condemnation—that is the essence of Kant's ethics. Self-abnegation and self-sacrifice—utter selflessness—and obedience to duty, not the pursuit of values, comprise Kant's altruism.[17]

Just as Kant's philosophy has entrenched altruism in our culture, it also has nearly destroyed the Western cultural spirit of the Enlightenment—

the Age of Reason sense of life that man could conquer the universe armed only with reason and its derivative products: science, technology, freedom from government-initiated coercion, and entrepreneurship. In one broad stroke, Kant turned rational self-confidence, self-assertiveness, and productive work for one's own sake and happiness into moral evils, and turned reason and man's mind into handmaidens of mysticism. In a famous line, he says, "I have therefore found it necessary to deny *knowledge*, in order to make room for *faith*."[18] Kant severed reason from reality and values from man.

Thus, Immanuel Kant is the source of the fundamental philosophic distrust of reason that permeates twentieth-century culture. He is the source of the hostility toward ethical egoism that motivates the hostility toward capitalism, which, in turn, motivates the hostility toward capitalism, which, in turn, motivates the hostility toward advertising. If reason, man's tool of survival, is impotent to know reality, then reason also is impotent to guide man's choices and actions. Thus, for Kant, faith is our means of knowledge, and duty is our guide to action. If our duty is to deny ourselves, then capitalism and advertising are anathema to morality.

Kant's philosophy is an assault on consciousness. "His argument," as Ayn Rand incisively summarizes it, "in essence [runs] as follows:

> man is *limited* to a consciousness of a specific nature, which perceives by specific means and no others, therefore, his consciousness is not valid; man is blind, because he has eyes—deaf, because he has ears—deluded, because he has a mind—and the things he perceives do not exist, *because* he perceives them.[19]

Kant's philosophy is an attack on the nature of man as a conceptual being. To the extent to which Kant's ideas motivate the critics of advertising, they are assaulting man's consciousness and attacking the nature of man as a conceptual being.

THE LIBERALISM OF THE ALTERNATIVE

Some writers on the "social" and economic effects of advertising have observed that the critics are motivated by contempt for capitalism.[20] Some have even identified the importance of a world view in shaping the positions of both critic and defender.[21] Most defenses of advertising, however, are based on a standard of social welfare, such as the "common good" or "advertising's contribution to society"—standards based ultimately on the morality of altruism, a key premise of the critics. Neil H. Borden explicitly states his research question in these terms: "Does advertising contribute to, or does it interfere with, the successful functioning of a dynamic, free, capitalistic economy, the aim of which is a high material welfare for the whole social group?"[22] Indeed, the defense and justification of free-market capitalism by many economists is based on the same premise.[23]

Ayn Rand, in a radical departure from the views of other writers, rejects the defense of capitalism based on altruism and a standard of the social or common good. She holds:

> The *moral* justification of capitalism does not lie in the altruist claim that it represents the best way to achieve the "common good." It is true that capitalism does—if that catchphrase has any meaning—but this is merely a secondary consequence. The moral justification of capitalism lies in the fact that it is the only system consonant with man's rational nature, that it protects man's survival *qua* man, and that its ruling principle is: *justice.*[24]

To appreciate the proper defense of advertising, we must understand the world view that includes and underlies this statement.

One, Secular World and Man's Volition

Ayn Rand's philosophy is a secular, one-world view in which reality consists solely of earth and the rest of the natural universe. There is no heaven or hell or world of Platonic Forms that is higher and more moral—or more real—than the "profane, materialistic" world in which we live. There is only *this* world, the Aristotelian world as revealed by our senses that includes consciousness as an attribute of certain living organisms, not as a faculty cut off from the material world.[25]

Rand rejects the mind/body dichotomy because man's mind and body are not separate or at odds with each other. "Man's mind," states Rand, "is his basic means of survival—his only means of gaining knowledge."[26] Indeed, human bodily survival requires thought and the acquisition of knowledge, because our simplest physical needs cannot be met without the exercise of reason. The fraud of modern historians is their denial of the mind in the achievements of allegedly materialistic entrepreneurs. Thought precedes action, and extensive thought has been required to create our Western, material civilization, especially the high material standard of living of the United States.[27] And advertising has been an important part of this creative process.

Thought and the acquisition of knowledge are not automatic, for the exercise of reason must be initiated by each individual. Rand rejects the doctrine of determinism, asserting that thinking is volitional. She states:

> Man has no automatic code of survival. He has no automatic course of action, no automatic set of values. His senses do not tell him automatically what is good for him or evil, what will benefit his life or endanger it, what goals he should pursue and what means will achieve them, what *values* his life depends

on, what course of action it requires. . . . Man's particular distinction from all other living species is the fact that *his* consciousness is *volitional*.[28]

"Free will" is the control that we have over the use of our minds. We can focus our minds fully on the task at hand, we can let random whims distract us, or we can exert effort to avoid focusing on whatever we are doing, that is, we can evade. Free will is our choice to think, to exercise our rational capacity, or not. Thus, Rand's theory implies that advertising cannot force consumers to buy products they do not need or want. Consumers must choose to buy them.

Objective Knowledge

"A process of thought," continues Rand, "is not automatic nor 'instinctive' nor involuntary—nor *infallible*."[29] To insure that the contents of our minds correspond to the facts of the external world, we need a method to guide us, to aid us in distinguishing true throughts from false thoughts. This method is logic. Thus, according to Ayn Rand, objective knowledge is achieved through the chosen use of reason and logic to attain correspondence between the contents of our minds and the facts of reality. Objectivity means volitional adherence to the facts by the method of logic.

In contrast to the doctrine of intrinsicism, Rand's theory of Objectivism holds that man's mind is active and contributes to the process of concept formation. The mind is not a mirror reflecting the essences of things,[30] but rather a processor of the data provided by reality; essences are a product of the human mind, but they must be determined in accordance with the laws of logic and based on the facts of reality. Knowledge, for Rand, is objective, not intrinsic (or subjective). Given the definite and limited nature of the human mind, then, an immplication of Rand's theory is that repetitive advertising may actually benefit consumers who occasionally forget advertisements they have seen before.

Objective Value

Rand's ethics is based on a theory of objective, not intrinsic (or subjective), value. Just as all factual knowledge of reality that we acquire is objective, not intrinsic in the things that we perceive (nor created out of thin air), so too is all evaluative knowledge objective, not intrinsic (or subjective). Values are a product of the relationship between the objects we evaluate and ourselves. What we evaluate as good

is neither an attribute of "things in themselves" nor of man's emotional states, but *an evaluation* of the facts of reality by man's consciousness according to a rational standard of value. (Rational, in this context, means: derived from the facts of reality and validated by a process of reason.) The objective theory holds that *the good is an aspect of reality in relation to man*—and that it must be discovered, not invented, by man.[31]

The objective theory of value would thus judge Eugene O'Neill plays, say, or the recycling of paper and plastic not by reference to the "revelations" of an authoritative elite, but only by their actual beneficial or harmful effects on the life of man.

Egoism

Man's mind is his basic means of survival, and "thinking is a delicate, difficult process, which man cannot perform unless knowledge is his goal, logic is his method and the judgment of *his* mind is his guiding absolute. Thought requires *selfishness*, the fundamental selfishness of a rational faculty that places nothing above the integrity of its own function."[32] According to Rand, man's life is the standard of moral value, and each individual's life is his own moral purpose. Each individual must be the beneficiary of his own thought and action. Thus, egoism is a requirement of man's survival. Why? Because life is the source of values.

Rand defines value as "that which one acts to gain and/or keep";[33] it presupposes two conditions: a beneficiary of the action and action in the face of an alternative. Only living organisms can have values because only living organisms meet these two conditions. Living organisms, acting in the face of the alternative of life, death, must acquire the values necessary to sustain their lives; if they fail to acquire the necessary values, they die. "It is only the concept of 'Life' that makes the concept of 'Value' possible. It is only to a living entity that things can be good or evil."[34] By contrast, inanimate matter, such as a rock, does not and cannot have values.

Life is not just the source of values, but also the standard of value. Plants require food from the soil and sunlight in order to survive; it is the life of the particular plant that determines and guides its pursuit of values within its environment. It is the life of a particular species that determines the species' goals and actions. Animals require locomotion to obtain the values they need for their survival; because animals possess consciousness, they must use their faculties of sensation or perception to guide their actions. Man, the highest animal of all, possesses not just a faculty of perception, but also a faculty of *conception*—reason—and, consequently, must use reason if he is to survive. "A plant can obtain its food from the soil in which it grows. An animal has to hunt for it. Man has to produce it."[35]

The difference between man and the lower animals is that he possesses the most intricate and highly developed mental faculty: a volitional consciousness. The lower animals and plants do not possess the freedom to destroy themselves; their values are automatic or "wired in." Man, however, can improve his life by choosing to learn how to rearrange the elements of his environment for his own benefit, or he can destroy his life, such as by attempting to live at the perceptual level of lower animals. Only man must choose to live, because he does not possess a wired-in, automatic code of values. This, in essence, is why man needs ethics—that is, an objective code of values to guide his choices and actions.

According to Rand, the standard of moral value is man's life—that is, man's life as a being that possesses the capacity to reason.

> Since reason is man's basic means of survival, that which is proper to the life of a rational being is the good; that which negates, opposes or destroys it is the evil.
>
> Since everything man needs has to be discovered by his own mind and produced by his own effort, the two essentials of the method of survival proper to a rational being are: thinking and productive work.[36]

As the standard of moral value, man's life is the supreme good or end in itself; each individual's life is his own moral purpose. The standard provides the abstract principle that guides the individual in the selection of concrete values necessary for his own happiness. The three cardinal values of Rand's ethics are reason, purpose, and self-esteem; the corresponding virtues are rationality, productiveness, and pride.

Since life is an end in itself, and reason is an attribute of the individual, so also is every individual's life an end in itself, not a means to the ends of others. Each individual, as beneficiary of his own actions, has the moral right to live for his own sake and his own happiness. Rational egoism calls for the end of human sacrifices—altruistic or otherwise—because no one has the right to sacrifice anyone to anyone, neither oneself to others, *nor others to oneself*. Thus, Rand's ethics embrace advertising as an institution not just of capitalism, but also of ethical egoism.

Capitalism

The political requirement of man's mind, the one consonant with his rational faculty, is freedom:

> A process of thought is an enormously complex process of identification and integration, which only an individual mind can perform. There is no such thing as a collective brain. . . .
>
> Since knowledge, thinking, and rational action are properties of the individual, since the choice to exercise his rational faculty or not depends on the individual, man's survival requires that those who think be free of the interference of those who don't. Since men are neither omniscient nor infallible, they must be free to agree or disagree, to cooperate or to pursue

their own independent course, each according to his own rational judgment. Freedom is the fundamental requirement of man's mind.[37]

Freedom is the absence of the initiation of physical force by others, especially the government, against the individual. Individual rights, especially property rights, are the means by which individuals are protected within a social system. When a government is restrained from violating individual rights, as by a constitution, and is held liable for encroaching upon the rights of its citizens, that government is set up to protect a system of free-market, laissez-faire capitalism. Any other system (for example, a mixed economy, or socialism) is inimical to and destructive of man's rational nature.[38]

The proper method of dealing with one another in a social setting, according to Rand, is through voluntary cooperation or trade. "The principle of trade is the only rational ethical principle for all human relationships, personal and social, private and public, spiritual and material. It is the principle of justice."[39] It is in this way that capitalism is "the only system consonant with man's rational nature." Capitalism is the only *moral* social system because it recognizes the conditions of man's survival as a rational being and, specifically, because it recognizes individual rights by banning the initiation of physical force. Rand, therefore, defends capitalism precisely because it rests on theories of individualism and egoism. Implicitly, then, advertising would have to be a morally good institution, not because it contributes to society's well-being, but because it appeals to the self-interest of individual consumers for the selfish gain of individual producers.

So also, the moral justification of advertising cannot and does not lie in the claim that it provides for the "common good." It is true that advertising does contribute to the betterment of every individual's life, as Borden and others have pointed out in exhaustive studies, but this, too, is merely a secondary consequence. The moral justification of advertising is that it represents the implementation of an ethics of egoism—the communication of one rational being to another rational being for the egoistic benefit of both.

The alternative world view, then, the one that deserves to be called "liberal" in the classical sense, provides the rational foundation of egoism, capitalism, and advertising; it can be summarized as follows. Reality consists of the one and only universe in which we now live, and our minds and bodies exist in this reality as an integrated union. Human consciousness is both conceptual and volitional, which means that the volitional exercise of reason is our only means to conceptual knowledge. Further, the proper use of reason to acquire both factual and evaluative knowledge requires the principle of objectivity. In morality, man's life is the objective standard of value, which means reason is the only proper guide to an individual's choices and actions. In addition, each individual's life is the purpose of ethics, and each individual is the proper beneficiary of his own actions. In a social context, individual rights, the basis of a moral social system, are protected by banning the initiation of physical force, and proper social cooperation is governed by justice and the trader principle.

Rational egoism is the ethics of man; laissez-faire capitalism is its implementation. Both are the foundations of the original American political and economic system.

Capitalism and Christianity

Contrary to the propaganda of modern religious conservatives, I must emphasize that capitalism and Christianity hold nothing at all in common. Capitalism was born during the Enlightenment of the eighteenth century, the Age of Reason. The founding fathers of the United States, most of whom were deists (some were atheists), were hostile both to the institution of the church and to what they called "priestcraft," by which they meant "that the clergy perpetuated superstition for their own ends: to control the minds of men."[40] As products of the benevolent Enlightenment, they also rejected their Puritan and Calvinist pasts. Control over the minds of men indeed was something that Jefferson would not tolerate.[41]

The secular, one-world view of Enlightenment thinkers led to the Declaration of Independence and the assertion that each individual has the right to pursue *his own* happiness, provided he follows the dictates of his reason, rather than of his "passions" (the eighteenth-century term for irrational emotions). Rational egoism and the protection of individual rights gave us capitalism and the material benefits we enjoy today.

As Ludwig von Mises points out, discussing the historical role of Christianity in the development of capitalism:

> The expectation of God's own reorganization when the time came and the exclusive transfer of all action and thought to the future Kingdom of God [Judgment Day], made Jesus's teaching utterly negative. He rejects everything that exists without offering anything to replace it. He arrives at dissolving all social ties. . . . The clearest modern parallel to the attitude of complete negation of primitive Christianity is Bolshevism. The Bolshevists, too, wish to destroy everything that exists because they regard it as hopelessly bad.[42]

There is one difference, however, Mises continues. The Bolshevists did at least offer some insight, indefinite and contradictory though it was, into the nature of the future kingdom.

Further, Mises states, Christianity since the third century has fought both for and against socialism.

But all efforts to find support for the institution of private property generally, and for private ownership in the means of production in particular, in the teachings of Christ are quite vain. No art of interpretation can find a single passage in the New Testament that could be read as upholding private property. . . .

One thing is clear, and no skilful interpretation can obscure it. Jesus's words are full of resentment against the rich, and the Apostles are no meeker in this respect. The Rich Man is condemned because he is rich, the Beggar praised because he is poor. . . .

Nothing, therefore, is less tenable than the constantly repeated assertion that religion, that is, the confession of the Christian Faith, forms a defense against doctrines inimical to property, and that it makes the masses unreceptive to the poison of social incitement. . . . On the contrary, it is the resistance which the Church has offered to the spread of liberal ideas which has prepared the soil for the destructive resentment of modern socialist thought. Not only has the Church done nothing to extinguish the fire, it has even blown upon the embers. Christian Socialism grew up in the Catholic and Protestant countries, while the Russian Church witnessed the birth of Tolstoy's teachings, which are unequalled in the bitterness of their antagonism to society. True, the official Church tried to resist these movements, but it had to submit in the end, just because it was defenseless against the words of the Scriptures.[43]

What Mises demonstrates, without himself making the point explicit, is that the ethics of altruism—the doctrine of self-sacrifice—which Christianity (in common with all other religions) has espoused throughout its history is incompatible with capitalism. Such a doctrine must inevitably move its proponents to work toward the destruction of capitalism. "A living Christianity cannot, it seems, exist side by side with Capitalism. Just as in the case of Eastern religions, Christianity must either overcome Capitalism or go under."[44]

THE CRITICS VS. REASON

At root, the critics' world view is an attack on reason. However, the correct understanding of reason at once erases the foundations on which the "social" and economic criticisms of advertising rest. Only three essential facts are required to uphold this statement:

First, reason is volitional, a fact that negates determinism and thus removes support for the view that advertising possesses the coercive power to force consumers to buy products they do not need or want. Second, rational values are objective, a fact that nullifies moral intrinsicism and thus removes support for the charge that advertising is offensive and therefore must be regulated or banned. Third, truth and certainty, through reason, are achievable; indeed, they must be achieved if man and civilization are to survive. This is a fact that obliterates the doctrine of pure and perfect competition and thus the charge that advertising is a tool of monopoly power.

To demonstrate these points will require the remaining pages of this book.

APPENDIX: THE FALLACIES OF MYOPIC MARKETING

Two errors in marketing derive from the false philosophic doctrines of intrinsicism and subjectivism. A discussion of the errors, especially as they relate to advertising, should prove helpful in understanding subsequent discussions of the criticisms of advertising.

I have termed the errors, respectively, "engineer's fallacy" and "salesman's fallacy," not because engineers and salesmen are the only ones who ever commit these errors, or that all engineers and salesmen commit them—they do not—but because engineers and salesmen typify the error within many companies and, as a result, clash with one another over how they think the business should be run. Indeed, in some companies, the clash becomes so divisive that name-calling stagnation results, with the engineers calling the salesmen crooks and the salesmen calling the engineers nerds and eggheads. That the errors lead to nearsighted, or myopic, marketing should become clear as the discussion progresses.[45]

Engineer's fallacy holds that a product is most effectively marketed by emphasizing its technical features while ignoring the customer's needs and wants and, especially, while ignoring the customer's ability or desire to understand these technical features. In addition to engineers, anyone who works in a technical profession, including but not limited to accounting, finance, and law, is prone to committing this fallacy. Salesman's fallacy holds that a product is most effectively marketed by promising whatever will get it into the customer's hands, usually by emphasizing the product's benefits while ignoring what is required to make good on the promises. In addition to salesmen, anyone who works in a people-oriented profession, including but not limited to advertising, public relations, personnel, and marketing in general, is prone to committing this fallacy.[46]

The product, according to engineer's fallacy, is intrinsically good, "in, by, and of itself," independently of what anyone may think of it, least of all what the customer may think of it.[47] If the product is intrinsically good, then it ought to sell itself. Indeed, "The product will sell itself" is the slogan of engineer's fallacy, and advertising and salesmanship are seen as social and economic waste. If the product does not sell, then it is the customer's fault for not exerting the effort required to understand such a valuable innovation.[48] Or if advertising and salesmanship are used, it is the fault of the advertising and sales departments—for misleading and deceiving the customer with sleazy puffery and sophistry. (Scratch an intrinsicist and you will find a subjectivist; engineers who must advertise and sell their products often commit all of the errors of salesman's fallacy, because the salesman's fallacy usually is the engineer's conception of marketing.) If the customer complains that the product is difficult to use or that the jargon used by the engineers is difficult to understand, the typical response of the advocates of engineer's fallacy is, "They'll get used to it," or "Well, they're just going to have to learn what these terms mean!" The customer must thus conform to the needs and wants of the engineers.

Engineer's fallacy is the fallacy of context dropping—the context of the customer for whom the product has been developed and the purpose for which the product is to be used. The person who commits the fallacy tends to design products only for himself and to market them as if the market consisted entirely of his clones. This myopic vision has caused computer programmers to become baffled by the intensity of anger expressed by their customers who discover a bug in the software the programmer sold to them. It has caused people such as Henry Ford, who considered advertising to be economic waste, to make statements like, "You can have any color car you want as long as it's black." And it has caused companies with technically good products to go out of business, by refusing to look at the market to adapt their products to the needs and wants of their customers. The many personal computer makers who are no longer with us come to mind, especially since most of them failed because their technical wonders were not easy to use—were not "user friendly," in the vernacular of the industry. Today, when applied to companies, we even have another term for engineer's fallacy; a company so managed, according to the popular business press, is said to be "engineering driven," rather than "market driven."

According to salesman's fallacy, the product, as well as the company that markets it, is malleable; the product and company do not have specific identities that must be adhered to when attempting to sell the product to customers.[49] The product consists of many benefits, some of which are psychological, and it must be presented to the customer in such a way as to motivate him to act; the challenge is to come up with the right benefits— the right promise—that presses the "hot button" to get the customer to buy. "Once the customers use the product," advocates of this error tend to say, "they'll thank me for selling it to them.'" (Scratch a subjectivist and you will find an intrinsicist; salesmen who are pressed to talk about the product's features talk as if it were a technical wonder, whether or not the prospect cares for or desires such a technical wonder. The salesman's typical conception of engineering is engineer's fallacy.) Thus, the slogan of salesman's fallacy is: "Promise them anything," or "I can sell anything to anyone," or "No prospect must walk away unsold." Salesman's fallacy readily lends itself to puffery and sophistry or worse, although it need not;

the basic form of the fallacy is overemphasis on benefits at the expense of features.[50]

Salesman's fallacy is the fallacy of subjectivism, for not only are the product and company seen as undefined and malleable, so is the customer (and the universe). The customer's needs and wants are not objectively real. Whatever the customer's wants, says the advocate of salesman's fallacy, we will find a way for our product to meet them. In this sense, salesman's fallacy also is the fallacy of context dropping—the context of the customer's objective needs and wants and the context of the company's employees who must fulfill the many subjective promises made by the salesman. The person who commits this fallacy lives entirely in a world of people, focused innocently or not only on the sale or commission to be made by manipulating others to buy his product, whether or not the customer needs or wants it.

This myopic vision has caused salesmen to overemphasize personal appearance and interpersonal skills—claiming, for example, that spit-shined shoes, a large supply of jokes, and the right amount of aggressiveness, rather than product and market knowledge, are the essence of successful selling. It has caused advertising agencies to omit mentions of a product's shortcomings—to hard-sell, as it were, as if the product were the greatest thing since sliced bread—only to be fired a few months later because their advertising does not sell the product. And it has caused companies to spend millions of dollars on advertising budgets and large sales forces, and little or no money on market research, only to find their sales and profits remaining flat or even declining, year after year. Today, when applied to companies, just as we have another term for engineer's fallacy, we have another term for salesman's fallacy; such companies, according to the business press, are said to be "sales driven," rather than "market driven."

A "market-driven" company is one that practices what has been called the "marketing concept."[51] Such a company views the customer as a rational human being who has needs that apply universally to all other human beings and wants that consist of values that are rationally optional—that is, tastes and preferences that are objectively valid but do not apply universally to all human beings. (For example, we all share the universal need of transportation, but a sports car and a sedan will each equally transport us to our destination; our choice of automobile, in most contexts, is rationally optional.) Such companies are not in business to make and marvel at technical wonders, or to ram products down the throats of their customers. They talk and listen to their customers, identifying their universal requirements for an improved life and their optional tastes and preferences; then they design products to meet those needs and wants.

That engineering- and sales-driven companies survive is not denied, but they do not survive for very long, or very well, without changing their management policy. Engineering-driven companies can survive as long as their primary customers are other engineers or other similarly technical people. When laymen begin to enter the market, such companies must become more aware of the layman's wants—his optional tastes and preferences. This usually means hiring marketing personnel. If top management understands the value of marketing, the transition to a market-driven company is relatively smooth. If not, then divisive conflicts between engineering and marketing result, and the company may still survive, but at a mediocre level of sales. That there are engineering companies that are market driven is not denied; Hewlett Packard is just one notable example from recent times.

Sales-driven companies and salesmen who practice the salesman's fallacy also can and do survive, but these companies and individuals are always hustling new business, always having to make cold calls. Practitioners of the salesman's fallacy exude the layman's image of the huckster. Consequently, after one or a few contacts with such companies and individuals, most customers take their business elsewhere. Hence, there is constant pressure to find new customers. Market-driven companies and market-driven salesmen generate loyalty to such an extent that many of them, after an initial "break-in" period, get the majority of their sales from referrals and repeat customers. Cold calling, according to those who are market driven, is for hucksters and novices. That there are companies known for their strong selling that are also market driven is not denied; Procter and Gamble is a notable example.

NOTES

1. Plato is the philosophic founder of the dichotomy and the Judeo-Christian religions institutionalized it in our culture. See the brilliant title essay in Ayn Rand, *For the New Intellectual* (New York: New American Library, 1961), 10–57, for the devastating effects of this dichotomy on the history and development of Western civilization. Cf. Leonard Peikoff, *Objectivism: The Philosophy of Ayn Rand* (New York: Penguin Books, 1991), 23–30.

2. Ayn Rand, *Introduction to Objectivist Epistemology*, expanded 2d ed., ed. Harry Binswanger and Leonard Peikoff (New York: New American Library, 1990), 52–54. Intrinsicism, I must emphasize, according to Rand, is a false doctrine and ultimately is a form of mysticism. Her own theory, and name of her entire philosophy, is called "Objectivism."

3. As a theory of concepts (or universals), intrinsicism is more commonly known in philosophy as "realism." Platonic realism asserts that concepts or universals exist intrinsically as archetypes in another dimension of reality, which in Christianity eventually became known as heaven. Aristotelian realism, on the other hand, maintains that there is only one reality, but that concepts or universals exist intrinsically as metaphysical essences *in* the concrete entities and actions we perceive. The Artistotelian form of realism is what I have describe above, because it is the

form today's nonphilosopher, albeit unwittingly, is most likely to espouse. Rand's identification of this doctrine pinpoints the metaphysical and epistemological root of the theory: namely, intrinsic essences.

Subjectivism is more commonly known in philosophy as "nominalism." This theory, which is the dominant one today among philosophers and other intellectuals, holds that concepts and essences are subjective inventions of the mind, mere "names" for the concretes of reality that have at best only vague and shifting "family resemblances" to one another.

Intrinsicism, however, not subjectivism, is the primary doctrine that underlies the criticisms of advertising. See Peikoff, *Objectivism*, 142–51, for a detailed discussion of the two false doctrines.

4. According to Ayn Rand, however, "consciousness, as a state of awareness, is not a passive state, but an active process." *Objectivist Epistemology*, 5. Consciousness possesses a specific identity, namely, to perceive the objects of reality. Man's faculty of perceiving reality is reason, a faculty that must be exercised by choice. The process of acquiring knowledge of reality is called concept formation, and the end products of the process are called concepts. Far from being a mirror that passively reflects embedded essences, the human mind is, figuratively speaking, an intellectual stomach that actively processes the food of external reality, turning it into the muscles and bones necessary for life and growth. Concepts and essences are not embedded in reality, as the intrinsicists maintain (nor are they fabricated out of thin air, as the subjectivists argue). Rather, they are objective products of the mind's identification of reality; they are "mental integrations of factual data computed by man—as the products of a cognitive method of classification whose processes must be performed by man, but whose content is dictated by reality." Ibid., 54. See chapter 6 for a presentation of Rand's theory of concepts.

Despite Aristotle's errors in formulating an intrinsicist theory of concepts, which indeed are a remnant of Plato's influence on him, Rand's philosophy falls within the Aristotelian tradition. I do not want to make it sound like Rand considers Aristotle to be a philosophical villain; rather, she considers him a hero.

5. As one critic, and former member of the Federal Trade Commission, put it: "I define 'persuasive' as those efforts to impart information which substantially all consumers already have, and by repetition of selected themes influence consumers favorably toward the advertised product. The argument that such efforts are socially (as opposed to competitively) wasteful is particularly compelling. . . . Such canceling out of advertising almost certainly occurs currently with respect to sales of nationally advertised analgesics, ready-to-eat cereals, gasoline, and many other product categories with exceptionally high advertising-to-sales ratios." Robert Pitofsky, "Changing Focus in the Regulation of Advertising," in Yale Brozen, ed., *Advertising and Society* (New York: New York University Press, 1974), 126.

6. Ayn Rand, "What Is Capitalism?," in *Capitalism: The Unknown Ideal* (New York: New American Library, 1966), 21–22. Also, see Peikoff, *Objectivism*, 241–48.

7. "The *subjectivist* theory [in ethics] holds that the good bears no relation to the facts of reality, that it is the product of a man's consciousness, created by his feelings, desires, 'intuitions,' or whims, and that it is merely an 'arbitrary postulate' or an 'emotional commitment'. . . . The subjectivist theory holds that the good resides in man's consciousness, independent of reality." Rand, "What Is Capital-

ism?," 21–22. Emphasis in original. The subjectivist theory of value is dominant today among philosophers and other intellectuals.

8. Michael Schudson, *Advertising: The Uneasy Persuasion. Its Dubious Impact on American Society* (New York: Basic Books, 1984), 10.

9. See, for example, Rudolf Carnap, *An Introduction to the Philosophy of Science*, ed. Martin Gardner (New York: Basic Books, 1966).

10. Karl Popper, *Conjectures and Refutations: The Growth of Scientific Knowledge* (London: Routledge and Kegan Paul, 1963), 115.

11. Milton Friedman, "The Methodology of Positive Economics," in *Essays in Positive Economics* (Chicago and London: University of Chicago Press, 1953), 41. Interestingly, the doctrine of pure and perfect competition has made its way into philosophy as an essential component of John Rawls's theory of egalitarianism, or "justice as fairness." The just, egalitarian state, according to Rawls, will be achieved when the doctrine of pure and perfect competition is fully implemented in society as a "fair game." What prevents this full implementation is the persistent greed of utilitarian capitalists. Utilitarianism, however, is the only moral defense of capitalism considered by Rawls. As a consequence, his work, among its many other faults, amounts to a massive straw man argument. John Rawls, *A Theory of Justice* (Cambridge, MA: Belknap Press of Harvard University, 1971).

12. W. T. Jones, *A History of Western Philosophy*, 2d ed., revised (New York: Harcourt Brace Jovanovich, 1975), 4:14–68.

13. Ibid., 5:220.

14. Ibid., 4:202–5, 218–49.

15. Karl Marx, *Capital: A Critique of Political Economy*, ed. Frederick Engels, trans. Ernest Untermann (Chicago: Charles H. Kerr, 1906), 1:163–73.

16. Ibid., 1909, 3:257.

17. Immanuel Kant, *Groundwork of the Metaphysic of Morals*, trans. and analyzed by H. J. Paton (New York: Harper Torchbooks, 1964), 61–73.

18. Immanuel Kant, *Critique of Pure Reason*, trans. Norman Kemp Smith (New York: St. Martin's Press, 1965), 29. Emphasis in original.

19. Rand, *For the New Intellectual*, 32. Emphasis in original.

20. Jules Backman, *Advertising and Competition* (New York: New York University Press, 1967); Leo Bogart, "Is All This Advertising Necessary?," *Journal of Advertising Research* 18 (October 1978): 17–26; Neil H. Borden, *The Economic Effects of Advertising* (Chicago: Richard D. Irwin, 1942); Harry R. Tosdal, *Selling in Our Economy* (Homewood, IL: Richard D. Irwin, 1957).

21. Kim B. Rotzoll, James E. Haefner, and Charles H. Sandage, *Advertising in Contemporary Society: Perspectives toward Understanding* (Cincinnati: South-Western Publishing, 1990), 13–27.

22. Neil H. Borden, *Advertising in Our Economy* (Chicago: Richard D. Irwin, 1945), 6.

23. Milton Friedman, *Capitalism and Freedom* (Chicago: University of Chicago Press, 1962).

24. Rand, "What Is Capitalism?," 20. Emphasis in original. Elsewhere Rand states: "The moral justification of capitalism is man's right to exist for his own sake, neither sacrificing himself to others nor sacrificing others to himself; it is the recognition that man—every man—is an end in himself, not a means to the ends of others, not a sacrificial animal serving anyone's need." Ayn Rand, "Faith and

Force: The Destroyers of the Modern World," in *Philosophy: Who Needs It* (New York: Bobbs-Merrill, 1982), 81.

25. See Peikoff, *Objectivism*, for more on this and other issues involving the philosophic foundations of egoism and capitalism.

26. Rand, "What Is Capitalism?," 16.

27. See Ayn Rand's now classic novel *Atlas Shrugged* (New York: Random House, 1957) for a dramatic moral vindication of allegedly materialistic business-men. The plot-theme of the novel is the mind on strike; the book dramatizes what happens to a civilization when the men of creative ability in all professions, especially in business, quit and disappear.

28. Ayn Rand, "The Objectivist Ethics," in *The Virtue of Selfishness: A New Concept of Egoism* (New York: New American Library, 1964), 19–20. Emphasis in original.

29. Ibid., 21. Emphasis in original.

30. Nor does it create concepts and essences out of thin air, which is the doctrine of subjectivism. See chapter 6 for Rand's objective theory of concepts.

31. Rand, "What Is Capitalism?," 22. Emphasis in original.

32. Leonard Peikoff, *The Ominous Parallels: The End of Freedom in America* (New York: New American Library, 1982), 308. Emphasis in original.

33. Rand, "Objectivist Ethics," 15.

34. Ibid., 15–16.

35. Ibid., 18.

36. Ibid., 23.

37. Ibid., 16–17.

38. See Ayn Rand, "Man's Rights" and "The Nature of Government," in *The Virtue of Selfishness*, 92–100, 107–15. In today's context, it must be emphasized that the right to life, according to Rand, applies only to actual human beings, not to potential ones—that is, not to fetuses. Nor does it apply to animals, because animals have no power of reason or the power to recognize rights.

39. Rand, "Objectivist Ethics," 31.

40. Ernest Cassara, *The Enlightenment in America* (New York: Twayne, 1975; reprint, Lanham, MD: University Press of America, 1988), 118.

41. "I have sworn upon the altar of God, eternal hostility against every form of tyranny over the mind of man." Quoted in ibid., 32.

42. Ludwig von Mises, *Socialism: An Economic and Sociological Analysis*, trans. J. Kahane (London: Jonathan Cape, 1936; reprint, Indianapolis: Liberty Fund, 1981), 375–76.

43. Ibid., 378–79. Mises, of course, uses the word "liberal" in its original sense, meaning freedom from government-initiated coercion. Cf. Ludwig von Mises, *Liberalism in the Classical Tradition*, trans. Ralph Raico (William Volker Fund, 1962; reprint, San Francisco: Cobden Press, 1985).

44. Mises, *Socialism*, 386.

45. The phrase "myopic marketing" comes, of course, from Theodore Levitt's article "Marketing Myopia," *Harvard Business Review* 38 (July/August 1960):45–56, in which he provides numerous examples of what I have called engineer's fallacy. See Philip Kotler, "From Sales Obsession to Marketing Effectiveness," *Harvard Business Review* 55 (November/December 1977):67–75, for a discussion of what I call salesman's fallacy. The identification of these errors is not original to me; for

several decades marketing textbooks have decried the production and product orientations of business management, on the one hand, and the sales orientation, on the other, as ineffective methods of running modern businesses. What I am demonstrating as new, however, is the connection between the two errors and the philosophic doctrines of intrinsicism and subjectivism.

46. Licensed professions, because of their monopolistic privileges—privileges that exempt their practitioners from having to meet their customers' needs and wants in a free, competitive marketplace—also exhibit the characteristics of engineer's fallacy. Medical doctors and lawyers are just the most notorious examples. Indeed, to the extent to which any private business is regulated by the government, it will exhibit the characteristics of engineer's fallacy, because the governmental regulations inhibit, by reducing incentives, and prevent, by direct regulation, the business from meeting the needs and wants of the market. Bureaucratic management is the institutionalization of engineer's fallacy. See Ludwig von Mises, *Bureaucracy* (New Haven, CT: Yale University Press, 1944).

47. "I have enough self-esteem and confidence in my product designs," says the proponent of engineer's fallacy, "without having to grovel like a neurotic dependent at the feet of other people. Market research is for people who have no principles or pride in themselves."

48. Advocates of engineer's fallacy sometimes will even impugn the customer's character. The customer, they say, is irrational or immoral for not recognizing the "obvious" value of the engineer's product.

49. "Perception is reality," says the proponent of salesman's fallacy, "so I just give my customers what they want—whether it's good for them or not. Besides, who can know what's good for my customers, anyway? Now if those eggheads back at headquarters would just get off their duffs and redesign the product like I told them, I could double my sales."

50. "Don't sell the steak, sell the sizzle," said an unnamed salesman long ago, no doubt in response to an engineer's overemphasis on features at the expense of benefits. The key to successful selling, however, is the communication of *both* steak *and* sizzle, the optimal proportion of which is determined by the actual needs and wants of the customer.

51. The "marketing concept" must not be confused with the "concept of marketing." The latter is the discipline and applied science of marketing. The former is an orientation of business management—a management philosophy, as it were—that no decision should be made, or action taken, whether by the president of the company or a stock boy, until its effects on the objective needs and wants of the customer have been properly considered.

Chapter 3

THE ALLEGED COERCIVE POWER OF ADVERTISING

Advertising forces consumers to buy products they do not need or want. This, in essence, is the first "social" criticism of advertising.

Advertising allegedly achieves this goal by making consumers change their tastes and preferences in such a way as to conform to the tastes and preferences of the advertisers. According to the charge, advertising either taps the internal urges of consumers to make them change their tastes or, as a powerful force in the environment, directly causes consumers to change their tastes. Advertising, the critics maintain, forces consumers to act in ways they would not if there were no advertising. The philosophic doctrine underlying this criticism is determinism, which denies the validity of free will.

There are two forms of this criticism. The first says that advertising deceives and manipulates consumers through subliminal advertising. The second says that advertising creates needs and wants by using techniques of persuasion, which the critics say is essentially the same as coercion. Let me now begin by discussing the charge of deception and manipulation.

"SUBLIMINAL" ADVERTISING ALLEGEDLY DECEIVES AND MANIPULATES

This first argument assumes that man is motivated by unconscious urges and instincts that he possesses innately; that is, man is determined to act the way he does because of internal stimuli. The essence of this criticism is Freudian psychology applied to the evaluation of advertising.

According to Freud, the id is our warehouse of primitive and impulsive drives, such as thirst, hunger, and sex. The critics point out that advertising allegedly—without our being aware of it—possesses the power to tap or trigger these impulsive drives. Consequently, advertising deceives, defrauds, and manipulates unwitting consumers into changing their tastes to conform to the desires of the greedy, selfish producers.

The manipulation is said to occur subliminally, below our threshold of awareness. Thus, in a movie theater in 1958, the words "eat popcorn" and "drink Coca-Cola" were flashed on the screen at a speed no one could perceive. During intermission the sales of popcorn supposedly increased 58 percent and the sales of Coca-Cola 28 percent.[1] By that time, of course, Vance Packard had already cried "hidden persuaders"; ever since, the enemies of capitalism and advertising have been celebrating.

The 1970s version of the subliminal advertising charge comes from a series of books by Wilson Bryan Key. In *Subliminal Seduction* the author claims to have seen the word "sex" embedded in the ice cubes of a glass used in an advertisement for Gilbey's gin.[2] He has since "seen" many other such "subliminal embeds" in advertising, including the sexual orgy in Howard Johnson's clam special mentioned in chapter 1, and has subsequently written two more books.

The first form of the "coercive power" argument does not rely exclusively on the charge of subliminal advertising, but it does rely on the advertiser's alleged ability to tap our subconscious minds and influence our behavior without our full awareness. An article in *TV Guide* acknowledges that advertisers do not use subliminal techniques. "No," it states, "advertisers aren't trying that now. But some are trying the next best thing: images flashed so quickly you barely have a chance to register them."[3] The idea is that rapid-fire scene changes in commercials can influence—that is, manipulate—consumers more effectively than slower paced commercials. Even though these scene changes are "liminal," that is, above our threshold of perception, they are assumed somehow to be able to manipulate us. Some writers, I must point out, would still call this technique *subliminal*.

Self-Contradiction

The notion of subliminal perception, however, is a self-contradiction, because it claims the ability to perceive something that is below our threshold of perception. Thus, the compound concept "subliminal perception" is invalid.[4] (Further, well-controlled experiments to test the plausibility of subliminal influence on behavior have failed to produce any evidence.[5]) To be sure, there are events in reality that are subliminal—that is, there are stimuli that can and do impinge on our sense organs but do so only at levels above or below the range our sense organs can register, such as ultraviolet light and ultrasound. We do not perceive these phenomena with our unaided eyes and ears. We know about them only through a volitional process of study and inference.

In effect, the proponents of subliminal advertising claim that advertisers inject consumers with imperceptible viruses to cause perceptible diseases, such as buying products of which the proponents of the subliminal advertising charge do not approve. Advertisers have enough trouble as it is getting consumers to pay attention to ads that are blatantly explicit, let alone to messages that are three thousandths of a second long or unrecognizably embedded in ice cubes.

Indeed, the charge that advertisers consciously and willfully use subliminal embedments in advertisements carries no more weight of evidence than the assertion that clouds contain sexual symbolism. The charge is an arbitrary assertion in the form of the fallacy *argumentum ad ignorantiam*. No one can prove that gremlins do not exist, nor does anyone have the obligation to do so. No one can prove a negative. Advertisers do not have the obligation to answer or rebut the charges of overly active imaginations, because there is no evidence that advertisers are so motivated. The burden of proof is on the asserter of the positive.[6]

The Unearned Popularity of the Charge

The popularity of the subliminal advertising charge, as well as the popularity of Freudian psychology, in my judgment, stems from the inability of many people to identify the nature and causes of their emotions and the causes of their actions. Such people readily believe that there are mysterious forces at work in the world, manipulating and controlling them. The source of these so-called inexplicable, internal urges, however—which advertising allegedly taps—is one's own thoughts.[7]

The popularity of the charge is aggravated by the many misuses of the word "subliminal"; some, no doubt, are deliberate on the part of the critics of advertising. Subliminal perception to some psychologists means either a low level of awareness or an awareness that occurs despite focused attention on something else—"liminal subliminal" perception, as it were.[8] If "subliminal perception," however, by itself is a contradiction in terms, *liminal subliminal* perception is worse than a contradiction. Some refer to the phenomenon of "déjà vu"—the "I've been here before" feeling of walking into a room you have never been in before—as subliminal perception. But déjà vu has been explained, at least in some of its forms, by psychologists as a near-instantaneous memory of the moment you first saw, that is, perceived, the room.[9] Still others call sexual innuendo in advertisements subliminal. But sexual innuendo is explicit; advertisers *want* consumers to pick up the sexual messages in those commercials. There is nothing subliminal or, as implied, devious about such techniques.[10]

There are other misuses.[11] The one use often presented as proof of the effectiveness of subliminal messages is that used in department stores to discourage shoplifting. Supposedly, some stores that have played "subliminal" messages such as "be honest" and "don't shoplift" over the store's music system have experienced declines in shrinkage. Declines in shrinkage may have occurred, but there are two problems with this alleged proof. One is that the messages are not subliminal; that is, if you were to put your ear to the speakers of the store's sound system, you would hear the messages. The second problem is that state laws require signs to be posted in the store, stating that such messages are being played. These "field experiments" hardly produce unconfounded results.[12]

Briefly during the 1950s, Freudian psychology did influence a number of marketing researchers, and today it still influences isolated researchers. Most of the findings from the 1950s, however, were laughable, such as the belief that women bake cakes because of their desire to have children. Or that single men prefer convertible automobiles because they represent to them a mistress, but married men prefer hardtops because they represent to them a wife. This Freudian influence, unfortunately, is what brought about the charge of subliminal advertising in the first place.

"PERSUASIVE" ADVERTISING ALLEGEDLY CREATES THE NEEDS AND WANTS IT AIMS TO SATISFY

The second form of the "coercive power" criticism says that advertising creates needs and wants by using techniques of persuasion, which the critics say is essentially the same as coercion. This charge asserts that advertising, as an element of the consumer's environment—that is, as an external stimulus—directly causes consumers to act. The essence of this criticism is behaviorist psychology applied to the evaluation of advertising. Accordingly, advertising is an external, environmental stimulus that controls our lives. Specifically, persuasive, emotional advertising, say the critics (including John Kenneth Galbraith), changes consumers' tastes and preferences, creating needs and wants they otherwise would not have.

False Dichotomy between Informative and Persuasive Advertising

In this argument, persuasion is equivalent to coercion. To be fair, the critics do not deny the value of all advertising—only the value of persuasive advertising. Their kind of advertising is called "informative," and their model is the price advertising of retail stores, such as "asparagus 99¢ a bunch" or "patio furniture on sale for $199." The critics usually even tolerate most newspaper and magazine advertising. Informative advertising, the critics say, is "rational."

What the critics cannot tolerate, however, is television advertising, especially competitive advertising of basically homogeneous products (such as bathroom tissue, liquid laundry detergent, and shaving cream). They also hate what advertisers call "reminder" advertising, which usually contains only a few words of copy, sometimes none. They especially despise the Mr. Whipple, "ring around the collar," and Noxzema "take it all off" commercials. Emotional advertising is persuasive and, therefore, "irrational."

The distinction, however, between informative advertising and persuasive advertising is a false dichotomy, stemming from the dichotomy in philosophy between reason and emotion. This is an example of the mind/body dichotomy applied to the evaluation of advertising.

The correct view is that all advertising is at once informative and persuasive. For example, a sign on a hot summer day that reads "lemonade—5¢" is informative; however, that simple informative message can very quickly become persuasive if, while walking down the street where the sign is posted, you are dying of thirst. On the other hand, an ad that has no copy in it at all—only, say, a photograph of the product—is informing consumers that the product exists (or still exists, because this type of advertising usually is providing the consumer with a reminder).

Determinism Is Untenable

The difficulty with this distinction between informative and persuasive advertising is that the doctrine of determinism, which underlies both forms of "coercive power" criticism, obliterates the distinction between force and persuasion. According to psychologist Edwin Locke, "If men [lack] volition, then persuasion [has] the same coercive power as direct physical force: 'persuasion' and force [just] represent two different methods of manipulating others."[13] Persuasion, according to the critics of advertising, is just another form of physical force—perhaps only a little less direct than pointing a gun at consumers. Thus, the critic concludes that persuasive advertising is bad.

Determinism, however, is a self-contradiction, because the advocates of determinism presumably also are determined, either by internal or external stimuli. They must believe what they do because they "can't help it"—just as an advocate of free will or Marxism or any other idea "can't help it." Determinists are determined to believe in determinism, and their claims to truth, therefore, are no more valid than anyone else's. Determinism is "a doctrine which is incompatible with its own content and which would make all assertions of knowledge and truth meaningless."[14]

Man is a being of volitional consciousness, which means that he possesses the capacity to reason but can choose to exercise that capacity or not. Free will, as Ayn Rand identified, means the ability or freedom to regulate conscious awareness—the ability to focus our minds or not, the ability to think or to evade.[15] If you cannot get inside the head of another person to make him think or focus his mind, then certainly advertising cannot get inside the minds of consumers to force them to run out and buy Noxzema shaving cream because of a sexy model. The consumer must choose to let the advertising in.

Further, there is a difference between selective perception and the decision to act. It is hardly controversial that consumers can tune out advertisements, especially television commercials, tuning back in at the precise moment program material resumes. Even if consumers choose to focus intently on particular commercials and absorb every word and nuance that is being communicated, they still have the free will to evaluate what has been communicated—accepting or rejecting the premise of the ad— and, still further, they have the free will to act or not to act on the basis of the evaluation. Determinism reduces the complexity of human choices and action to the status of a reflex.

Tastes and Wants Not Dependent on Advertising

This means, speaking precisely and technically, that advertising cannot change tastes, create needs or wants, or even create demand. Advertising can make consumers aware of needs, it can stimulate their wants, it can stimulate demand, and it can make it possible for consumers to enjoy a larger number and wider range of tastes. But tastes, needs, wants, and demand all originate within the consumer. Advertising is just the sign that says "lemonade—5¢." Or, to put it in the language of cause and effect, advertising can be the *necessary* condition for the existence of specific wants, but not the *sufficient* condition. Unless advertising is the necessary *and* sufficient condition, it cannot be said to cause or determine wants.

Consider the issue this way: Suppose I wheel into the room before you a platter of sizzling T-bone steaks. If it has been several hours since you last had a meal, you might experience a strong desire to eat; you may even begin to salivate. On the other hand, if you happen to be a vegetarian, you might react with revulsion or even contempt. Clearly, the cause of wants or desires is in the person who has the want; the cause of the want is a value judgment made by the consumer about the object being desired or avoided. If the physical presence of the T-bone steaks cannot make a vegetarian want them, how can an advertisement do it? As Austrian economist and Nobel laureate F. A. Hayek points out, it is a non sequitur to move from the existence of products and product advertising to the conclusion that those products and their advertising create the consumers' wants. In this illogical thinking, an important step—the value judgment— is missing.[16] So much for Galbraith's so-called dependence effect.

Another problem with this form of "coercive power" criticism is that the terms "need" and "necessity" are seldom defined. Critics, when they can be pinned down, usually define "need" as "bare physical subsistence." At this point, they acknowledge that consumers need food, but deny that they need Big Macs, T-bone steaks, or caviar. A proper definition of need is: the objective requirements for the survival and happiness of a rational being. In this sense, man will always need better and wider varieties of food, faster and more comfortable ways to travel, objects of ornamentation and contemplation (jewelry and art). Man's needs are limitless. The job of advertising is to persuade consumers to prefer or want the marketer's specific brand that meets one of these generic needs.

Now Galbraith would have us believe not only that our wants in modern society are artificially created by advertising, but also that, in a primitive society, "it is not necessary to advertise food to hungry people."[17] But, as one writer points out in an article entitled "Galbraith's Wicked Wants," the lowly potato, an obvious remedy to Europe's recurrent famines, was not accepted as a staple for two hundred years. As late as 1740 in the American colonies, the potato was said to be unhealthy and to shorten man's life. A little "want creation" advertising three or four centuries ago, this writer points out sarcastically, could have helped mankind considerably.[18]

Luxuries and Necessities

But, other critics go on, has not advertising turned microwave ovens and videocassette recorders into necessities that not long ago were considered luxuries? Has advertising not changed our tastes by creating a necessity that otherwise would not have existed? The answer is no, at least in the deterministic sense that the critic means, because it is consumers who have turned these products into necessities. A luxury is a product that only a few people can afford to own and, consequently, choose to own. A necessity, when contrasted with a luxury, is a product that most people can afford to own and, consequently, choose to.

We have always had a need for faster, more convenient methods of cooking and a need for entertainment available at one's convenience. The marketers of today's microwave ovens and VCRs, to be sure, have made it possible for consumers to meet these needs in a better and cheaper way, and advertising certainly has contributed to the process. (This is the necessary condition.) But as prices for these products have declined over time, and as consumers' incomes have risen, consumers' attitudes—their value judgments—toward the products have changed.[19] Their freely reckoned evaluations no longer declare the products to be luxuries, but gradually over time to be necessities. (This is the sufficient condition.) Far from being passive receptacles that respond in knee-jerk fashion to advertising, consumers' minds actively perceive the changing facts of the marketplace and then evaluate them. Over time, luxuries become necessities.[20]

In any event, the critics here usually are thinly disguised elitists who cannot tolerate the fact that advertising, marketing, and capitalism very rapidly turn the expensive toys of the select few into everyday comforts of the masses. Luxuries, in a progressing, capitalistic economy, rapidly become necessities. The poor, it turns out, get richer, and the rich—either in wealth or in ideology—unfortunately in today's intellectual climate become less tolerant.

FRAUD, PUFFERY, AND THE FEDERAL TRADE COMMISSION

But, the critics continue—they cannot be faulted for lack of polemical energy—what about the alleged widespread use of deception and fraud by today's advertisers, as is implied by the first form of the "coercive power" criticism that charges advertising with being inherently deceptive and manipulative?

Honesty Sells

Let me just say this: the first principle of good advertising is "the primacy of the product"—that is, without a good product, you have nothing—but the second principle is "honesty sells." In the nineteenth century, advertising agents told their clients: "Let's try honesty for a change" as a means of increasing sales and profits.[21] And an advertising agent, by publishing in 1869 the first directory of American newspapers, single-handedly brought a halt to the common practice of exaggerating newspaper circulation, sometimes by as much as five times the true figure. This agent, needless to say, made money selling his directory.[22]

In short, the free market makes honesty profitable. In a truly free, laissez-faire economy, all sellers are exposed equally, without protection, to the value judgments of consumers. In such a contest the more rational—meaning the more explicitly consistent and honest seller—will win; consumers will see with their own eyes and minds the sharp contrast between the honest and dishonest. They will see the dishonest sellers for what they are: promisors of false value, fakers of reality. Consequently, they will give their business to the more honest sellers—the ones who, to use a practitioner cliché, "promise only what they can deliver" and "deliver what they promise." In this way, the free market moves sellers to ever higher levels of honesty.

In a less-than-free, interventionist economy, however, such as we have today, someone else's judgment—a bureaucrat's—interferes with the consumer's ability to evaluate sellers. The bureaucrat has now stamped certain sellers as "good" and "honest," according to some minimum standard established by the regulatory authority. The sellers no longer have to strive to maintain the highest levels of consistency and honesty—because they have already met the minimum standards. The picture now is clouded—the sharp contrast is gone—and the consumer's power of judgment has been undercut; in this way, the hampered market degenerates to lower and lower levels of mediocrity and, in the case of advertising, to lower and lower levels of puffery, sophistry, or just plain empty advertising.[23]

During pre-capitalist times—prior to the Industrial Revolution—lies, deception, and trickery were commonly associated, fairly or unfairly, with the practice of horse trading. With the advent of capitalism and, especially, of media advertising, which economist George Reisman equates to posting a surety bond with the public,[24] honesty and trust in business relationships became normal. To the extent that we are now moving back toward a more primitive society, dishonesty and distrust—the practices of horse trading—naturally follow. The relationship between honesty and capitalism can be seen today by comparing the somewhat capitalistic United States with the noncapitalistic Third World countries. An appropriate symbol of this difference is the use of packaged goods and brand names. American consumers trust what the marketers say is in the packages; Third World consumers do not, and to this day do their buying by visual inspection.

Fraud, Puffery, and Sophistry

What about the alleged deception and fraud? First of all, public prosecution by the Federal Trade Commission (FTC) does not mean that an advertiser deceives and defrauds consumers. As with most antitrust cases, prosecution by the FTC likely represents public crucifixion of an innocent businessman.

Fraud and the FTC. Fraud, as defined by the common law of deceit, involves the following five conditions: the communication of a false material fact; knowledge on the part of the deceiver that the fact is false; intention to deceive; reliance on the part of the victim that the statement was true; and objective injury or damages to the victim. These conditions indicate that the mere falseness of a statement or a statement that misleads—without the other four conditions being present—does not violate individual rights. The FTC, however, dispenses with the knowledge and intent conditions and de facto assumes injury if a fact *may be* construed by the consumer to be false or misleading. I emphasize the words "may be" because the FTC only has to show a tendency or capacity to deceive to win its cases. And it is the five commissioners who decide whether or not the consumer may be deceived. In recent years, consumer surveys have been conducted to support the commissioners' decisions, but as few as 14 percent of the consumers surveyed need construe an ad to be false or misleading before the commission declares it deceptive.[25]

Prior to the 1970s, the commission established a standard of deception based on what an "average consumer" would find deceptive. In the 1970s, the activist FTC liberalized the "average consumer" standard to the "apparently naive and uncritical consumer" and, eventually, in the late sev enties, to the "ignorant, unthinking, credulous, and gullible consumer." Deception is not difficult to prove when you have such a standard.[26]

Suffice it to say that everything that can be said about antitrust laws in general can be said in specific about the rulings of the Federal Trade Commission. Namely, they are instances of nonobjective law and represent prior restraint; therefore, they are immoral and unconstitutional because they violate individual rights.[27]

Puffery. Either puffery or sophistry, but not fraud, is the worst I would say about only a small portion of today's advertising—and much of that is encouraged by the nonobjective nature of the law. Puffery is extravagant praise. It is the combination of exaggeration and evaluation. The surest sign of puffery in advertising is the use of superlatives: best, finest, greatest, most wonderful product on earth, and so forth. Often, the word "we" is omnipresent in such advertising, which practitioners call "brag and boast" advertising. Hence: "*We* [patting themselves on the back] are the best, finest, most wonderful."

Puffery is not a form of rational persuasion. Nor is it *effective advertising*. The joke about puffery is that it is on the puffers! As advertising man David Ogilvy puts it, "Facts will always outsell flatulent puffery." How does he know? He relies on years of research that have tested factual ads against puff-filled ads, using coupon and direct mail advertising as the means to generate measurable responses; the factual ones always—to this day—outpull the ones filled with puffery.[28] The more fundamental explanation is that rational beings respond more favorably to reasoned, factual arguments than to fallacious exaggerations and evaluations; consumers naturally want to know exactly what they are being asked to buy. Only facts can give us that needed information.[29] Indeed, the principle "the more you tell, the more you sell" is one that all good copywriters follow. The evaluation of facts in good advertisements is left to the consumer.[30]

Puffery, or "seller's puff," as the courts refer to it, is (and ought to be) legal because exaggerated opinions do not state specific facts; statements of puff, therefore, can be neither true nor false.[31] The concept of puffery, however, is not well understood. Although it is a species of sophistry, the concept has been extended improperly to cover legitimate, rational persuasion. A marketing textbook, for example, refers to the following as puffery: "Coca-Cola is the real thing," "Our gasoline puts a tiger in your tank," and "Our weight reduction plan is easy."[32] And for decades, the critics of advertising have castigated the cosmetics industry for its alleged puffery and sophistry in describing tubes of congealed castor oil and wax (lipstick) as "Moonbeam Enchantment."

Sophistry. None of the four examples above, however, is puffery or sophistry. Sophistry is the use of fallacious reasoning in the process of making an argument. An example of sophistry (which also is not puffery) would be an ad that uses what practitioners call "borrowed interest"—the use of something that has inherent interest, such as a cute puppy or child, or a sexy model, to promote a product. But the interest—the puppy or child—is unrelated to the product. The specious reasoning is, in effect: "Buy our printing press because of the sexy model sitting on top of it."[33]

The slogan "Coke is the real thing" is a statement of material fact, that Coca-Cola is *the* original cola and not an imitation. The "tiger in the tank" is a *metaphor* for a material fact—the ingredients in the gasoline that will give your car more power.[34] At this point, let me pause to ask an impertinent question: do the people who equate these slogans to puffery know how to use their conceptual faculties? Can they abstract from the literal-mindedness that their statements imply? Apparently not.[35] Continuing: the "ease" of the weight-reduction plan implies that it will not be torturously difficult to follow, as some can be. Further, the ad says nothing about absolving consumers of the need for will power—and consumers well know that will power is a major part of the battle in weight reduction.

Indeed, the critics of advertising dispense completely with the fact that man possesses a conceptual consciousness when they deny the validity of image-creation advertising for such products as cosmetics, fragrances, and beverages. The two words "Moonbeam Enchantment" evoke a pleasant emotion in consumers who buy that particular lipstick; the words do so because consumers place value on the image projected by the associations connected with the two words. The emotion is evoked by the tube of congealed castor oil and wax—*and the brand name*. Both causes are real. Consumers respond to and buy both. The castor oil and wax are the product's features; the moonbeam enchantment (the emotional image) is the benefit. The emotion, to be sure, is intangible, but rational beings are quite capable of perceiving and acquiring intangible, psychological values.[36]

FTC: No Protector of Consumers. Earlier, I said that much of the puffery and sophistry that exists today is encouraged by the nonobjective nature of the law governing advertising. If your ads must not be misinterpreted by the "ignorant, unthinking, credulous, and gullible consumer" or your copywriters must comply with up to thirty-four regulations governing what legally may be said to children, advertisements over time are likely to contain fewer and fewer facts. The Federal Trade Commission, consequently, hardly can be viewed as a watchdog capable of protecting the consumer; rather, it is more like a pit bull that chases away sincere attempts at informative, factual advertising.

In a free market, no marketer or advertiser can survive without two values: favorable word-of-mouth communication and repeat purchasers. The source of these values is a quality product and honest dealings; they add up to what is usually called good will or a favorable reputation.[37] In a free market, it is the competition for a high-quality reputation that protects consumers from unscrupulous advertisers and salesmen. An excellent reputation is one of the highest values a marketer can achieve—and it takes years to earn, by satisfying customers repeatedly through honest dealings and quality products. The FTC (and other regulatory agencies) undermine the efforts of honest marketers by putting all advertisers—honest and dishonest—on the same footing; the regulations make all honest advertisers seem equally suspect and all dishonest ones, who meet the minimal standards, equally respectable.

Thus, the consumer under regulation—in comparison to under a free market—faces the more difficult task of trying to distinguish the two types of advertiser. Indeed, under regulation all incentive to strive for more rigorously honest and factual advertising has been removed. If the seal of approval from the FTC has already been stamped on advertising, why bother to improve? The regulations, which when adopted by the FTC were considered minimum standards, now have become maximums. Add to this the regulations that force advertisers to avoid misleading the "ignorant, unthinking, credulous, and gullible consumer," and the *rational* consumer now must pay for the "FTC watchdog" by suffering increasing amounts of puffery, sophistry, and just plain empty advertising.[38]

I said "much of" the puffery and sophistry that appears in the advertising we see today is encouraged by the regulations, but not all of it. One agency executive disputed the often heard "client's lament": "Half my advertising's wasted; the trouble is, I don't know which half."[39] The executive said the more correct slogan should be: "Half the people who work in advertising don't know what good advertising is!" I agree with this latter statement, because much of the puffery and sophistry that appear in advertisements today are put there deliberately by advertising people, thinking that it is good advertising.[40]

Much of the puffery and sophistry, however, comes from smaller advertisers who either try to do their advertising themselves (and do not know what good advertising is) or hire smaller, less competent agencies. The top agencies—and top advertisers—do know what good advertising is. Some people point to the winners of awards as examples of good advertising, but top agencies and advertisers know that all an award means is that the advertisement has won a popularity contest. Effectiveness at selling the product is the purpose of advertising, and the communication of a unique selling proposition is the standard by which advertisements are judged objectively.[41]

Advertising to Children. Because advertising does not possess the coercive power the critics say it does, it cannot force products upon the poor, helpless children of the world. Indeed, under the common law that protects minors, children are hardly helpless. In most states, minors can void a purchase at their election, even after they reach the age of adulthood and even if they committed fraud in the process of acquiring the product as a minor. The adult seller, however, is bound to his commitment.

In this issue, it is important to distinguish the advertisement—a mere statement of words—from the action of a sale and purchase. Selling a product to a child without the parent's consent or contrary to the parent's wishes constitutes a violation of the *parent's rights*. Parents are responsible for their children, for raising them to the age of adulthood; they are responsible for what their children eat, what they wear, what they do before and after school—and what they watch on television and buy in stores. If parents do not like what their children are watching on television, then it is their responsibility to turn off the set. If parents do not like or approve of what their children are buying, it still is their responsibility to veto such behavior.

However, if parents make it known to a seller that they do not wish to have certain products sold to their children, then the parents may have legal recourse—but it is legal recourse as a violation of their (the parents') rights, not the child's. And a rational court of law, no doubt, would throw out as frivolous those cases involving the sale of bubble gum and sugared cereal; what this issue revolves around is the sale of dangerous products, such as poisons or guns, or big-ticket items, such as automobiles or grand pianos. The sale of the latter items brings in the minor's right to void any such purchase. Children, through their parents and their own rights as minors, are thoroughly protected under the common law.

What children are not protected from, however, are the words of other people—words of their parents, their teachers, their friends and relatives, and the words of television programs and advertisements. Yes, words can be harmful, but mere statements of words—provided they do not constitute fraud (or libel and slander)—do not violate individual rights. Therefore, the mere statement of words, including statements used in advertisements, should be free of legal restraint. And, in the list of other people above whose words can potentially harm children, I daresay that the words of television programs and advertisements are dead last in a rating of potential harm.

Objective Law. In a free-market, capitalistic society, the only legitimate, *objective* protection of everyone's—marketers' and consumers'—individual rights in connection with advertising is the respect for, and enforcement of, the common law against fraud. The five stringent conditions—false material fact, knowledge, intent, reliance, and injury—that must be demonstrated to prove fraud are properly stringent in order to make and keep the law *objective*.[42] Anything less than that turns both marketers and consumers into victims of subjective law, that is, of "rule by men" rather than of "rule by law." Anything less than a stringent, objective law to protect the freedom of speech turns advertising into a pawn of the government censors. It establishes the principle that the government has the right to regulate the flow of information in society. Anything less than the stringent conditions of common law fraud establishes the principle that censorship is legal

NOTES

1. "Subliminal Ad Tactics: Experts Still Laughing," *Marketing News*, March 15, 1985, 6–7.

2. Wilson Bryan Key, *Subliminal Seduction: Ad Media's Manipulation of a Not So Innocent America* (New York: New American Library, 1973), 3–10.

3. David H. Freedman, "Why You Watch Some Commercials—Whether You Mean to or Not," *TV Guide*, February 20, 1988, 3–7.

4. Invalid concepts are "words that represent attempts to integrate errors, contradictions or false propositions. . . . An invalid concept invalidates every proposition or process of thought in which it is used as a cognitive assertion." Ayn Rand, *Introduction to Objectivist Epistemology*, expanded 2d ed., ed. Harry Binswanger and Leonard Peikoff (New York: New American Library, 1990), 49.

5. Timothy E. Moore, "Subliminal Advertising: What You See Is What You Get," *Journal of Marketing* 46 (Spring 1982): 38–47.

6. Wilson Bryan Key's motivation certainly must be questioned. His books provide no evidence whatsoever that advertisers deliberately retouch photographs, of which he accuses them in the sex-in-the-ice-cubes example. "He asks his students to describe their *feelings*," he told one advertising professor some years ago. Key's research, according to this professor, "was conducted using his students at the University of Western Ontario—but *none*, Mr. Key says, ever 'discovered any of the subliminal details in the advertisement.' Of course, with Mr. Key's expert 'guidance,' all soon are able to 'see' the objects he points out." Jack Haberstroh, "Can't Ignore Subliminal Ad Charges," *Advertising Age*, September 17, 1984, 44. Emphasis in original.

7. Ayn Rand, "The Objectivist Ethics," in *The Virtue of Selfishness: A New Concept of Egoism* (New York: New American Library, 1964), 27–30; Aaron T. Beck, *Cognitive Therapy and the Emotional Disorders* (New York: New American Library, 1976).

8. George A. Miller and Robert Buckhout, *Psychology: The Science of Mental Life*, 2d ed. (New York: Harper and Row, 1973), 99–100.

9. Graham Reed, *The Psychology of Anomalous Experience: A Cognitive Approach*, rev. ed. (Buffalo, NY: Prometheus Books, 1988), 105–111, 166–167; Vernon M. Neppe, *Psychology of Déjà Vu: Have I Been Here Before?* (Johannesburg: Witwatersrand University Press, 1983), 18, 63–65.

10. Whether the use of sexual innuendo constitutes effective advertising or not is a different issue. "The test is *relevance*. To show bosoms in a detergent advertisement would not sell the detergent. Nor is there any excuse for the sexy girls you sometimes see draped across the hoods in automobile advertisements. On the other hand, there is a *functional* reason to show nudes in advertisements for beauty products." David Ogilvy, *Ogilvy on Advertising* (New York: Crown Publishers, 1983), 25–26. Emphasis in original. Critics who raise sex as an issue in advertising are showing their colors as advocates of the mind/body dichotomy: they think sex is too earthly and profane to be flaunted in advertisements. See ibid., 26–30, for examples of the *tasteful* and *relevant* use of sex in advertisements.

11. Martha Rogers, "Subliminal Advertising: The Battle of the Popular Versus the Scholarly," in Stanley C. Hollander and Terrence Nevett, eds. *Marketing in the Long Run* (Lansing: Michigan State University Press, 1985), 69–82.

12. I cannot bring myself to comment in the text on the ever-popular "subliminal learning tapes." My students, however, always mention them. Consequently, I feel obliged to report the standard answer I give my students: I have not yet met any students who have become geniuses by listening to subliminal learning tapes, especially while sleeping!

13. Edwin A. Locke, "Behaviorism and Psychoanalysis: Two Sides of the Same Coin," *The Objectivist Forum* (February 1980): 12–13.

14. Edwin A. Locke, "The Contradiction of Epiphenomenalism," *British Journal of Psychology* (1966): 204. Cf. Leonard Peikoff, *Objectivism: The Philosophy of Ayn Rand* (New York: Penguin Books, 1991), 69–72.

15. Rand, "The Objectivist Ethics," 18–22; Peikoff, *Objectivism*, 55–69.

16. F. A. Hayek, "The *Non Sequitur* of the 'Dependence Effect,'" *Southern Economic Journal* (April 1961): 346–48.

17. John Kenneth Galbraith, *American Capitalism* (Boston: Houghton Mifflin, 1956), 97.

18. Jean Boddewyn, "Galbraith's Wicked Wants," *Journal of Marketing* (October 1961): 14–18. Cf. George Reisman, "The Revolt against Affluence: Galbraith's Neo-Feudalism," *Human Events*, February 3, 1961.

19. This condition—declining prices and rising incomes—occurs only in a *progressing*, predominantly capitalistic economy, one in which the proportion of capital investment is greater than that of consumption; this greater proportion of capital investment leads to increased innovation and, consequently, to an increased productivity of labor. The increased productivity of labor, in turn, leads to lower costs and prices. Over time, real income rises. See George Reisman, "Classical Economics Versus the Exploitation Theory," in Kurt R. Leube and Albert H. Zlabinger, eds., *The Political Economy of Freedom: Essays in Honor of F. A. Hayek* (Munich: Philosophia Verlag, 1985), 207–25; idem., *Capitalism: A Treatise on Economics*, forthcoming.

20. This process, it must be emphasized, occurs only in an economy in which businessmen enjoy sufficient freedom to save their profits and to reinvest them in further cost-saving innovations. In the Dark and Middle Ages, in which freedom was scarce and capital consumption high, luxuries remained luxuries. Only under capitalism—or the remnant of capitalism that is left in the twentieth century—can we experience the rapid decline in real prices and progression of luxuries to necessities.

21. This statement has been attributed to various advertising agents in the 1880s. The client usually was a merchant, asking the advertising man what new could be done in their advertising. Frank Presbrey, *The History and Development of Advertising* (Garden City, NY: Doubleday, 1929; reprint, New York: Greenwood Press, 1968), 303.

22. Ibid., 275. The publication was George P. Rowell's *American Newspaper Directory*.

23. These last two paragraphs are an application of Ayn Rand's statement: "When opposite basic principles are clearly and openly defined, it works to the advantage of the rational side; when they are not clearly defined, but are hidden or evaded, it works to the advantage of the irrational side." Ayn Rand, "The Anatomy of Compromise," in *Capitalism: The Unknown Ideal* (New York: New American Library, 1966), 145.

24. Reisman, *Capitalism*.

25. For example, see *Benrus Watch Co.*, 352 F.2d 313 (8th cir. 1965).

26. This 1970s "activism" of the FTC was begun in 1969 by the Republicans; Nixon appointee Casper Weinberger was the first activist FTC chairman. Kenneth W. Clarkson and Timothy J. Muris, "The Federal Trade Commission: Letting Competition Serve Consumers," Law and Economics Center, University of Miami (LEC Working Paper #81–2,n.d.), 8. In less recent history, of course, it was the Republicans who gave us antitrust laws in the first place.

27. For the philosophic critique of antitrust laws, see Ayn Rand, "America's Persecuted Minority: Big Business," in *Capitalism*, 44–62. For an economic critique, see Dominick T. Armentano, *Antitrust and Monopoly: Anatomy of a Policy Failure* (New York: John Wiley and Sons, 1982). See Lowell Mason, *The Language of Dissent* (Cleveland: World Publishing, 1959), 162–86, for examples, as discussed by a former FTC commissioner, of the nonobjective nature of administrative laws applied to advertising.

The Constitutional argument against regulatory agencies, as far as I am concerned, still stands—namely, that the mere existence of administrative agencies is a violation of the separation of powers clause of the Constitution; combined in one agency are the executive, legislative, and judicial functions of government. "Extensive exercise of the three distinct powers are placed in the same hands, with the result that instead of the greatest practical separation we have a most impracticable union of powers. It is this precise thing that the framers of the Constitution quite unanimously agreed was the very definition of tyranny." Ward E. Lattin, *Federal Administrative Regulatory Agencies and the Doctrine of the Separation of Powers* (Washington, DC: Georgetown University Press, 1938), 27.

28. "Very few advertisements contain enough factual information to sell the product. There is a ludicrous tradition among copywriters that consumers aren't interested in facts. Nothing could be further from the truth. Study the copy in the Sears, Roebuck catalogue; it sells a billion dollars' worth of merchandise every year by giving *facts*." David Ogilvy, *Confessions of an Advertising Man* (1963; reprint, New York: Atheneum, 1980), 95–96. Emphasis in original. To review the research in this area, see John Caples, *Tested Advertising Methods*, 4th ed. (Englewood Cliffs, NJ: Prentice-Hall, 1982).

29. This is another application of, or rather perspective on, Ayn Rand's principle quoted above in note 23.

30. Cf. the "new ways of praise and criticism" advocated by child psychologist Haim G. Ginott in *Between Parent and Child: New Solutions to Old Problems* (New York: Avon Books, 1965), 43–59. The general principle—whether you are trying to sell products to consumers or trying to raise a mentally healthy child—is: describe the facts and let the other person (customer or child) draw the evaluative conclusion.

31. In some cases, apparent puffery can be both factual and true. Advertisements for the Ford Escort for many years claimed that it was the "best-selling" car in the world. A footnote in the ad explained exactly what was meant by "best-selling": largest number of cars of one model sold worldwide.

32. Louis W. Stern and Thomas L. Eovaldi, *Legal Aspects of Marketing Strategy: Antitrust and Consumer Protection Issues* (Englewood Cliffs, NJ: Prentice-Hall, 1984), 375.

33. And sophistry is *not* effective advertising; facts, also, will outsell flatulent sophistry. Humor that distracts the consumer from grasping and remembering the selling message of an advertisement is sophistry. The "disease called entertainment" is how Ogilvy describes it.

34. Yes, it is exaggeration, but only in the sense of hyperbole, which is a figure of speech not intended to be taken literally. This usage of metaphor in advertising is a direct descendant of Western "tall talk." "Any Western tall-talker would have been proud to call a shampoo 'Halo' or to name an automobile the 'Fury.' " Daniel J. Boorstin, *The Americans: The Democratic Experience* (New York: Vintage Books, 1974), 145.

Speaking of the nineteenth-century American experience, Boorstin states: "In America, the word 'tall' meant not only high or lofty, but 'unusual,' 'remarkable,' or 'extravagant.' And these were precisely the distinctions of the American experience. No language could be American unless it was elastic enough to describe the unusual as if it were commonplace, the extravagant as if it were normal. The extravagance of the American experience and the inadequacy of the traditional language made tall talk as necessary a vehicle of the expansive age of American life as the keelboat or the covered wagon. . . . Tall talk described the penumbra of the familiar. It blurred the edges of fact and fiction." Daniel J. Boorstin, *The Americans: The National Experience* (New York: Vintage Books, 1965), 290.

"Booster talk," the language of anticipation, as Boorstin discusses it, is closer to puffery. Yet, considering the context of rapid innovation and progress throughout nineteenth-century America, even "booster talk" seems excusable. Speaking of this "language of anticipation," Boorstin states: "Now, especially in the booming West, men acquired a habit of innocent overstatement. . . . To describe the American habit as simply the 'glorification of the commonplace' misses something peculiarly American. As tall talk confused fact and fiction in interestingly uncertain proportions, so booster talk confused present and future. . . . Free to name as they pleased, Americans often cast their nomenclature in the mold of their hopes." Ibid., 296–97. Thus, towns were called cities, colleges were hailed as universities, and "ramshackle, flea-bitten inns and taverns" were described as hotels. "Americans thought they were not exaggerating but only anticipating—describing things which had not quite yet 'gone through the formality of taking place.' These were not misrepresentations but optimistic descriptions." Ibid., 297. Such is the experience of rapid progress under capitalism.

35. This literal-mindedness of the critics of advertising is precisely what led me, as a first clue, to conclude that the attacks, at root, are on man's conceptual level of consciousness.

36. Fragrances and beverages are special cases, because they appeal directly, and only, to our senses of smell and taste. Either we like the smell or taste, or we do not. The physical function that these products perform for us is extremely limited: fragrances make us smell nice; beverages quench our thirst and provide minimal nutritional benefit. Beyond that, fragrances and beverages predominantly perform for us a *psychological* function, by appealing directly to our conceptual faculties—in the form of an image created by the advertising (much as a novelist evokes an image through skillful, descriptive writing)—and thus by appealing to our emotions. The advertising of such products, therefore, is almost entirely image advertising, and differentiation is achieved through the creation of a specific image.

Consider the case of fine jewelry. Ornamentation is the only physical or functional value that we experience when we buy and wear it. The real benefit, however, that we receive from fine jewelry is psychological; it is the feeling of pride—a sense of oneself, especially the sense that "I am worthy of such extravagance." Among close friends, especially those involved in romantic relationships, the giving and receiving of jewelry take on an even greater psychological meaning. Image advertising simply attempts to capture and communicate these psychological moments.

37. Alan Greenspan, "The Assault on Integrity," in Ayn Rand, *Capitalism*, 118–21.

38. Financial advertising—because it is so highly regulated not only by the FTC but also by the Securities and Exchange Commission—is the best example of "just plain empty advertising." The toaster oven giveaway ads for new bank branch openings come to mind, as well as the "tombstone" ads—so called because tombstones are what they look like—of new security issues. The semi-deregulatory climate of recent years has allowed banks to practice product development and some degree of freedom in pricing; consequently, the toaster ovens have given way in bank advertising to price wars over certificates of deposit. Still, it is difficult to produce informative advertising when regulations do not permit you to say anything.

39. The origin of this statement has been attributed to various businessmen, most commonly John Wanamaker in the United States and Lord Leverhulme in England.

40. Let us not leave this discussion without reminding ourselves that advertising does not hold a monopoly on puffery, sophistry, or misleading and deceptive communication. The content of political speeches and political advertising is so boringly accepted today as such that mention of it seldom raises an eyebrow. However, let me challenge the reader to look more closely at the headlines of such newspapers as the *New York Times* and *Wall Street Journal*, and compare their messages to the content of the articles. I think you will find—occasionally, not always, as is the case with advertising—a certain amount of discrepancy between the two; you will also, no doubt, find some puffery and sophistry in each publication. This, incidentally, should not be too surprising, because reporters and advertising copywriters learn their skills in the same schools of journalism.

41. Indeed, it is notorious in the advertising industry that award-winning advertisements are poor salesmen. See Caples, *Tested Advertising Methods*, 31–33.

42. Indeed, an advertisement almost never can be fraudulent, primarily because in contract law an advertisement is not an offer to make a contract, only an invitation to make the offer. A salesman, however, can commit common law fraud.

Chapter 4

THE ALLEGED OFFENSIVENESS OF ADVERTISING

Advertising is offensive. This, in essence, is the second "social" criticism of advertising.

Frequent targets of this charge are Mr. Whipple and his Charmin bathroom tissue commercials, the "ring around the collar" commercials of Wisk liquid detergent, and the Noxzema "take it all off" shaving cream ads. Advertising, in other words, allegedly offends the consumer's sense of good taste by insulting and degrading his intelligence. Further, advertising promotes low- and poor-quality products and encourages harmful and immoral behavior. Worst of all, the critics assert, it promotes products like cigarettes, beer, and pornographic literature that have no redeeming moral value. Advertising, therefore, because it promotes harmful and immoral products and encourages harmful and immoral behavior, is itself immoral.

In its early stages, the criticism does not attribute the power of physical force to advertising. However, because of their underlying intrinsicism, the critics frequently equate their tastes to moral values and their moral values to alleged rights deserving legal protection from the "coercive" power of advertising. Thus, in its final stages, the "offensiveness" charge collapses to one or both forms of the first "social" criticism.

THE MORAL ISSUE

Advertising allegedly is offensive to good taste.

What unites all advocates of this criticism is their lack of explicit discussion and especially definition of the concepts "taste" and "good taste." Even more significantly, they fail to discuss the relationship between these two concepts and morality, because their intrinsicism does not permit them to see the essential difference between tastes and moral values. What complicates matters when discussing this criticism is that today's intellectual climate is one of subjectivism, in which all tastes and values are said to be optional, that is, subjective. Although the critics may be subjectivists in other areas of their lives, they are intrinsicists when it comes to advertising. Intrinsicism is a doctrine that denies the existence of rational options.

Let me begin this discussion, then, by asking: *what is taste?*

Tastes Are Morally Optional Values

Literally, in the physiological sense, tastes are the sensations we experience when something comes into contact with our tongues. For example, my taste for hamburger is quite strong—equally as strong as my distaste for liver. More generally, tastes are concrete values that are morally optional. They are concrete in the sense that they are evaluations of perceptually given concrete objects, such as items of food, articles of clothing, or pieces of furniture; they also can be evaluations of perceptually given concrete actions, such as playing basketball, taking leisurely drives in one's car, or eating dinner in a fine restaurant (as opposed to, say, eating dinner at home or in a coffee shop). Tastes *qua* values hold for us no wider significance than the emotional associations we experience during their acquisition and use.

Tastes are morally optional, according to a rational standard of ethics, in the sense that they are discretionary, rather than universal, necessary, or obligatory, as are moral values. What one man pursues as a taste is not a moral requirement for all men to pursue; or, to put this another way, no one man's tastes can claim moral superiority over any other's. While productive work is a universal moral value, and all men must pursue it in order to survive, whether I *ought* to prefer hamburger or liver is entirely optional.[1] Many of our tastes are acquired in early childhood and remain with us without change for a lifetime. Remembering that these values are just tastes—when, say, meeting another person from a different background than one's own—can help prevent us from making inappropriate moral evaluations.

For example, I learned to drive an automobile at the age of fourteen in the wide-open spaces of the midwestern United States. Today, consequently, I prefer driving cars to taking subways, buses, and other forms of mass transportation, because I still fondly recall the emotional associations connected with "taking drives" (on a Sunday afternoon, for instance); in other words, I find driving to be relaxing. A lifelong New Yorker, however, might have different tastes—and might not even have a driver's license. This last, to me, evokes the initial emotional reaction: "He's crazy." However, when I calmly examine the rational standard of mental health (and ethics), I have to admit that the New Yorker's tastes are not warped. His tastes can be explained—to be sure, tastes have causes—but my tastes do not have to be adopted by everyone. This is what it means to say that "tastes are optional."

This also, I submit, is the correct meaning of the Latin proverb "*de gustibus non est disputandum,*" commonly translated as "tastes are not disputable" or "there is no disputing about taste."[2] There is no disputing about tastes in the physiological sense because all foods—as opposed to poisons—are right and good for us. Our taste for any one particular food is optional. Hence, I like hamburger, you like liver. By extension, and provided the context is carefully defined, we can also say: I like strong sex appeals in my television commercials, you like PBS pledge breaks.[3] Our tastes in advertising are not disputable, because execution in advertising is optional.[4] However, if you think that sex appeals in television commercials are offensive, then my answer to you is: I'm sorry you feel that way, but you have your tastes and I have mine. And we each go about our own business.

Unfortunately, the critics of advertising do not stop here, because the context is never carefully defined. To them, tastes are disputable—because to them tastes and moral values are identical. Consequently, the charge against advertising mushrooms. Now advertising is offensive because it promotes immoral (tasteless) products and encourages immoral or harmful (tasteless) behavior. And the advertising itself, therefore, is immoral—that is, tasteless.

Intrinsicism. The root of this charge against advertising is the false philosophic doctrine of moral intrinsicism, or the doctrine of intrinsic value. I use the term "intrinsicism" as it has been defined by Ayn Rand. This doctrine, to repeat a quotation from chapter 2, holds that moral value, or the good

> is inherent in certain things or actions as such, regardless of their context and consequences, regardless of any benefit or injury they may cause to the actors and subjects involved. It is a theory that divorces the concept of "good" from beneficiaries, and the concept of "value" from valuer and purpose—claiming that the good is good in, by, and of itself.[5]

The Ten Commandments of the Judeo-Christian ethics are examples of moral intrinsicism. The commandment "thou shalt not lie" does not have an amendment attached to it that says "depending on context and consequences." It says the act of lying is intrinsically or inherently evil, period, meaning that if a homicidal maniac comes to your door looking for your children, your moral duty is to answer him truthfully when he asks if they are there. Thus, in the marketplace, if certain products possess value "'in, by, and of themselves," and if certain people happen to know which products are intrinsically valuable, then these people—the ones with the "good taste"—will insist that there are certain products that consumers should not need or want.

This doctrine of intrinsic value is what underlies the problem in classical economics known as the "paradox of value," the alleged paradox that gold is more highly valued by consumers than iron, although iron is more useful in production than gold. Intrinsicism is the doctrine that the Neoclassical and Austrian economists rejected when they formulated the theory of marginal utility—and, consequently, resolved the paradox of value. It also underlies the medieval notion of what was called the "just price." This is the view that prices and market value are not the result of an interaction between consumer value judgments and the products supplied by producers, that is, a result of demand and supply, but rather the result of some intrinsic quality that exists in each product.[6]

For the moral intrinsicist, value judgments are automatic because values are self-evident. If material objects possess an intrinsic value, you simply open your eyes and look at them to grasp their value. Purpose and context are irrelevant in the formation of values, and specific material objects and specific actions by their nature, according to the intrinsicist, are either moral or immoral. And the intrinsicist happens to be the one who knows which ones are which.

But there is an obvious problem. Depending on which intrinsicist you talk to, cigarettes and cigarette advertising are immoral; liquor and liquor advertising cause drunken driving and are, therefore, immoral; and the use of women, blacks, children, men, whites, Hispanics, Asians, Italians, Yuppies, golden retrievers, and even tubby tabbies—all at various times and in various advertisements have been attacked as immoral exploitation. The critics contradict one another over which ads are immoral, because they each have their own set of intrinsic values about which are the "just" goods and which are the "just" ads. The critics, of course, do not stop at calling these immoral; they obliterate the meaning of individual rights, attribute to advertising the power of physical force, and then proceed to advocate legislation to regulate such "immoral" activities.

As Ayn Rand states it, however, "material objects as such have neither value nor disvalue; they acquire value-significance only in regard to a living being—particularly, in regard to serving or hindering man's goals."[7] Any specific actions—taken out of context of the actor—have neither value nor disvalue. A Cadillac, for example, is intrinsically neither moral nor immoral. Further, the decision to purchase a Cadillac is usually not a moral issue, although it could be—if, for example, the purchaser would be starving his children to pay for the car. Needless to say, cigarettes, liquor, and cigarette and liquor advertising by themselves are neither moral nor immoral; the advertising and sale of these products do not "hinder man's goals," and they certainly do not violate anyone's rights.

The Issue of Options. The issue here is subtler than it seems at first. The moral intrinsicist denies the existence of options. Consequently, every object and action must be either moral or immoral. In fact, however, there are many choices in our lives in which morality is not an issue at all—because the morality of the issue has already been settled. A moral issue, according to Ayn Rand, is one that calls for volitional choice in a situation that has long-term consequences for one's life.[8] The decision, for example, whether a young person ought to pursue a productive career or remain living with his parents, depending for support on their income, is probably a moral issue, because of the long-run consequences on his life as an adult, rational being. But the context and purpose must be carefully specified before judging such issues. I can think of instances in which such a choice would not be a moral issue—if, say, a tragic accident rendered the youth quadraplegic.

The decision, however, of whether to drive a car to work or to take a bus is not usually a moral issue, because either choice is morally optional, that is, either way would be moral. This issue—like thousands of others we encounter in our daily lives—is one of taste. Moral values are intellectual, conceptual values that shape a man's character. Tastes are associational, perceptually based values that shape the more concrete aspects of a man's personality. Moral values are abstract and universal; tastes are concrete and individual.[9] The choice, then, of whether to buy a Big Mac or T-bone steak for dinner, or neither—contrary to what vegetarians may say—is morally optional. So too is the choice of whether to buy a Ford or Toyota—contrary to what the protectionists say. The selection of specific brands or types of goods and services in the marketplace is almost entirely a matter of moral option—that is, of taste.

Tastes (or, at least, most of them) are formed through the semiautomatic mental process of perceptual association. Moral values, on the other hand, such as honesty and integrity, are acquired (or should be acquired) through the volitional process of conceptual integration.[10] They are formed, first, through a long, deliberate process of identifying and digesting the facts of man's rational nature, specifically, the requirements of his survival and well-being; second, moral values must be applied deliberately to the concrete choices and actions of one's own life. The appraisal in moral evaluation states that a particular choice or action will benefit or harm our long-term well-being as a rational animal; making this appraisal requires that we hold in our minds the context of all our other values, including our concrete, optional values, thus requiring an enormous act of conceptual integration. The connection between our universal, moral values and our optional, concrete values? Moral values are the universal guidelines that direct an individual's choices and actions in particular situations, thus providing the means by which to distinguish what is optional from what is not.

Consider this example: I grew up using—as if it were a taste, or morally optional value—the expression "to Jew a price down." As a child and youth, I had heard the expression frequently and adopted it as a phrase that had "a nice ring to it" to describe a tough bargainer. (I knew virtually nothing about Judaism or the existence of a Jewish culture.) However, when I moved to New York City as a young adult, I noticed that whenever New Yorkers referred to bargaining or negotiation, they never used my pet expression. I eventually came to realize that my "taste" for this expression was not morally optional at all, but was an unjust insult to a much-maligned and productive group of people. By rethinking the issue, integrating the new data I had acquired in the first few months of working in New York, I came to realize that I was violating at least two of my own moral values: justice, for falsely maligning the Jewish people, and productiveness, for accepting and spreading the denigrating connotations of an expression toward normal business activity.

Conversely, I grew up thinking that alcohol consumption and gambling are morally evil. My adult moral values, however, have taught me that these two activities (when pursued in moderation) are in fact optional. Thus, the alleged tastes we acquire in childhood can sometimes turn out to be serious moral issues, and the moral values we are taught in childhood can turn out to be optional tastes.

Today it is true that almost no one makes the distinction between optional and non-optional values. On the one hand, many people say that all values are optional, which is the doctrine of subjectivism. On the other hand, many say that all values are (non-optional) *moral* values, which is the doctrine of intrinsicism. My discussion of taste and moral values, I think, indicates the complexity of the broad field of value theory, and the amount of path-breaking work that remains to be done. Suffice it to say, for the remainder of this chapter, that my tastes (or yours) do not have to be adopted by everyone.

"Good Taste" Is Discriminative Ability

This brings us to the notion of "good taste."

Taste, in this sense, is an achievement. It is the ability and willingness to make fine distinctions among similar objects according to a specified standard. Thus, a person who has good taste in wine is one who discriminates good from bad according to various criteria, such as appearance, color, smell, taste, touch, and finish. A person with poor taste cannot make such discriminations and, perhaps, does not want to learn how. In this example, however, the person with good taste is not—contrary to what some wine connoisseurs might say—morally superior to the person with poor taste, because the basic value of wine consumption is a concrete value that has no wider significance to either person's life.[11] The person with the good taste in wine is superior only in the sense of being better at evaluating wines.[12]

In determining what is, or who has, good taste, a standard must be specified. The standard may be one of morality; usually, it is not. For example, when we say that someone has "good taste in friends," we could mean that the friends have a good moral character, as evidenced, say, by their courage and integrity. More likely, however, we mean that they are attractive, good-looking people (especially if they are members of the opposite sex) or that they all like football. The latter two examples are concrete, morally optional values.

In current usage, "good taste" seems to fall into three broad categories; it can mean (1) etiquette, or manners, the standard of which is efficiency and respect in social relations, (2) beauty, the standard of which is a sense of harmony,[13] or (3) any number of miscellaneous usages, depending on the standard that is specified, such as good taste in wine or choice of friends. The statement, "The party was in such good taste," can encompass all three of these categories, meaning, for example: the host and hostess exhibited flawless etiquette, the decor of the ballroom was harmoniously integrated, and the wine at dinner was exquisite. Some critics who denounce advertising for its alleged bad taste actually are accusing the advertisers of poor etiquette, such as by advertising sexually related products at times when children are present.

All too often, however, the statement "You have good taste" simply means that your tastes match mine—without any emphasis on, or recognition of, the other person's achievement or discriminative ability; this, at best, is lazy thinking, at worst, subjectivism. Nevertheless, in almost all discussions of advertising and good taste, the most significant error committed is either the failure to specify the standard of judgment or, in the case of the critics of advertising, the assumption that all standards of good taste are moral—and, sometimes, esthetic—standards.

The Standard of Good Advertising. With this in mind, let me bring back Mr. Whipple of "Please don't squeeze the Charmin" fame, "ring around the collar," Palmolive's Madge, and any other of your "favorite" commercials. These ads, according to many people, are irritating, insulting, degrading, and repetitive to the point of torture. They are, however, good advertisements; they meet the standard and fulfill the purpose of good advertising. The standard of good advertising is the communication of what advertisers call a "unique selling proposition."[14] The Charmin ads, when they were on the air, communicated that Charmin is one of the most irresistibly, squeezably soft bathroom tissues on the market; the Wisk "ring around the collar" ads communicate that Wisk, when poured directly on tough stains, can help prevent public embarrassment.[15] The purpose of good advertising is not to irritate people, but to sell products.

   The evaluation of these ads is not a moral issue, nor is it an issue of taste, although taste frequently plays a large role in most people's judgments of advertising. If you do not like Mr. Whipple and feel resentment at these so-called irritating ads, then you are probably not a regular user of the products advertised. Regular users of a brand, as study after study has shown, tend to enjoy, or at least be more tolerant of, that brand's advertising. People who do not use a particular brand tend to find the ads offensive and irritating.

   However, your resentment of the ads—and I want to emphasize this point—is an emotion, and emotions are not causeless. Your resentment is probably based on some tastes (or optional values) that you hold about one of three things: the product itself, the personalities of the actors in the commercials, or the life-style portrayed. When I have questioned people about their reasons for disliking certain advertisements, time after time I have found one of these three causes to prevail. But dislike of certain products or certain types of people or life-styles is not the criterion by which to judge advertisements.

   The standard of good advertising is the presence of a unique selling proposition—a message about what the product is and can do for consumers—and the purpose of good advertising is to sell the product. Mr. Whipple, "ring around the collar," and Madge all did excellent jobs for their products on both counts; consequently, they must be evaluated as good advertisements. Now it is still okay to dislike Mr. Whipple, if your taste in store managers runs in a different direction. Just please do not confuse your emotional reactions to advertisements with objective judgments.[16] In this sense, it is possible to say, and not have it be a contradiction, "This is a good ad, but I don't like it."[17] Indeed, in all issues of good taste, it is not a contradiction to say: this is a good wine, a good (moral) person, a good automobile, but I don't like it (I don't like wine), him (he doesn't like football, nor does he even have a driver's license!), or it (I prefer economy cars). The distinction here is the difference between a conscious evaluation based on an explicitly identified standard and an emotional reaction based on a different, sometimes subconscious and therefore unidentified standard.

   You may, of course, dislike certain advertisements on moral grounds, even though the ads still technically can be judged good according to the standard of good advertising. Advertisements for religion fall into this category, as well as the many appeasement-oriented ads that go out of their way to make peace with the morality of altruism, with special interest groups, with government regulators, or even with communist countries, such as the People's Republic of China. Ads for seedy massage parlors and "escort" services fall into this category. So do the Calvin Klein ménage-à-trois ads. And, if such ads existed, "hit man for hire" would be immoral.

Mr. Whipple and the Wisk "ring around the collar" ads, however, do not fall into this category.

"Good Taste" in Advertising. As for Mr. Whipple: good taste is precisely what the Charmin bathroom tissue commercials achieved. Toilet paper and bathroom elimination are not pleasant subjects for anyone to discuss. Using a standard based on respect (which actually makes this an issue of good etiquette in advertising), the Charmin bathroom tissue commercials presented Charmin's selling message in a humorous, "slice-of-life" buying situation. They did not show the product in use, which by any standard would indeed be in poor taste; nor did they show the spinning of a toilet paper spool; nor did they even show a bathroom. (And the words "toilet paper" disappeared from advertising copy decades ago, because they were considered to be in poor taste.) The clever manner in which Procter and Gamble's advertising agency solved the delicate problem of communicating Charmin's softness calls for praise, not condemnation or ridicule. (An argument could be made that some of the old "ring" ads violated the standard of good etiquette, by showing a man's wife being embarrassed in front of other people, but the critics of these ads have seldom been this delimited about what offends them.)

I have spent this much time defending certain unpopular advertisements because some students of intellectual issues seem to think that, in a completely rational world, entrepreneurs would create advertisements far different from what we see today. They would not. In essentials, their ads would follow the same basic principles of good advertising as those used in the Mr. Whipple or "ring around the collar" ads, the most important being: communicate a unique selling proposition about your product, and do not let your execution upstage the selling message.

Good taste in advertising is the ability to communicate persuasively while respecting the values of man the rational being—and the specific cultural values and tastes of the target audience for whom the ads are intended. The former set of values provides the moral context of communication, while the latter provides the motivational values with which to make the communication persuasive. The principles of persuasive communication hold that communicators should appeal to these values, not just respect them; casting insults, however, will obviously work to the communicator's disadvantage.

This standard of good taste, please note, applies not only to advertisers, but also to salesmen, teachers, journalists and other writers, and public speakers. Advertisers do not hold the monopoly on good or alleged bad taste, and in a contest of who most respects the former set of values—the values of man the rational being—I would say that advertisers, given today's intellectual climate, win hands down. In a contest of the latter, advertisers again still probably win, because advertising is an institution of popular culture that thrives on appealing to its audience's cultural and optional values.[18]

The Alleged Esthetic Issue

A further error in connection with taste can be dispensed with in short order, namely, that critics insist on evaluating as if it were art. *But advertising is not art*, and it is wrong to apply the standard of good art to advertising. To be sure, certain elements of art, or tools of the artist, are used in the development of advertisements, just as certain elements of acting are used in teaching.[19] But the standard of good teaching is not acting ability. The most significant difference between art and advertising is that advertising does not project its creator's metaphysical value judgments.[20] If it does, such advertising on the face of it is *bad advertising*.[21]

Advertising's goal is to sell one specific, concrete product to a specifically defined segment of consumers, by communicating the features and benefits of the product in a way that appeals to the tastes of the consumers. Advertising's goal is to be as narrow and concrete as possible, without missing any members of its target audience. (Marketers, if they could afford it, would custom-make their products; but complete customization is impossible, so marketers develop an average product for each segment of the market. As a result, not everyone in the world is a prospect for any given marketer's product.[22]) The goal of art is to project fundamental values that apply to all of mankind, regardless of time, place, or culture. Advertising and art, in this sense, are like night and day.

The Issue of Product Quality

An issue that requires more extensive discussion is the relationship between product quality and taste.

Critics often fail to distinguish the quality of an advertisement from the quality of the product advertised. Thus, they see an ad for a low-quality product (usually one they themselves do not like or use) and conclude that the advertising also is of low quality. Worst of all, critics sometimes equate low quality to immorality and, therefore, charge advertisers with promoting immoral products. Other times, they assert that certain products, regardless of their quality, are immoral and, therefore, so too is the product's advertising. Let me now discuss the nature of product quality and its relationship to moral values and taste.

Product quality is the degree to which a product meets the needs and wants of the consumers for whom it is intended. To evaluate which product in a given category has the higher quality, we must identify the needs and wants that are being addressed. For example, Henry Ford's Model T automobile for many years satisfied the need of economical transportation. But in 1927, General Motors recognized that the consumers' wants—that is, their optional values or tastes—can be as important as their universal, physical needs.[23] Henry Ford said, "You can have any color car you want as long as it's black." General Motors replied, "We have a car for every taste, a price for every pocketbook." In this competition, General Motors won—because GM had the higher quality products.

In an automobile, color is not a frivolous, subjective feature to be dismissed from consideration in judging product quality. Nor is it frivolous if an automobile has the ability to evoke a sense of status or prestige in its owner, comfort, a sense of moving up in the world, or any number of other intangible, psychological emotions that products can arouse.[24] Intangible, psychological benefits are as objective—in the sense that they are real, they exist—as such tangible and precisely measurable physical features and benefits as economy, durability, craftsmanship, and performance. The difference is that the range of psychological benefits that a particular product might possess is wider than the range of its physical features and physical benefits; further, psychological benefits cannot be measured as precisely as physical features and benefits.[25]

Judging product quality can be challenging, because four conditions must be specified before an evaluation can be made: (1) the relevant product category must be defined—that is, we must be certain we are not comparing apples to oranges; (2) the universal need the product is trying to meet must be identified—yes, food is a universal need, but so is protein, so are pleasure and friendship, so are novelty and variety, and so forth; (3) the optional wants or tastes of consumers, which play a much larger role in product quality than most people realize, also must be identified; and (4) price must be either held constant or brought explicitly into the discussion.[26]

Social Value vs. Philosophical Value. Price, or economic value, is an expression of what Rand identifies as "socially objective value," "the sum of the individual judgments of all the men involved in trade at a given time, the sum of what *they* valued, each in the context of his own life."[27] This idea subsumes an additional, closely related concept: market value. Market value—as distinct from price—is the relative ranking of one product to another. For example, the market today ranks romance novels more highly than the Romantic novels of the nineteenth century. The social value of, say, a Harlequin romance is higher than that of a Victor Hugo novel. Now the price of any individual romance or Romantic novel may not differ, but the market value does, because more people today want and, consequently, buy romance novels. The market value of romance novels, therefore, results in greater sales and profits.

Social value, however, is not the same as philosophical value. "Philosophically objective value" is "a value estimated from the standpoint of the best possible to man, that is, by the criterion of the most rational mind possessing the greatest knowledge, in a given category, in a given period, and in a defined context."[28] The automobile, for example, is a means of transportation that is superior to the horse and, consequently, exhibits in its relationship to man a greater philosophical value. Victor Hugo novels can also be shown to have greater philosophical value than Harlequin romances. Obviously, the philosophical value of a product may or may not coincide with its social value; in a free market, however, there is a tendency over time for philosophically valuable products to acquire greater and greater social value.[29] Philosophical value, therefore, I submit, is the root of product quality.

Rand's distinction between social and philosophical value replaces a much confused distinction in economics. Sometimes, economists distinguish between what they call "exchange value" (or price) and "noneconomic value"; other times, they distinguish between "subjective" and "objective" use value. The former distinction seems to correspond, although not exactly, to Rand's, but the latter is false, because all use value is *objective*.

Objective use value is alleged to be a product's technical or engineering features, such as the heating value of an oil furnace, as expressed in BTUs; subjective use value is alleged to be the subjective feelings we experience as a result of product use, such as the warmth one feels in an oil-heated room. An automobile, however, as indicated above in the competition between Ford and General Motors, is much more than functional transportation. It also is the source of a bundle of psychological benefits, which often, when evaluated by consumers, take the form of morally optional values or tastes. But these intangible, psychological benefits are not *subjective* use values, because they are just as *objective* as the tangible features and physical benefits of durability, performance, and craftsmanship. Objectivity and the notion of objective value require that both physical features and psychological benefits be subsumed under the concept of product quality. The relationship between features and benefits is one of cause to effect: features cause benefits.[30] Product quality is the degree to which a product possesses philosophically objective value, but this *includes* the product's so-called subjective use value.[31]

The Price/Quality Comparison. Within the category of automobiles, the latest state-of-the-art luxury sedan exhibits a greater value—or product quality—than the latest economy hatchback. This is so because technological innovations, the source of increased benefits to mankind, typically are introduced first on luxury models, later trickling down to less expensive models (also because more features—and therefore more benefits—are included on luxury models). In this context, price and quality tend to correlate because technological innovation costs more in labor and materials.

However, within the luxury car category, for example, or the hatchback category, for that matter, each brand attempts to meet the tastes—the optional values—of some specific segment of consumers. As a result of competition, both technology and price tend to equalize over time; that is, over time competitors tend to offer nearly identical technical features in their products, and they also tend to price their products approximately the same. This is an essential characteristic of what is called a "mature market." Thus, when technology and price are held constant (or are approximately equal across competitors—they are never exactly the same), one brand of automobile marketer works on, and consequently strives primarily to deliver to its customers, excellent craftsmanship, another strives primarily to deliver performance, another comfort, another status and prestige. In this way, as the consequence of competition, tastes become relevant in judging product quality. The marketer who knows the optional values of the market and delivers ahead of anyone else a product that satisfies those tastes is the marketer of a higher quality product, just as General Motors in 1927 offered a higher quality product than Ford. But competition based entirely on taste is unstable, because, as marketers well know, technical advantage produces greater profits in the long run.

Consequently, the relationship between price and quality in the above narrowly defined product categories is less certain. If one brand is priced above the average of the category, this may be the result of an added, innovative feature that the competition does not or cannot offer, one that has increased the company's costs of production. Consequently, this brand will have a higher quality than the others. If nothing of value stands behind this higher price—that is, the product quality is the same as the competition's but the price is higher anyway—then the whole price/quality package is inferior and competition eventually will drive either the price down or the product off the market.

On the other hand, if a brand is priced below the average, this may be the result of an innovation in production that has led to a decrease in costs and, consequently, to a cut in price. This brand, then, will have a price/quality package that is superior to the competition's. If the price cut results from an elimination of features or benefits that the competition offers at the higher price, then the product is inferior, but its inferiority is compensated for by the lower price. Market leaders, to complicate matters further, frequently succeed in cutting price while at the same time adding improved features, thus offering a higher quality product at a lower price.

As can be seen, evaluation of product quality is complicated, requiring careful specification of the category under discussion and the standard by which the product is to be judged. The standard is always the best possible to man, but this includes *both* technical features *and* tastes. It is a common mistake of laymen and engineers alike to equate quality with durability, craftsmanship, performance, economy, or any number of other specific product attributes that they happen to value. In a given product category, "the best possible to man" actually means the best possible to *one specific segment of men*. Some segments of automobile consumers primarily value durability, some primarily value craftsmanship, some primarily value the feeling of status and prestige their cars give them. No one technical feature or taste defines the standard of product quality for a given category; the consumers' actual needs and wants provide the means of evaluation.

Product evaluation is complicated because products are complicated—and products are complicated because consumer needs and wants are complicated. Consumers want a certain amount of durability, but they do not want too much of it if the price of the automobile must increase beyond their reach;[32] they also want comfort, status and prestige, and changes in fashion.[33] The marketer's challenge is to provide the optimum bundle of features and benefits—the optimum bundle of values—that meets these varied tastes. Frequently, there is a trade-off among the many possibilities.

Discussions of product quality among laymen often are fruitless because the above four conditions are seldom specified. One person values craftsmanship in the furniture he buys, another values durability; but the two argue for an hour before they realize they are comparing apples to oranges. Or another pair argue without realizing that one is trying to evaluate products at the same price level while the other is evaluating products at different price levels. Laymen who are unfamiliar with the product category under discussion are doomed to talking at cross-purposes. They would be more objective if they conducted their discussions by stating, for example: "I value craftsmanship in furniture, given my present context and budget. You value durability, given your present context and budget. The issue of craftsmanship vs. durability is optional, that is, is an issue of taste. You have your tastes and I have my tastes—that is why we have different furniture." The question of which furniture has the greater philosophically objective value can be answered only with a greater knowledge than these two discussants are likely to have—and the furniture may well have the same level of quality after all, although the discussants would never know it, or admit it.

Thus, at any given level of technological advancement, the marketer and advertiser work almost entirely in the realm of optional values or taste, because no product is developed to satisfy everyone's needs and wants. Every product is a unique bundle of values created specifically for one unique segment of consumer tastes. Another way of putting this is that there is "no one best" product for everyone—provided we understand that the phrase "one one best" does *not* mean "it's all subjective." There is also "no one best" advertisement for everyone, provided, again, we understand that this statement does not endorse subjectivism.

Services and Intellectual Products. The concept of "philosophically objective value" implies the existence of a value that is philosophically *subjective*—that is, a disvalue, a value that is irrational and inimical to the best possible to man. However, because values do not exist intrinsically in things or actions as such, no physical, tangible good or concrete act can be said to be evil. Even arsenic, a lethal poison, is a benefit to man when it is fed to rats, and killing another person in self-defense can be justified morally. It must be remembered that "poison" and "moral evil," and "killing" and "moral evil," are not synonymous—neither poison nor killing per se is evil.

Immorality is a volitional act that violates the principles necessary to sustain and enhance man's life as a rational being—an act that harms one's own life or undeservedly harms the lives of others. An advertisement that reads "arsenic for sale—it tastes good on your Wheaties" certainly would be immoral. But this kind of advertising—the hysteria of the environmentalists notwithstanding—does not occur today.[34] Besides, the immorality in this example is not the arsenic, but the act of the advertiser that encourages almost certain death. Indeed, because there is no such thing as intrinsic value, no *physical good* offered for sale on the market—and judged "in, by, and of itself" independently of context and purpose—can possess negative value. All goods possess more or less philosophically objective value.

Services and intellectual products, on the other hand, require special discussion, because they can possess negative philosophical value. Services are actions, labor or machine-produced activity performed for another person. Therefore, we can say that some services, because of the nature of their purpose, such as a prostitution ring or a hit man service, can be harmful to man's rational nature. And some intellectual products, such as supermarket tabloids notorious for printing falsehoods about celebrities, also can be harmful to man's rational nature. Thus, we can say, provided the context is defined carefully, that certain services and intellectual products, and, therefore, their advertising—for example, "hit man for hire"—are "inherently" immoral.

This discussion leads to the conclusion that just as we can talk about "disvalues," such as murder, so in the marketplace can we talk about negative product quality—the degree to which a product (here meaning service or intellectual product) meets the irrational and immoral desires of a segment of consumers. Presumably, there are "better," or rather more effective, hit men than others; it does not make sense, however, to say that the more effective hit man offers a "better quality" service, any more than we would rationally say that Hitler was a "better quality" dictator than Mussolini. "Disquality" is probably too cumbersome a neologism to use to describe this phenomenon; nevertheless, some concept seems necessary to indicate negative product quality.[35]

It is this concept of negative product quality that people are thinking of when they refer to a supermarket tabloid that caters to the corrupt tastes of the public. The false, scandal-mongering smears of such tabloids is not correctly described as inferior product quality; it is inferior *moral* quality. And the tastes of the public to whom the tabloid is catering are not morally optional values; "taste" in this context is being used in its moral sense. The public's tastes are corrupt, just as the publisher is who seeks to satisfy them. It is in this sense that marketers can become subjectivists, catering to the subjective tastes of the public.

A better example of this occurs in the marketing of education, education being an intellectual product. Student knowledge and skills have declined dramatically over the past decades. Educators have responded not by trying to meet the objective educational needs of students, but by giving them what their subjective tastes dictate: television (slickly produced videotapes), minimal work (usually in the form of group projects), and easy As (grade inflation). This is not just poor, but positive, product quality; it is negative product quality (disquality?) that is destroying the students' minds.

My point here is that marketers and advertisers are sometimes accused of subjectivism because they cater to the tastes of the public. I would say that this charge is justified only in some cases of services and intellectual products. In cases of physical, tangible goods—which is the area in which the charge is most often heard—I cannot imagine marketers at all catering to the irrational tastes of the public. After all, what would that entail? Food that makes you sick? (The hysteria of the environmentalists again must be ruled out.) An automobile that does not move? Consumers can, and do, buy services and intellectual products that, figuratively speaking, make them sick or do not move, for example, public education and books filled with false and immoral ideas! In the area of goods, marketers can cater to lower or higher levels of consumer tastes, but the tastes are all within the realm of morality and, consequently, are moral.

And fads, it must be stated emphatically, are neither irrational nor immoral nor worthless in any sort of way. The hula hoop and, yes, even the Pet Rock were and are *rational* values.[36]

Thus, judging product quality and a product's advertising is not an activity to be taken lightly. It certainly cannot be based on one's emotional reactions to the product or to its advertising. Objective standards, such as those discussed in this chapter, must be established and validated through a process of logical reasoning. Then, and only then, can each product and advertisement be judged, by applying the standards rigorously without the tainting influences of one's emotions.

This last the critics do not come close to achieving, because they have no inkling of objective standards.

THE LEGAL ISSUE

The critics who complain that advertising offends their tastes do not stop at criticizing. They want to regulate or make illegal what they consider offensive. They do this by elevating their tastes to the status of morality and immorality—that is, what they find to be distasteful is automatically, without further examination, assumed to be immoral, and what they find to be immoral, they maintain, ought to be regulated, taxed, or banned. Aside from the confusion of distaste with immorality, the primary question here is: what constitutes an illegal act? At what point should one draw the line between the legal and the illegal?

Acts That Initiate Physical Force Must Be Banned

According to Rand, an act should be considered illegal only when it violates individual rights, and rights are violated only by *initiating* physical force against others.[37] Rand's basic political and legal principle is: acts that initiate physical force must be banned; acts that result from the mutual consent of adults—whether moral or immoral—should be legal. The proper function of government is the protection of individual rights. "The government acts as the agent of man's right of self-defense, and may use force only in retaliation and only against those who initiate its use."[38] Thus, taking money from another person without that person's consent is the initiation of physical force; prosecuting and imprisoning the thief is the government's legitimate retaliatory use of force. The legal, consequently, is the voluntary, the contractual; the illegal is the initiation of force, or initiated coercion.

As shown in chapter 3, advertising is not coercive. Consequently, non-fraudulent advertising, including persuasive advertising, appeals to the reason and volition of consumers to obtain their voluntary consent to buy the advertiser's products. The use of persuasive advertising is just that: an appeal to consumers for their voluntary cooperation in joining together with producers to engage in contractual relations. Further, an advertisement, as stated in chapter 3, is in legal terms usually only an *invitation* to the consumer to *make an offer* to buy the seller's product; thus, an advertisement by itself is not considered a legal offer. This point makes it difficult to prosecute advertisers successfully under common law fraud—and rightly so, because advertising, contrary to what the Supreme Court says, is a form of free speech.

Since advertising is not inherently or intrinsically a form of coercion, and since it cannot get inside the heads of consumers to force them to act against their will, it cannot and does not violate the rights of consumers. The relationship between advertisers and consumers is strictly voluntary.

Censorship

In contrast, it is the critics of advertising who initiate the use of physical force—in the form of laws—against consumers by telling them what products they can or cannot buy and on what conditions they can or cannot buy them. And it is the critics who also initiate the use of physical force—in the form of laws—against producers by telling them what products they can or cannot advertise and on what conditions they can or cannot advertise them. Such government-initiated coercion—in the form of nonobjective laws—violates individual rights. It does not matter whether the laws prohibit or regulate the advertising of cigarettes, distilled liquor, presweetened cereals, or pornographic literature; if advertising is not a form of coercion, it cannot be held liable for infringing anyone's rights. On the contrary, it is the advertiser's rights and the consumer's rights that are infringed by legislation that prohibits or regulates advertising. Such legislation, in which a government action prohibits or regulates the flow of information within society, properly goes by another name, censorship. The meaning of censorship, however, and its relationship to advertising and the right of free speech are not well understood. Let me clarify the key concepts involved.

Freedom of speech presupposes property rights.[39] The right of free speech is the freedom of each individual to express himself in any form or in any medium he chooses—with or on his own property, or with or on the property of others who have voluntarily agreed to let the individual use their property as a platform on which to speak. The individual's only obligation is to refrain from defrauding, defaming, or in any other way infringing on the freedoms of others—by initiating physical force against them. Falsely yelling "fire" in a crowded theater is *not* an expression of free speech that is restricted by the "public interest"; it is criminal assault. Penalizing noisy home crowds, on the other hand, through a rule agreed upon by the owners of the National Football League, *is* an expression of the NFL owner's right of free speech, because no initiation of physical force is involved in the rules of professional football, and because both players and fans voluntarily accept the conditions of the NFL owners when they set foot on the owner's property.

Censorship is always an action *by the government* to restrict what an individual or corporation is allowed to say.[40] (And a corporation is a voluntary association of individuals.) Censorship is never a private action. It is not censorship, for example, when a privately owned publishing company refuses to print an article of mine or when a newspaper refuses to carry an advertisement its owners find offensive. A publisher's refusal to run an article or advertisement is merely the expression of his right of free speech—the publisher's right to use *his* property as a vehicle for the ideas *he* values. The difference between a governmental action and a private action is the difference between coercion and voluntary cooperation—the difference between a gun and the free market.[41]

Censorship is the government's use of its legal and regulatory authority to control the flow of information within society. An occasionally cited historical experiment vividly demonstrates how the taxation of advertising amounts to censorship. In 1712, a tax was imposed on newspapers and newspaper advertising in Great Britain; it was initially imposed to control seditious libel but was continued for 141 years to raise revenue for the license bureau. At the time it was imposed, Britain's annual newspaper circulation was 2.5 million, the American colonies at the time had only 1 newspaper (3 in 1719, 25 in 1765). In 1853, when the law was abolished, Britain had a population of 27 million people, but only 500 newspapers with an annual circulation of 91 million; the United States, in contrast, which had enjoyed a free market in newspaper publishing throughout the period, had a population of 23 million, but 2,300 newspapers with an annual circulation of 423 million. The Stamp Act of 1765 was the only time, until recently, that a tax was imposed in the United States on media and media advertising—and that led ultimately to a certain tea party in Boston, followed by a violent revolution![42]

Advertising—the Supreme Court's recent rulings notwithstanding—differs not a whit in its essence from any other kind of media communication protected by the First Amendment of the U.S. Constitution. All newspaper and magazine articles, as well as all radio and television programs, are commercial speech produced for the explicit purpose of inducing a "commercial transaction"; all media communication, in other words, contains "purely commercial messages." The wording of headlines, the copy structure of news articles, and the choice of reporters—all are designed by editors and publishers to stimulate the sales of newspapers and magazines.

The notion that commercial speech is somehow different from other forms of speech protected by the First Amendment stems from the old and false doctrine that government is the guardian of the "public interest." According to this doctrine, advertising (as opposed to newspaper articles and editorials) can be regulated, taxed, or prohibited, if such action would serve some "compelling state interest." The "compelling interest" in the past has been the protection of the public's so-called right to be informed, that is, the protection of an allegedly helpless public against possibly deceptive, profit-making messages. Today, when attempts are made to tax advertising, the "interest" is simply the empty state and federal treasuries.

The "public interest," however, is a euphemism for whatever the state declares to be in its interest, which varies according to which pressure group controls the political party that controls the legislature, or which subcommittee chooses to examine which particular issue. Whatever the interests of the state may be, they are indeed compelling, because while ordinary citizens become criminals when they use physical force for any reason other than self-defense in life-threatening or emergency situations, the unique nature of government, again, is that it holds the legal monopoly on the use of physical force.

Moreover, the "public" has no "right to be informed"; there are no public or group rights, only individual rights. The public is not some superorganism or supernatural entity, separate from or better than its individual members, as this doctrine holds; the public has no rights that individuals do not have. This doctrine in fact rests on the morality of altruism, and the "public interest" arises from the collectivist notion of the divine right of kings—because the king supposedly knows what is best for his subjects, who must dutifully sacrifice themselves for the greater good of the kingdom; today, it is the divine, mythical public that claims the right to sacrifice advertisers.[43]

Rights, however, are not privileges to be granted and withdrawn at the whim of any courtier, special interest group, or majority that happens to be in power in Washington or the state capital. Rights are the inalienable conditions of human existence and the basic requirements of peaceful association; they are violated, one more time, as Rand was the first to make explicit, only through the *initiation* of physical force.

The New Prohibitionism

The specific assaults that occur today on tobacco and alcohol advertising raise the specter of a new prohibitionist mentality. In effect, these critics charge that consumers have no free will and, consequently, are helpless pawns of the advertisers; in addition, they charge that certain products, such as tobacco and alcohol, are intrinsically evil and, consequently, their advertising must be regulated, taxed, or banned.

Both of these charges are false. Human beings, as demonstrated in chapter 3, are not determined to act the way they do by either heredity or environment; we—each one of us—control our own destinies. Determinism is a self-contradiction because, to be consistent, the advocates of determinism would have to admit that they themselves are determined to believe in determinism; such an admission, however, invalidates all knowledge, including the knowledge that determinism is true. No one—advertiser, politician, parent, or teacher—can get inside our minds to make us want to smoke (or not to smoke) cigarettes. (A gun, of course, can make us do things we otherwise would not choose to do, but advertising is not a gun.) Those who smoke do so by choice.

Further, material objects and actions do not possess intrinsic value; no product, taken out of the context of its use and of the person using it, is inherently dangerous or harmful. Skydiving, it would seem to most of us, is a dangerous activity, but to some it is highly valued, even at the risk of an early death. And for the health of obese people, why not declare chocolate mousse "dangerous"? Value, as Rand identified, is a relationship between the material object and the person doing the valuing; it results from the free choice of the individual to evaluate the object in relation to his goals.[44] Tobacco and alcohol, in other words, are not intrinsically evil or harmful. The regenerative powers of the human body, for example (a smoker's lungs supposedly recover to normal after fifteen nonsmoking years), and the Paracelsus principle of toxicology ("the dose makes the poison") put the lie to this doctrine.

When advertising is subordinated to the edicts of the tax authorities and government regulators—whether federal or state—morality, individual rights, and the unique achievement of the United States Constitution go out the window. If the moral purpose of government is the protection of individual rights, using physical force only in retaliation and only against those who initiate its use, then it is our right of self-defense that we delegate to the government. The government's power, however, was originally restricted by the Constitution and the Bill of Rights. These two documents were the founding fathers' means of subordinating politicians to moral law. It is this achievement—the protection of our political freedoms—that is being challenged and destroyed by every increase in government power. It is this achievement that is being threatened through the recent proposals to tax and ban advertising.

I have not discussed (nor am I going to discuss) the economic effects of advertising taxation or regulation. To be sure, as economists have pointed out many times, taxes and other regulations shift resources away from capital accumulation and toward consumption, and in the long run will certainly fail to achieve the bureaucrats' alleged goals.[45] My point—my unique selling proposition, as it were—is simply this: the taxation, regulation, and prohibition of advertising is censorship. It is the initiation of physical force against law-abiding citizens. Therefore, it is immoral and contrary to the intent and meaning of the First Amendment of the U.S. Constitution.

APPENDIX

HOW TO EVALUATE AN ADVERTISEMENT

Given the above comments about taste and moral issues in advertising, allow me to provide guidelines for making an objective evaluation of particular advertisements. The guidelines are for judging advertisements *qua* advertising; thus, I am assuming that the ads you are evaluating fall within the realm of morality. Most do. You can, if you wish, also use this format for evaluating immoral ads on the technical grounds of what constitutes good advertising.

First, assume that you are *not* a member of the target audience. The odds are that you are not. Next, *set aside* your own emotional reactions to the ad—your own tastes, preferences, and personal biases. This includes your reactions to the personalities of the actors, your reactions to the lifestyle that is being portrayed, and, especially, your reactions to the product.

If you are not a user of a product, or even a prospect, remember: you still can evaluate an advertisement as good—and not like it.

Now, answer these questions:

(1) What are the advertiser's objectives? To inform you of the product's features and benefits? To change your attitude about the product, from negative or neutral to positive? Or simply to remind you that the product is still on the market? Only direct-response advertising aims at getting an immediate action out of you, to dial an 800 number, for example, or to send for more information. Another way of putting the question is: what does this advertiser want the audience to know, feel, or do?

(2) Who is the target audience? At what kinds of people, with what needs and tastes, who are watching the same television programs as you or reading the same magazine, is this ad aimed? There are many products on the market today that are aimed at highly specific target audiences; that is why you are not likely to be a member of any given target audience.

(3) What is the selling message? What is the ad saying to the target audience? What product features and benefits is it communicating? Do *not*, however, take the message too literally; advertising messages are abstractions communicated to many people at one time, and copywriters reserve the right to use metaphors. Therefore, ask yourself, what is the abstract meaning of the advertisement's metaphors, such as the "Marlboro man" or the "tiger in your tank"?[46]

(4) What is the execution? Execution is the concrete means by which the selling message is presented to the audience. Thus, it includes the slogan, the organization of the copy, the specific choice of words that make up the copy, the art and layout of all the visual elements of the ad, the photography or illustration, and the choice of models or actors. For broadcast ads, execution also includes the jingle and any other sounds that may be used; in television, the movement of people and objects that takes place on the screen.

Finally, given the advertiser's objectives and target audience that you have now identified, rate how well the selling message and execution have been integrated by the advertiser. That is, how well do the selling message and execution work together communicating to the target audience to achieve the advertiser's objectives?[47]

To the extent that the execution, such as humor, a sexy model, or a cute baby, upstages the selling message, the advertisement is bad. This is the bane of Madison Avenue: viewers of entertaining television commercials love the humor and music, but cannot remember the product. This does not mean that effective television commercials have to be boring; it just means that their creation is a difficult achievement.[48] To the extent that the selling message is unique (and not upstaged by the execution), that is, it contains information that the competition either does not now communicate or cannot communicate (because their product does not offer the particular feature or benefit in question), the ad will be good.[49] Uniqueness is important for differentiation, and its best source is the product itself—the principle is the "primacy of the product." The most effective advertising is that which has been created for products that are better and/ or cheaper than the competition's.[50]

Does evaluating advertisements now seem a little less easy than you originally thought? You certainly cannot objectively evaluate ads while sipping beer in front of your television set. Indeed, the evaluation of radio and television commercials is especially difficult; in thirty or sixty seconds they are gone. Even if you record the commercials, you will have to play the tape a number of times to make a proper assessment. Add to this the difficulty in actually determining what the advertiser's objectives and target audience are. Only the agency executives have all the relevant information with which to make an evaluation. The rest of us can only be approximate in our judgments.

HOW TO ARGUE AGAINST THE CENSORSHIP OF ADVERTISING

Given the above theoretical foundation for the argument against the censorship of advertising, I would like to offer some tips to laymen—and to marketing and advertising professionals—on how to argue with the critics. First, allow me to discuss tips on content, followed by additional tips on method.

How to Argue Content

(1) *Name the actions of the critics and legislators for what they are: a call for censorship*. Make certain, however, that you spell out clearly the meaning of censorship. Censorship is an action *by the government* that restricts what an individual is allowed to say; it is not a private action. It is the use of physical force by the government to control the flow of information within society.

(2) *Assert firmly that human beings have the free will to choose their own values*. Consumers are not helpless pawns of the tobacco, alcohol, or any other industry.

(3) *Challenge and reject the idea that material objects and actions possess intrinsic value or disvalue*. Tobacco and alcohol, for example, are not intrinsically evil or harmful, nor are they the equivalent of arsenic, as the critics of advertising would have us believe. The critics' argument rests on this idea of inherent or intrinsic value. Reject it or we are on our way back to the era of Prohibition.

(4) *Reject the notion that the "public has a right to be informed."* There are no public or group rights, only *individual* rights. As stated above, the

"public" or "society" is not some superorganism separate from or better than its individual members. The rights of a corporation derive from the voluntary association of its individual owners and are, therefore, merely an extension of private, individual rights. Consequently, if human beings have free will and tobacco is not inherently or intrinsically evil, then today's tobacco advertisers defraud no one. In effect, the critics are charging tobacco advertisers with seditious libel against the king's surgeon general![51]

Methods of Argument

(1) *Argue principles, not consequences.* Argue by stating clearly the above principles, not by citing umpteen studies of the consequences of advertising bans in various countries around the world. Principles are universals that capture the essence of an issue and thereby apply to all situations past, present, and future. Empirical studies, on the other hand, are concretes that only show what happened at one point in time in one location. Principles, not concretes, win debates. The more rational the principles, and the more explicitly they are argued, the more likely the rational side will win.[52]

Censorship is the initiation of physical force that violates the rights of law-abiding citizens. It is immoral and contrary to the intent and meaning of the First Amendment of the Constitution, period. That is a unique selling proposition, and the critics cannot touch it without evasion. State the principles proudly, then let the critics weasel around for answers.

(2) *Repeat the message again and again.* Of course, I should not have to make this point to marketing and advertising professionals. Yet, when it comes to serious political and legal issues, it seems that marketers and advertisers forget everything they know about persuasive communication. The critics apparently understand this principle of method and, consequently, have not shut up. Send the message to anyone who will listen, but especially to the average person. To congressmen, yes—but, quoting Ralph Nader, who, although no friend of advertising, nevertheless understands this principle: "If you are weak on the streets, you are weak." And advertising today is "weak on the streets."

(3) Above all, *do not appease or apologize; state the message with all the moral outrage you can muster.* Or, to put it another way: long live the memory of Neville Chamberlain! Do not suggest that the tobacco companies, for example, concede defeat. Appeasement did not stop Hitler; it will not stop the juggernaut of censorship. Do not, under any circumstances, suggest to the critics that you could live with a modest reduction in tax deductions, but not with a ban on advertising. You cannot live with either, because either way you will have given up the principle and will have allowed the critics to obliterate your right of free speech.

Do not apologize for refusing to put health warnings in tobacco ads until the government required them. Apology is an admission of guilt, of having done something wrong. Marketers and advertisers have done nothing wrong, you have violated no one's rights. Tobacco, again, is not arsenic, and apology certainly will not stop the revenge the critics are seeking. Both appeasement and apology only serve to undercut your standing and fuel the critics.

Moral conviction and moral integrity are needed to defend advertising against the claque of social engineers who are trying to take away the advertiser's right to free speech. Moral outrage that such a sham of justice could be perpetrated in a free society needs to be expressed by anyone, but especially by marketers and advertisers, who wish to defend advertising. The critics now speak with moral conviction and outrage. It is time marketers and advertisers responded in kind. A strong moral stand by marketers and advertisers would undercut the claque's momentum. A strong moral stand would let the critics know that they do not have a monopoly on moral conviction. A strong moral stand would give the marketing and advertising industry the confidence it needs to fight back against these modern, hatchet-brandishing Carry Nations.

NOTES

1. This example assumes that I have a normal, healthy body and that there exists a rational science of nutrition. If my doctor, however, discovers that my cholesterol count is high and my level of iron low, he could rationally insist that I eat something other than hamburger. Values are contextual, and what is optional is one context may not be optional in another. But in this context, I would also insist upon the rational option of taking iron pills, rather than enduring the nausea of trying to swallow liver!

2. "There is no accounting for tastes" and "everyone to his liking" are other versions of the proverb. Alfred Henderson, *Latin Proverbs and Quotations* (London: Sampson Low, Son, and Marston, 1869), 77; Burton Stevenson, *The Home Book of Proverbs, Maxims and Familiar Phrases* (New York: Macmillan, 1948), 2,282. In its broadest sense taste *is* disputable, because a "taste" for murder violates more than a few moral principles. Taste, however, is not often used in this moral sense.

Moreover, *de gustibus et coloribus non est disputandum*—about tastes and colors there is no disputing—is a lesser known Latin expression. Just as there is no objectively superior (physiological) taste, there is no objectively superior color. This version of the proverb, I think, demonstrates that its origin and most common usage is in the area of optional values.

See note 17 below for a brief discussion of the so-called problem of taste in esthetics.

3. The context is that neither of us is an advertising agency executive assigned to judge which of two commercials better meets the standard of good advertising; rather, we are average consumers sitting in front of our television sets, sipping

beer, and generally preferring to watch either entertaining advertisements or advertisements for products we happen to like and use.

4. Execution is the specific form—the copy and art—in which a selling message is communicated in an advertisement. There is, of course, nothing wrong per se in using either sex appeals or hard-selling pledge breaks in television commercials—because there is nothing *morally* wrong either with sex or with hard-sell tactics. The principle is: whatever execution you choose for your advertisements, it must not upstage the selling message. That the Public Broadcast System (and therefore its pledge breaks) is funded in large part by government-expropriated tax money, and that its operation is approached with a prissy, altruistic self-righteousness, is a different—and decidedly *moral*—issue.

5. Ayn Rand, "What Is Capitalism?," in *Capitalism: The Unknown Ideal* (New York: New American Library, 1966), 21.

6. But market value is not subjective, as the Neoclassical and Austrian economists concluded. It is what Ayn Rand identifies as "socially objective value"; "What Is Capitalism?," 24–25. See the discussion of product quality later in this chapter and the discussion that market value is primarily psychological value in chapter 7.

7. Ayn Rand, "From the Horse's Mouth," in *Philosophy: Who Needs It* (New York: Bobbs-Merrill, 1982), 96.

8. Moral values are "values which are volitionally chosen, and which are fundamental, that is, shape the whole course of a man's action, not merely a specialized, delimited area of his life." Leonard Peikoff, "Character," in Harry Binswanger, ed., *The Ayn Rand Lexicon: Objectivism from A to Z* (New York: New American Library, 1986), 68.

9. A man's character is the moral values that he accepts and acts upon, whereas his personality is all of his values—moral and abstract, as well as optional and concrete—that make him uniquely different from all other men.

10. Most people today, unfortunately, acquire their moral values not through independent, conceptual thought, but through a passive process that might be called "preconceptual, cultural osmosis."

11. On the other hand, if the person with the poor taste in wine were somehow to become the master at a winery, his refusal to learn how to judge wines certainly would become a moral issue. But then the issue is no longer that person's good or poor taste in wine, but his refusal to learn what is required for his productive career. Wine is just a concrete application of the principle. Context, again, determines whether a particular concrete value is moral or optional.

12. To imply otherwise, or to insinuate through manner or tone of voice that such a person is superior in ways other than in judging wine, is a characteristic of snobbery.

13. See Ayn Rand, "Beauty," in Binswanger, ed., *Ayn Rand Lexicon*, 48–49.

14. Rosser Reeves, *Reality in Advertising* (New York: Alfred A. Knopf, 1968), 46–49.

15. For informative histories of these two advertising campaigns, see "Marketing Classics: 'Please Don't Squeeze the Charmin,'" *Marketing Communications*, March 1980, 4–5, and Bill Abrams, "'Ring around the Collar' Ads Irritate Many Yet Get Results," *Wall Street Journal*, November 4, 1982, 31. The slogan "ring around the

collar," incidentally, was born when market research at Lever Brothers reported dirty shirt collars as a major laundry problem.

16. Direct-mail advertisers discuss what might be called "the junk mail premise," which states that if you are not interested in a particular product, the direct-mail advertising you find in your mailbox is just junk. If you are interested in the product and are seriously considering buying it, you will read every word of the copy and report to your friends that the ad was the finest piece of informative advertising you have ever read. In critics and laymen alike, consistency, unfortunately, has never been widespread where judgments of advertising are concerned. General advertisers use an earthier example: "You may find the Preparation H commercials offensive, but hemorrhoid sufferers do not."

Indeed, "everyone's an expert on advertising"—meaning, *thinks* he's an expert— is the agency executive's lament. It is amazing how cavalierly laymen from all walks of life, and from all philosophical perspectives, toss off judgments about advertising's alleged quality. For the reason of some as yet undiscovered principle of psychology, a little prime-time television turns every viewer into an "expert" on what constitutes good and bad advertising.

17. This parallels Rand's statement in esthetics that "it is not a contradiction to say: This is a great work of art, but I don't like it." Ayn Rand, "Art and Sense of Life," in *The Romantic Manifesto: A Philosophy of Literature* (New York: New American Library, 1971), 43.

In the history of esthetics, the eighteenth-century "problem of taste" resulted from the failure to distinguish esthetic judgment—this is good art—from esthetic response—I don't like it. Giorgio Tonelli, "Taste in the History of Aesthetics from the Renaissance to 1770," in Philip P. Wiener, ed., *Dictionary of the History of Ideas* (New York: Charles Scribner's Sons, 1973), 4:353–57, Monroe C. Beardsley, "History of Aesthetics," in Paul Edwards, ed., *The Encyclopedia of Philosophy* (New York: Macmillan and the Free Press, 1967), 1:26–27.

This confusion, I submit, along with the failure to recognize the existence of rational options, also has contributed to the subjectivist interpretation of *de gustibus*, namely, that all tastes and values are subjective.

18. But advertising is not an institution of, nor does it influence, high culture. As David Ogilvy states, "Advertising *reflects* the mores of society, but does not *influence* them. Thus it is that you find more explicit sex in magazines and novels than in advertisements. . . . There used to be an unwritten law against showing women in advertisements for cigarettes. It was not until long after people got used to seeing them smoke in public that this taboo was lifted. I was the first to show women in liquor advertisements—30 years after they started drinking in public." David Ogilvy, *Ogilvy on Advertising* (New York: Crown Publishers, 1983), 26. Emphasis in original.

19. See Ayn Rand, "Art and Cognition," in *The Romantic Manifesto: A Philosophy of Literature*, 2d rev. ed. (New York: New American Library, 1975), 74–75.

20. Ibid., 74. See also Ayn Rand, "The Psycho-Epistemology of Art," for her theory of art and the meaning of the concept of metaphysical value judgments, in ibid., 19–20.

There is a benevolent sense of life that is communicated by most advertising, but that benevolence actually derives from the nature of capitalism. Capitalism is inherently benevolent, because it is pro-man and pro–this earth. Advertising is just the messenger.

21. If advertising is a form of art, and it also is "just salesmanship," then why do we not judge salesmen according to the standard of good art? Because advertising is not art, but those who wish to judge advertising as art most assuredly also do not want to view it as salesmanship.

22. Many laymen hold the mistaken view that successful products must appeal to all, or at least most, consumers in the world. The textbooks properly call this the "majority" fallacy.

23. Technically, in this context, wants or tastes are values that consumers pursue in order to satisfy their universal, *psychological* needs, such as novelty and variety. However, many different concrete values, all of which are optional, can satisfy the same psychological needs. When one value prevails for a period of time in the marketplace, it is said to be "in fashion." See George Reisman, *Capitalism: A Treatise on Economics*, forthcoming, for a discussion of the economic value of the needs for novelty and variety.

24. Lest the reader think I am endorsing neurotic dependence, "prestige" simply means recognition and "status" is a certain level of recognition within a hierarchy of prestige. The consumer's desire for these two values may be, and often is, completely rational.

25. Cf. my discussion of market value as psychological value in chapter 7.

26. Price is not an attribute of product quality; rather, it is the quantity of money the buyer agrees to pay the seller in exchange for the product's quality. Price, from the perspective of the buyer, represents the amount of production the buyer has achieved in the past—production that has contributed to the satisfaction of the market's past needs and wants—that today he is willing to give up in exchange for the new product.

27. Rand, "What Is Capitalism?," 24–25. Emphasis in original.

28. Ibid., 24.

29. Ibid., 26.

30. This relationship between features that exist physically in the product and benefits that exist psychologically in the minds of consumers is analogous to the alleged dichotomy in philosophy between the primary and secondary qualities of sense perception. It is incorrect to say that primary qualities are objective but secondary qualities are subjective. Both are real, both exist, as do product features and benefits. Ayn Rand, *Introduction to Objectivist Epistemology*, expanded 2d ed., ed. Harry Binswanger and Leonard Peikoff (New York: New American Library, 1990), 279–82.

31. The concept of "utility," however, seems only minimally "useful" in the context of economics and marketing, for utility, most of the time, seems to be no more than a synonym for "value," and the law of marginal utility can readily be called the law of marginal *value*. When defined as the capacity of a thing to satisfy a human need, utility can imply the existence of intrinsic value, although it need not. Indeed, everything in the universe possesses the capacity to satisfy a human need; therefore, we can say that everything in the universe is potentially "that which one acts to gain and/or keep." In this latter sense, "utility" is a derivative of the concept of "value," as is "quality," and might best be described as "potential value." This last is analogous to the concept of "energy" in physics, which is often

described in physics textbooks as "potential work." "That which one acts to gain and/or keep" is Rand's definition of "value." Ayn Rand, "The Objectivist Ethics," in *The Virtue of Selfishness: A New Concept of Egoism* (New York: New American Library, 1964), 15.

32. Clothing in the Middle Ages had to last a lifetime. Does this mean that it was superior to the clothing that today lasts only a few years? (Clothing that had to last a lifetime, incidentally, did not tolerate too many washings!)

33. "It should be noted that there is nothing irrational in a desire for fashion changes. On the contrary, it represents boredom with stagnation and a desire for novelty, which are characteristics of a rational consciousness. Cattle, for example, are incapable of desiring fashion changes." George Reisman, "The Myth of Planned Obsolescence," *Il Politico* (University of Pavia) 38 (1973):489.

34. See George Reisman, "The Toxicity of Environmentalism," *The Freeman* 42 (September 1992):336–50, for a devastating critique of the environmental movement.

35. "Disutility" perhaps could be used here, because, according to the *Oxford English Dictionary*, it means injuriousness or harmfulness. Disutility, however, as in the "disutility of labor," is also used to mean a lower *positive*, rather than negative, value.

The word "disquality" actually exists in the *O.E.D.*, meaning "defect," but it is listed as a nonce word. I could not find it in any American dictionaries.

36. Goods, incidentally, are called "goods" because they are *good for man*—in some context and for some purpose. So what is *good* about a Pet Rock? It makes a wonderful conversation piece on the coffee table.

37. Ayn Rand, "Man's Rights," in *The Virtue of Selfishness*, 95.

38. Rand, "What Is Capitalism?" 19. Cf. Ayn Rand, "The Nature of Government," in *The Virtue of Selfishness*, 107–15.

39. Rand, "Man's Rights," 97.

40. Ibid., 98–99. Cf. Ludwig von Mises, *Theory and History: An Interpretation of Social and Economic Evolution* (New Rochelle, NY: Arlington House, 1969), 24.

41. This is the distinction between political power and economic power. Political power is always the power of governmental coercion, initiated or retaliatory, because the government holds the legal monopoly on the use of physical force; political power is always the power of a gun. Economic power, on the other hand, is consumer dollar power, the power of an entrepreneur to grow rich by repeatedly satisfying the needs and wants of consumers, offering them better and cheaper products than the competition; economic power has nothing at all to do with coercion, but everything to do with *voluntarily* offering *values* to consumers. Ayn Rand, "America's Persecuted Minority: Big Business," in *Capitalism: The Unknown Ideal* (New York: New American Library, 1966), 46–47.

42. Frank Presbrey, *The History and Development of Advertising* (Garden City, NY: Doubleday, 1929; reprint, New York: Greenwood Press, 1968), 74–76, 119, 131, 150. This "experiment" was alluded to earlier in chapter 1. "Annual circulation" is the total number of newspapers distributed during one year.

43. Ayn Rand, "Collectivized Rights," in *The Virtue of Selfishness*, 103.

44. Rand, "What Is Capitalism?," 21–27.

45. For example, see J. J. Boddewyn, "Advertising Taxation Is Here to Stay," *International Journal of Advertising* 2 (1983):291–300.

46. For Marlboro, the message is: "you're not effeminate if you smoke filter-tipped cigarettes" (only women used to smoke filter-tipped cigarettes). As pointed out in chapter 3, the message for the tiger is: this gasoline adds power to your engine.

47. This criterion is based on Seiden's "concept/execution test," in Hank S. Seiden, *Advertising Pure and Simple* (Chicago: American Marketing Association, 1976), 26–33.

48. They do not have to be exciting or entertaining, either, much to the chagrin of creative departments. Some of the most effective advertisements, such as "talking heads" in television commercials and all-copy ads in print media, are downright dull, by creative standards. Such ads are usually produced for clients with small budgets. Creative departments must constantly fight their desire to entertain, reminding themselves often that their raison d'être is salesmanship.

49. This is simply a paraphrase of Rosser Reeves's "unique selling proposition." Reeves, *Reality in Advertising*, 46–49.

50. "A gifted product is mightier than a gifted pen." Quotation attributed to an unnamed advertising man from the 1930s, quoted in ibid., 55.

51. And the critics, no doubt, would gladly bring back the Alien and Sedition Laws—especially the sedition law—of 1798.

52. Ayn Rand, "The Anatomy of Compromise," in *Capitalism*, 144–49.

Chapter 5

THE ECONOMIC FOUNDATIONS
OF ADVERTISING: THREE VIEWS

For many years, two schools of thought have dominated the debate over the economic effects of advertising. They are the "monopoly power" school of thought, associated with mainstream, or orthodox, "Neoclassical" economic theory, and the "market competition" school, associated with the "Chicago" school of economic theory.[1] One other school of thought that has been conspicuously ignored in this debate is the "Austrian" school of economics.[2]

What unites the monopoly power and market competition schools of thought—and, simultaneously, distinguishes the Austrian school—is the former two schools' acceptance, and the latter's rejection, of perfect competition as the correct description of a free and competitive marketplace. Along with their acceptance of perfect competition, and related to it, the former two schools also embrace mathematics and statistics as essential tools with which to develop economic theory; the Austrians reject any such use as an unjustified transfer of physical science methodology to the human sciences.

The Neoclassical school views perfect competition as a normative ideal against which business practices are evaluated. According to this theory, advertising disturbs the static equilibrium of perfect competition and introduces "imperfect" elements of monopoly into the competitive marketplace. The Chicago school, on the other hand, views perfect competition as an analytical model, that is, as a mental construct in which change has been eliminated. When economists of the Chicago school examine current business practices in light of this "mental construct," they generally conclude that such activities as advertising actually help move the economy in the direction of perfect competition. Advertising, by communicating information to consumers (advertising is inherently informative, say these writers), is a means of market entry that increases the price elasticity of demand for the advertised brand. Consequently, advertising contributes to the establishment of one crucial condition of perfect competition: namely, perfect knowledge.

This curious acceptance of the doctrine of pure and perfect competition by two apparently opposed schools of thought requires elaboration. The Austrian school of economists, in contrast, provides the economic foundation of a correct theory of competition and, thus, of marketing and advertising.

THE NEOCLASSICAL SCHOOL

The Neoclassical school of economic thought, which is espoused today by nearly all influential economists around the world, has accepted the doctrine of pure and perfect competition in one form or another since its late-nineteenth-century British origin.

The Origin of Perfect Competition

The doctrine of pure and perfect competition evolved over a period of nearly one hundred years, originating unfortunately in two ideas of the classical economists: the notion of the natural price and the idea of a "stationary state." However, perfect competition and Adam Smith's conception of competition differ significantly.[3] Indeed, the theory of pure and perfect competition is almost entirely a product of the mathematical economists, who postulated the well-known conditions of perfect competition to satisfy—or, more precisely, to try to make reality fit—the equations they formulated.

According to George Stigler,[4] the concept of pure and perfect competition was first formulated by Augustin Cournot in his 1838 book *Researches into the Mathematical Principles of the Theory of Wealth.* Over the years, the theory gradually was refined by William Stanley Jevons, Francis Edgeworth, Alfred Marshall, and John Bates Clark. The culmination and statement of it that today we find in almost every economics and marketing textbook came in Frank Knight's *Risk, Uncertainty and Profit,* published in 1913. Thus, pure and perfect competition is defined as a state of affairs in which both producer and consumer act rationally to maximize, respectively, profits and utility, and every party to the competitive process "makes merely passive adaptations without any control on his part over either the price or the character of the product, and without any sense of rivalry with his competitors."[5]

By contrast, classical economists (and, today, laymen and students of marketing and advertising) have a different idea of competition. They view it as an active behavioral process in which each competitor seeks to influence market conditions, attempting to turn them to his favor; thus, competition is a rivalry among producers for a finite source of revenue—namely, the consumer's dollars. When this competitive process is not interfered with by the government, it becomes an "ordering force" like gravitation, moving capital and labor toward their most productive and beneficial uses.[6]

To meet the requirements of mathematical analysis, however, especially the requirements of calculus, the Neoclassical economists made price a constant, rather than a variable to be controlled by the producer. This relegated competition solely to passive reactions to variations in demand and supply. Pure and perfect competition, therefore, to use a different analogy from physics, is more like the perfect vacuum in which bodies fall freely without friction; it is a "static equilibrium," as it is commonly described.[7]

In addition to the assumption of economic rationality in both producer and consumer,[8] the doctrine of pure and perfect competition requires several other assumptions: an indefinitely large number of buyers and sellers, so that no single producer can influence total supply and no single buyer can influence total demand; product homogeneity, so that the customer has no reason to prefer one product over another; free entry and exit for all producers, including perfect mobility of all resources—no barriers to entry or exit, in other words; and perfect information about product costs, price, and quality available to all buyers and sellers—to prevent any one buyer or seller from having an unfair or monopolistic advantage over everyone else.[9]

Obviously, the doctrine of pure and perfect competition has no place for such elements of "friction" as marketing or advertising. The marketer produces heterogeneous products, controls his prices, and disseminates information through advertising—all in an attempt to influence the consumer to prefer his products over everyone else's. Marketing and advertising, therefore, violate several assumptions of the concept. As a result, Neoclassical economists assert the marketing and advertising thwart the optimum allocation of resources that pure and perfect competition aims for and, consequently, are inherently anticompetitive, monopolistic, and wasteful.

Imperfect and Monopolistic Competition

Discontent with the concept of pure and perfect competition led in the 1930s to a modification of the theory, presented almost simultaneously by Joan Robinson, in her book *The Economics of Imperfect Competition*, and Edward Chamberlin, in his book *The Theory of Monopolistic Competition*. Pure and perfect competition, it was widely recognized at the time, said little about reality, the closest things to it being the stock and agricultural markets; even in those markets, it was argued, the assumptions do not hold. "The root of the difficulty," says Chamberlin, "is that under conditions of pure competition there would be no selling costs," only production costs.[10] Since all members of the market have perfect knowledge, they incur no expense in buying and selling products. But since this obviously is not true, says Chamberlin, pure and perfect competition analysis must underestimate demand as well as the costs of supply.

At this point Chamberlin introduces the distinction between production costs and selling costs. The distinction is an old one, stemming from the ancient world's mistaken view that only manual labor is productive; Chamberlin simply popularized it in economics during the 1930s. It holds that selling costs are expenditures incurred by businesses to stimulate the product's demand and thereby to create a market for it, whereas production costs are expenditures incurred to make or fabricate the product and transport it to the consumer. Selling costs do not alter the physical product or, according to Chamberlin, add value to it; they merely affect the demand for it. Production costs, on the other hand, affect supply. Advertising, of course, is a selling cost. Thus, advertising and other selling costs are brought explicitly into the discussion of economic phenomena under the theory of imperfect and monopolistic competition—but only at the price of being blamed for possessing monopoly power.

The concepts of imperfect and monopolistic competition attempt to provide a theory of value that more accurately describes the real world; the effect of the theory, however, was to extend the concept of monopoly to apply virtually to the entire economy.[11] Imperfect and monopolistic competition, unlike pure and perfect competition, does not assume perfect information, product homogeneity, or lack of control over price. It does assume a modified economic rationality and a large number of buyers and sellers. Producers and consumers, under the new theory, are no longer passive "price takers," as they are under pure and perfect competition; under imperfect and monopolistic competition they are "price searchers," actively exerting an influence on the prices of products.

Consumers, under the new theory, can and do prefer specific brands, thus becoming "brand loyal," as the economic criticisms of advertising charge. Consequently, consumer demand for particular products becomes less elastic—that is, less sensitive to changes in price—than occurs under pure and perfect competition. The prices of such products, further, are increased by producers to levels higher than otherwise would occur under perfect competition, prices that, in turn, lead to lower output than otherwise would occur. Thus, an element of monopoly—increased price and reduced output—is introduced into the market according to the theory of imperfect and monopolistic competition. Market conditions are basically competitive, but they also contain elements of monopoly or a tendency to establish monopoly power.

The doctrine of pure and perfect competition gave rise to the theory of imperfect and monopolistic competition, but the theory of imperfect and monopolistic competition is the immediate source of the "monopoly power" arguments against advertising—because marketing and advertising introduce such imperfect, monopolizing elements of the economy as product differentiation strategies, advertising to induce brand loyalty, and price setting (or price "administering," as the textbooks call it) to reduce output and establish monopolistic practices.

Indeed, these "imperfections" in the market economy lead to less than optimal allocation of resources and thus, so the theory claims, require government intervention to correct the "inherent flaws" of the free market. The rise of the theory of imperfect and monopolistic competition is held by Neoclassical economists to be the kiss of death to capitalism. "Positive economic theory," says one writer, referring to the Robinson/Chamberlin view, "now demonstrated that laissez faire was dead, and that the only way in which its conditions could be approximated was through conscious intervention. . . . The free market could be sustained only by economic planning!"[12] And one of the primary activities that must be controlled and regulated by the government is marketing, especially advertising.

The distinction between production costs and selling costs implies that advertising adds to the cost of the product. If, however, says Chamberlin, the added cost can be recovered by increased sales volume, which would be the result of an advertising-created larger market, then the added cost would result in no loss of welfare, and perhaps would result, through the reduction of imperfect market knowledge, in a movement toward pure and perfect competition. (This, precisely, is the point of view taken by the Chicago school of economists.) If, on the other hand, advertising alters consumer tastes through manipulation or persuasion, then it leads consumers to prefer one brand over another and thus helps to bring about the monopolistic elements of competition.[13]

This last—the altering of tastes through manipulation or persuasion, which is the essence of the "coercive power" argument against advertising—illustrates how the "social" and economic criticisms of adverting mutually reinforce one another, in this instance with both camps equating persuasion to coercion.

THE CHICAGO SCHOOL

In many respects the Chicago school of economics is similar to the Neoclassical school. Both grew out of late-nineteenth-century British Neoclassicism. Both hold that economic theory is best formulated in mathematical terms and "empirically" tested by the experimental and statistical methods of the physical sciences. And both advocate and defend the doctrine of pure and perfect competition. However, the Neoclassical school is an ardent advocate of government intervention into the economy to regulate such imperfections of the free market as advertising.

In other respects, the Chicago school is similar to the Austrian school. Both are advocates of an unregulated free market—the Austrians being more uncompromisingly laissez-faire than the Chicago school—and both hold generally favorable attitudes toward marketing and advertising.[14] But the Austrians reject the doctrine of pure and perfect competition as well as the view that the mathematical and statistical methods of the physical sciences are the model on which economic science should be built.

In addition to Frank Knight, who gave the doctrine of pure and perfect competition its current form, other economists who have elaborated the Chicago school's basic principles are Jacob Viner, Henry Simons, Lloyd Wynn Mints, George Stigler, and Milton Friedman.[15] To understand the school's evaluation of advertising, an understanding of its epistemology is essential. One reason for this is to demonstrate its rejection of the theories of imperfect and monopolistic competition; the other is to demonstrate its blatant Platonism. Milton Friedman, in a now classic article, eloquently expresses this methodology, even to the extent of using Plato's allegories of the cave and the divided line.[16] This second point is relevant because the Austrian economists are explicit Aristotelians. An understanding of each school's philosophical foundation is essential to an understanding of their differences.

Friedman's Methodology

"The ultimate goal of a positive science," says Friedman, "is the development of a 'theory' or 'hypothesis' that yields valid and meaningful (that is, not truistic) predictions about phenomena not yet observed."[17] Friedman holds that theory consists of two elements. The first is a systematic language that has no substantive content; theory is merely a system of logical or mathematical concepts into which empirical, factual material can be filed and organized. The language is a set of tautologies that acquires meaning or content only when converted to substantive hypotheses. Substantive hypotheses are the second element of theory; they are tested through empirical studies. When factual evidence fails to contradict a hypothesis, the data collected are filed into the language categories for future reference. The validity of a substantive hypothesis is tested by its ability to predict experience. A hypothesis that predicts experience is said to support the theory; one that does not, does not support the theory.[18]

Thus far, Friedman's epistemology does not differ significantly from that practiced by most "social" scientists today, including the Neoclassical economists; it derives straightforwardly from the philosophy of logical positivism. Friedman's "systematic language" is more commonly called "theoretical constructs," and his "substantive hypotheses" are often called "operationalized variables." Where Friedman throws in a unique twist, however, is in his discussion of the realism of assumptions and in the conclusion that prediction is the ultimate test of a hypothesis. This conclusion leads directly to his fundamentally free-market orientation in economics and to the Chicago school's generally favorable attitude toward advertising. A look at Friedman's views on assumptions and prediction is now in order.

Criticism "Largely Irrelevant"

"Truly important and significant hypotheses," says Friedman, "will be found to have 'assumptions' that are wildly inaccurate descriptive representations of reality, and, in general, the more significant the theory, the more unrealistic the assumptions."[19] A theory, says Friedman, is an abstract model, precisely defined, complete within its boundaries, and fully consistent with the laws of logic or mathematics. Euclidean geometry and the economics of perfect competition, says Friedman, are two such complete, abstract models. Substantive hypotheses, however, in order to be empirically testable, must necessarily be concrete and incomplete approximations of the model, for "completeness is possible only in a conceptual world, not in the 'real world.' "[20] The "real world," according to Friedman, is made up of complex phenomena that can never be captured completely in a testable hypothesis, nor, for that matter, in a theory. A theory, however, attempts to abstract some features of the real world and incorporate them into a consistent model or representation. The model—that is, the assumptions underlying the hypotheses—is, by nature, therefore, substantially different from any phenomena of the real world. For example, the concept of perfect competition differs substantially from real world competition, as Euclidean geometry, so says Friedman, differs from its real-world applications. The world of conceptions and thought—the world of Platonic Forms—is complete and perfect; the world of real phenomena is incomplete and imperfect.

How, then, is theory verified? By operationalizing the theory into substantive hypotheses, which immediately become incomplete approximations of it, and by testing the hypotheses to determine whether or not they can predict previously unobserved phenomena. If they predict more times than not, then the theory is supported, even though the theory itself is a "wildly inaccurate" description of reality. Friedman explains the discrepancy between theory and the real world by using the "as if" device. Real-world observations may not reveal a world of perfect competition, says Friedman, but "under a wide range of circumstances individual firms act *as if* they were seeking rationally to maximize their expected returns"[21]— that is, *as if* they knew the principles of perfect competition.

The Chicago School's Defense of Perfect Competition

The most significant implication of Friedman's views on assumptions is his alleged defense of the doctrine of pure and perfect competition against the attacks of the advocates of imperfect and monopolistic competition. As discussed above, the theory of imperfect and monopolistic competition came into existence because of economists' disillusionment with the unrealistic assumptions of perfect competition. The assumptions, however, says Friedman, are *necessarily unrealistic*. Lack of realism, he maintains, is not a valid criticism of the theory. Indeed, "such criticism is largely irrelevant."[22] The theory of imperfect and monopolistic competition, according to Friedman, would be more useful if it could demonstrate a greater generality than the theory of perfect competition. Alas, says Friedman, the theory only "introduces fuzziness and undefinable terms into the abstract model where they have no place."[23] He concludes:

> The theory of monopolistic competition offers no tools for the analysis of an industry and so no stopping place between the firm at one extreme and general equilibrium at the other. It is therefore incompetent to contribute to the analysis of a host of important problems: the one extreme is too narrow to be of great interest; the other, too broad to permit meaningful generalizations.[24]

The rejection of monopolistic competition and defense of perfect competition is what enables Friedman and the Chicago school to advocate the free market—because perfect competition is what they (and the Neoclassical economists) define as laissez-faire capitalism.[25] If monopolistic competition is not an adequate model with which to analyze the phenomena of the market, but perfect competition is, then logically it follows that the free market is the most efficient allocator of resources. The Chicago school thus rejects the Neoclassicists' advocacy of economic planning and intervention, which the Neoclassicists allege is necessary to make the market more "competitive."

Advertising as Information

The rejection of the theory of imperfect and monopolistic competition would seem to defend advertising against the criticism that it is inherently monopolistic. Indeed it does, say economists of the Chicago school. This is not to say, however, that the real world does not have imperfections. It does. But these imperfections are being removed daily from the market through the process of normal business transactions, that is, through competition, which, in the real world, is an *active* rivalry, rather than a *passive* adaptation to demand and supply. One of the key elements aiding the removal of these imperfections, especially the removal of imperfect knowledge, is advertising.

The function of advertising in the economy, and its theoretical justification, according to the Chicago school of economists, is precisely its *perfecting* qualities. Advertising reduces consumer ignorance by communicating product information, even if it is only the information that "product X exists."[26] It reduces the dispersion of competitive prices, thereby stabilizing the conditions of demand and supply. Advertising reduces what are called "search" or "transaction costs"—the time and effort consumers would have to expend, were there no advertising, to acquire product information.[27] Advertising, continue the Chicago economists, is demanded and supplied jointly with the product, just as buttons are demanded and supplied jointly with a coat. And should they so desire, consumers can buy privately branded products without also having to buy, or pay for, advertising, just as consumers can buy coats without also having to buy, or pay for, the buttons that come with them.[28]

Further, advertising, by increasing the amount of information consumers acquire about the various products on the market, increases the elasticity of demand of the advertised product. Because inelasticity, according to both the Chicago and Neoclassical schools of economists, is a characteristic of monopoly, advertising, according to the Chicago economists, *reduces* monopoly power—which is opposite the conclusion drawn by the Neoclassical economists. Thus, markets are made more perfect and brought closer to the model of perfect competition by advertising.

Advertising, through and through, according to the Chicago economists, is information, not persuasion.[29]

THE AUSTRIAN SCHOOL

On the surface, it may appear that the Chicago school provides a valid defense of advertising. While Chicago economists, through their many studies, have taken the edge off the criticisms leveled at advertising by the Neoclassical school, they fundamentally still accept the premises of the critics—namely, that a Platonic Garden of Eden is the standard of evaluation of economic activity. Ultimately, a defense of advertising based on unreality must collapse.

The Austrian school of economists, in contrast to both the Neoclassical and Chicago schools, rejects perfect competition as either a normative or analytical model. Austrian economic analysis studies the real—Aristotelian—world of concretes in which we live.[30]

Perfect Competition Is Out

The Austrians reject perfect competition because "competition is by its nature a dynamic process whose essential characteristics are assumed away by the assumptions underlying static analysis."[31] At best, states Ludwig von Mises, the notion of a static equilibrium, which he refers to as "the imaginary construction of an evenly rotating economy," is "a limiting notion, a mere mental tool," not a real entity.[32] Mises continues:

> The imaginary construction of the evenly rotating economy is a mental tool for comprehension of entrepreneurial profit and loss. It is, to be sure, not a design for comprehension of the pricing process. The final prices corresponding to this imaginary conception are by no means identical with the market prices. The activities of the entrepreneurs or of any other actors on the economic scene are not guided by consideration of any such things as equilibrium prices and the evenly rotating economy.[33]

In this static economy, or "final state of rest," "the market process would cease to operate."[34]

The preoccupation with static analysis, suggests F. A. Hayek, has created "a peculiar blindness" in the minds of present-day economists "to the role played in real life by such institutions as advertising."[35] Needless to say, the attempts in the 1930s of Chamberlin, Robinson, and their followers to develop a new theory of competition without relying on the unrealistic conditions of perfect competition are, according to the Austrians, not a solution. Indeed, Israel Kirzner points out, "the authors of the new theory [of imperfect and monopolistic competition] failed entirely to correctly identify the source of [the existing theory's] unrealistic character. Instead of attacking the equilibrium emphasis in the theory of pure competition, these authors introduced *different* equilibrium theories."[36]

The Market Process

The aim of economic theory, according to the Austrian economists, is to describe the market as it exists in the *real world*. This real-world market is an active, ever-changing *process,* not a "static state." "What distinguishes the Austrian School," states Mises,

> is precisely the fact that it created a theory of economic action and not of economic equilibrium or non-action. . . . The Austrian School endeavors to explain prices that are really paid in the market, and not just prices that would be paid under certain, never realizable conditions. It rejects the mathematical method, not because of ignorance of mathematics or aversion to mathematical exactness, but because it does not emphasize a detailed description of a state of hypothetical static equilibrium. . . . It has never mis-

understood that statistical data belong to economic history only, and that statistics have nothing to do with economic theory.[37]

Further, states Mises, "the impracticability of measurement is not due to the lack of technical methods for the establishment of measure. It is due to the absence of constant relations. . . . [Economics] is not quantitative and does not measure because there are no constants."[38]

What Mises means by this last statement is that there are no constant relations in human behavior, in the deterministic sense that physical matter exhibits constant relations from one time and place to another. Man has free will; human beings can change their minds. This precludes the measurement of exact mathematical relationships among human actions. (While Mises acknowledges the existence of free will, he does not go out of his way to emphasize it.) The absence of constant relations in human behavior precludes the establishment of quantitative propositions, but this does not preclude the identification of universal scientific propositions that apply to human behavior. This, says Mises, is precisely what a sound science of economics achieves.

What static equilibrium theory provides, however, says Mises, is a theory of "economic quantities," not a theory of human action. What the quantitative researcher accumulates are the (often trivial) data of economic history, not principles of economic theory.[39] "Scientism"—a pretense at science—is what Hayek calls attempts by social and behavioral scientists to imitate the methodologies of the physical sciences.[40]

The aim of economic theory, according to Mises, is to study market phenomena, that is, "the determination of the mutual exchange ratios of the goods and services negotiated on markets, their origin in human action and their effects upon later action."[41] He continues:

> The market is not a place, a thing, or a collective entity. The market is a process, actuated by the interplay of the actions of the various individuals cooperating under the division of labor. The forces determining the—continually changing—state of the market are the value judgments of these individuals and their actions as directed by these value judgments. The state of the market at any instant is the price structure, that is, the totality of the exchange ratios as established by the interaction of those eager to buy and those eager to sell. There is nothing inhuman or mystical with regard to the market. The market process is entirely a resultant of human actions. Every market phenomenon can be traced back to definite choices of the members of the market society.[42]

Several points can be made about the above quotations. One: the proper method of economic analysis, according to Mises, is the methodical reduction of aggregate concepts to their individual components, or "methodological individualism," as it has been called.[43] Two: Mises is obviously not describing a hypothetical "static equilibrium," but the real-life changing market in which everyone participates. And three: prices are ratios of exchange that must cover a product's costs of production, not equal its marginal costs. These points require elaboration.

(1) Methodological individualism is the method of tracing the origins of all institutions of the market economy to their source in individual human choices and actions. Hence, the market itself is always seen by Austrian economists not as an ineffable, mystical entity or "final state of rest," but as individual buyers and sellers making value judgments about which ends to pursue and which means to employ to achieve them, all in the context of mutual cooperation over a period of time. Indeed, the use of such a method reveals that the institution of advertising—in which a selling message is communicated to many people at one time—is nothing more than salesmanship, or mass-media selling. Thus, an understanding of how advertising works, or of whether advertising exerts monopoly power, should begin by understanding the personal selling process.

(2) While the activities that constitute the real-world market process might *tend* to move the economy toward some imagined final state of rest or equilibrium, that state is never reached. Therefore, the proper object of study, according to Mises, is such self-evident givens as product heterogeneity, consumer ignorance, large buyers and sellers who influence prices, and the general interdependence of buyers and sellers in a constantly changing market. In short, the market is a process of continual *dis*equilibrium. This does not mean, however, that the market process is inherently imperfect or monopolistic. What does not and cannot exist, according to Mises, must not be used as the standard by which to judge what does. Consequently, advertising is embraced by the Austrians as a legitimate institution of the market process.

(3) Prices in the real world, according to the Austrians, must be set high enough to cover a product's full (average) costs of production. While prices in some businesses may approach or equal their marginal costs, which the doctrine of pure and perfect competition maintains should occur routinely, such real-world businesses are certainly on the road to ruin, for real-world, free-market businesses *suffer losses* when their prices are set equal to marginal costs.

In a market economy, prices are quantities of money for which a good can be exchanged.[44] What ultimately determines the quantities of money to be exchanged are the value judgments of the buyer and seller, not the arcane formulas of the perfect competition doctrine. Valuing commodities in money, however, does not mean that prices are a measure of fixed or intrinsic value, as is implied in the doctrine's quantitative propositions, because constant relations, as exist in physical nature, do not exist among human choices and actions. "There is nothing in prices," states Mises, "which permits one to liken them to the measurement of physical and chemical phenomena."[45] Hence, real-world market prices cannot be likened to the final equilibrium prices of pure and perfect competition.

Further, the value of money itself—that is, its purchasing power—in market exchanges is not neutral. The value of money varies, sometimes greatly, in accordance with changes in the demand for and supply of money, and its variations affect goods and services unevenly over time.[46] This implies that there is a need to examine *real* prices in any attempt to charge advertising with the monopoly power to increase prices. Adjusting for the quantity (and quality) of goods that an hour of labor time will buy has rarely, if ever, been done in the many "empirical" studies of advertising's alleged ability to increase prices.[47]

The Intellectual Division of Labor

A major problem of economics, continues Hayek, is the problem of the division of knowledge,

> which is quite analogous to, and at least as important as, the problem of the division of labor.... [But] price expectations and even the knowledge of current prices are only a very small section of the problem of knowledge as I see it. The wider aspect of the problem of knowledge with which I am concerned is the knowledge of the basic fact of how the different commodities can be obtained and used, and under what conditions they are actually obtained and used.[48]

This problem of the division of knowledge—the problem of how less-than-omniscient producers communicate with less-than-omniscient consumers, and vice versa—is partially solved through media advertising.

Mises concludes: "The market process is the adjustment of the individual actions of the various members of the market society to the requirements of mutual cooperation. The market prices tell the producers what to produce, how to produce, and in what quantity."[49] Thus, the price system functions, in the words of Hayek, as a system of "telecommunications," a system by which information is communicated to all market participants so they may adjust their plans and actions harmoniously with those of everyone else.[50]

The Importance of the Entrepreneur

It is the entrepreneur—and competition, in the sense of rivalry—that are "assumed away" by the theory of static equilibrium. States Mises:

> The concatenation of the market is an outcome of the activities of entrepreneurs, promoters, speculators, and dealers in futures and in arbitrage....
> The driving force of the market process is provided neither by the con-

sumers nor by the owners of the means of production—land, capital goods, and labor—but by the promoting and speculating entrepreneurs. These are people intent upon profiting by taking advantage of differences in prices. Quicker of apprehension and farther-sighted than other men, they look around for sources of profit. . . . The entrepreneurs take into account anticipated future prices, not final prices or equilibrium prices. They discover discrepancies between the height of prices of the complementary factors of production and the anticipated future prices of the products, and they are intent upon taking advantage of such discrepancies.[51]

Consequently, competition is "the striving of individuals to attain the most favorable position in the system of social cooperation."[52]

In real life, just as human beings are not omniscient—that is, no one possesses "perfect knowledge"—prices and costs are not "given" to anyone; they *result* from the "concatenation" of the market process. Consequently, there exist in the market during any period of time discrepancies between the prices consumers are willing to pay for finished products and the costs of factors of production that entrepreneurs would have to incur to produce the products. Entrepreneurs alertly perceive ahead of anyone else an opportunity to profit from this gap in knowledge and, consequently, proceed to take advantage of the opportunity. Their reward for success is entrepreneurial profit; their penalty for failure is entrepreneurial loss.[53]

Alertness to profit-making opportunity, along with the ability and willingness to take advantage of it, is the essence of entrepreneurship;[54] perceiving opportunities and acting on them ahead of anyone else make entrepreneurship inherently competitive.[55] These very actions of entrepreneurs, however—that is, buying factors of production at costs that are lower than the prices for which they sell the products to consumers—change the price structure of the market, thus creating more discrepancies from which entrepreneurs can profit. In this way, entrepreneurs are the "driving force" of the market process.

Indeed, the actions of entrepreneurs give rise to the tendencies toward uniformity that are observed in the market economy: namely, the tendencies toward a uniform rate of profit on invested capital, a uniform price for the same good throughout the world and over time, and a uniform wage rate for workers of the same degree of ability.[56] But in any given moment these observed uniformities are *not* static equilibriums. They are arithmetic means that result and are calculated from the actions of individual buyers and sellers; their ultimate referents in reality are discrete quantities that are dispersed around the means. These uniformities are anything but "static," because in the next instant the data on which they are based—human choices and actions—will have changed.

Advertising as Entrepreneurship

In the absence of omniscience (or "perfect knowledge"), according to the Austrian economists, advertising is essential to successful entrepreneurship. To take advantage of a profit-making opportunity, entrepreneurs buy advertising along with their other factors of production and focus on selling their finished products at prices greater than their costs.

Advertising is the production of consumer awareness. It is the entrepreneurial function of *making* consumers aware of the product and of its features and benefits. If an entrepreneur seeks to open a gasoline station, for example, quoting Kirzner:

> it is not enough to buy gas and put it in the ground. The entrepreneur puts it in the ground in a form that the consumer recognizes. To do this requires much more than fabrication. It requires communication. It requires more than simple information. It requires more than writing a book, publishing it, and having it on a library shelf. It requires more than putting something in a newspaper in a classified ad and expecting the consumer to see it. You have to put it in front of the consumer in a form that he *will* see. Otherwise, you're not performing your entrepreneurial task.[57]

Advertising, consequently, in order for the entrepreneur to become competitive and to take advantage of the profit-making opportunity, must be more than "informative"; it must also be "persuasive." States Mises, speaking approvingly of advertising:

> Business propaganda must be obtrusive and blatant. It is its aim to attract the attention of slow people, to rouse latent wishes, to entice men to substitute innovation for inert clinging to traditional routine. In order to succeed, advertising must be adjusted to the mentality of the people courted. It must suit their tastes and speak their idiom. . . .
>
> Like all things designed to suit the taste of the masses, advertising is repellent to people of delicate feeling.[58]

Rarely in the history of economic thought, if at all, has an economist spoken so favorably about the institution of advertising. The Neoclassical economists, if they speak of advertising at all, attack it and demand severe regulations or bans on it to protect, no doubt, the "delicate feelings" of the select few. The Chicago economists generally defend advertising, but do not go so far as to defend persuasive advertising. Only the Austrian economists defend advertising, including its persuasive varieties, as a legitimate function of business entrepreneurship.

THE DOCTRINE OF PURE AND PERFECT COMPETITION

The fundamental theory on which the economic criticisms of advertising rest is the doctrine of pure and perfect competition. Over forty years ago, marketing intellectuals attempted to reject it as a grossly incorrect description of reality. They rejected the two schools of economics that espouse the doctrine, but, unfortunately, did not discover, or at least embrace, the Austrian school; nor did they reject the fundamental premises of the doctrine or its normative implications.

This doctrine is pernicious, invasive, and seemingly resistant to challenge. It is the standard by which business activities have been judged for at least a century and continue to be judged today. It is the foundation upon which our antitrust laws are based and upon which most regulatory agencies operate. (This includes the Federal Trade Commission, which regulates advertising.) It permeates almost all economics and business courses taught in today's colleges and universities; in the field of finance, the doctrine underlies the much-touted "[perfectly] efficient-markets" hypothesis (also known as the "random walk" theory), which holds that it is not possible to make money in the stock market.[59] And perfect competition forms the core of what is called "industrial organization theory," the basis of popular discussions of competitive strategy by such writers as Michael Porter.[60] Although it originated as an alleged answer to socialism, perfect competition has even been accepted by socialists as an ideal by which resources should be allocated in the worker's paradise.[61]

As long as this doctrine is accepted by business intellectuals and economists, marketing and advertising have no sound theoretical foundation. This doctrine must be examined in detail and rejected at its source in epistemology. The next chapter refutes the doctrine of pure and perfect competition, first by presenting a *reductio ad absurdum* argument, followed by a thorough discussion and refutation of the doctrine's epistemological premises.

NOTES

1. Albion refers to these two, respectively, as the "advertising = market power" and "advertising = information" schools of economic thought. Mark S. Albion, *Advertising's Hidden Effects* (Boston: Auburn House, 1983), 15–21.

For representatives of the Neoclassical school, see Nicholas Kaldor, "The Economics of Advertising," *Review of Economic Studies* 18 (December/January 1949–50: 1–27; Joe S. Bain, *Barriers to New Competition* (Cambridge, MA: Harvard University Press, 1956); and William S. Commanor and Thomas A. Wilson, *Advertising and Market Power* (Cambridge, MA: Harvard University Press, 1974).

For representatives of the Chicago school, see George J. Stigler, "The Economics of Information," *Journal of Political Economy* 69 (June 1961): 213–25; Lester G. Telser, "Advertising and Competition," *Journal of Political Economy* 72 (December 1964): 537–62; and Philip Nelson, "Information and Consumer Behavior," *Journal of Political Economy* 78 (March/April 1970): 311–29.

2. For representatives of the Austrian school, see Carl Menger, *Principles of Economics,* trans. James Dingwall and Bert F. Hoselitz (1950; reprint, New York: New York University Press, 1981); Friedrich von Wieser, *Natural Value,* trans. Christian A. Malloch (London: Macmillan, 1893; reprint, New York: Augustus M. Kelley, 1989); Eugen von Böhm-Bawerk, *Capital and Interest,* trans. George D. Huncke and Hans F. Sennholz (South Holland, IL: Libertarian Press, 1959); and Ludwig von Mises, *Human Action: A Treatise on Economics,* 3d rev. ed. (Chicago: Henry Regnery, 1966).

3. See Paul J. McNulty, "A Note on the History of Perfect Competition," *Journal of Political Economy* 75 (June 1967): 396–97.

4. George J. Stigler, "Perfect Competition, Historically Contemplated," *Journal of Political Economy* 65 (February 1957): 1–17.

5. Stefan Stykolt, "Economic Competition," in Julius Gould and William L. Kolb, eds., *A Dictionary of the Social Sciences* (New York: Free Press of Glencoe, 1964), 216.

6. The classical economists, unfortunately, are not always consistent in the contrast between "free competition," on the one hand, and "government-imposed monopoly" or "government intervention into the competitive process," on the other. This distinction, however, is implied in the spirit of their writings.

7. McNulty, "History of Perfect Competition," 397–99; idem, "Economic Theory and the Meaning of Competition," *Quarterly Journal of Economics* 82 (November 1968): 643–50.

8. The concept of "economic rationality" has almost as interesting a history as the doctrine of pure and perfect competition. The classical economists and utilitarians used the term to represent human motivation by self-interest and the ability of entrepreneurs and consumers rationally to calculate pleasure/pain ratios to guide their choices and actions; this concept, however, rests on the false doctrines of psychological egoism (man, by nature, pursues self-interest) and psychological hedonism (man, by nature, pursues pleasure). The Neoclassical economists used the concept as an abstract model with which to guide their own scholarly work in determining the optimum allocation of resources within an economy; to Neoclassical economists, "economic rationality" means that the ends of action are given (that is, entrepreneurs and consumers do not choose their own goals) and that entrepreneurs and consumers possess perfect rationality (meaning that they cannot make mistakes) and perfect information (they are omniscient).

The enemies of capitalism, naturally enough, jumped on the latter concept and caricatured it as an exaggerated, hyperrational, "lightning calculator" known as "economic man," the profit and utility maximizer. Unfortunately, the critics also lumped the classical and Neoclassical economists together; the net effect has been the widespread conclusion that capitalism rests on a ridiculous theory of human nature and that most economic behavior, therefore, because it involves the pursuit of self-interest, is *irrational.* See Alfred F. Chalk, "Economic Man," in Gould and Kolb, eds., *Dictionary of the Social Sciences,* 223–25.

9. A distinction sometimes is made between pure competition, on the one hand, and perfect competition, on the other. Pure competition is said to be a condition in which the buyers and sellers have no control over price, but may not have perfect

information, whereas in perfect competition they do. The distinction, however, is usually not maintained, and one term or the other is used to denote the concept. Stykolt, "Economic Competition," 216.

10. Edward Hastings Chamberlin, *The Theory of Monopolistic Competition: A Re-Orientation of the Theory of Value,* 8th ed. (Cambridge, MA: Harvard University Press, 1962), 174.

11. Technically, "imperfect" competition assumes "imperfect" knowledge, whereas "monopolistic" competition assumes control over price. Today, however, as in the "pure" and "perfect" concepts, little distinction is made between the two.

12. Ben B. Seligman, *Main Currents in Modern Economics: Economic Thought Since 1870* (1962; reprint, Chicago: Quadrangle Books, 1971), 3:720.

13. Chamberlin, *Monopolistic Competition,* 118–23.

14. There does exist a connection between the Chicago and Austrian schools, not least of which is Frank Knight's introduction to the 1950 translation of Carl Menger's *Principles of Economics,* in which he acknowledges an intellectual debt to Menger. In addition, Austrian economist F. A Hayek held the position of professor of social and moral science at the University of Chicago from 1950 to 1962.

15. Seligman, *Main Currents,* 673.

16. Milton Friedman, "The Methodology of Positive Science," in *Essays in Positive Economics* (Chicago: University of Chicago Press, 1953), 3–43. See John Ridpath, "The Philosophical Origins of Antitrust," *The Objectivist Forum* 1 (June 1980): 6–14, for a discussion of Frank Knight's explicit Platonism.

17. Friedman, "Methodology of Positive Science," 7. The term "positive science," as used by Friedman, means, in the tradition of the philosophy of logical positivism, descriptive, nonnormative, value-free science. The assumption is that ethics, esthetics, or anything else involving a discussion of values is not science.

18. Ibid., 7–9.

19. Ibid., 14.

20. Ibid., 25.

21. Ibid., 21. Emphasis in original.

22. Ibid., 41.

23. Ibid., 38.

24. Ibid., 39.

25. Milton Friedman, *Capitalism and Freedom* (Chicago: University of Chicago Press, 1962).

26. Friedman has written little on advertising, but he does say that advertising is largely informative. Even when advertising is persuasive, says Friedman, it is a responder to consumer tastes, not a shaper of them. Milton Friedman, *From Galbraith to Economic Freedom,* pamphlet (London: Institute of Economic Affairs, 1977), 14–15.

27. Stigler, "Economics of Information."

28. Telser, "Advertising and Competition"; idem, "Advertising and the Consumer," in Yale Brozen, ed. *Advertising and Society* (New York: New York University Press, 1974), 25–42; idem, "Towards a Theory of the Economics of Advertising," in David G. Tuerck, ed., *Issues in Advertising: The Economics of Persuasion* (Washington, DC: American Enterprise Institute for Public Policy Research, 1978), 71–89.

29. Nelson, "Imformation and Consumer Behavior"; idem, "Advertising as In-

formation," *Journal of Political Economy* 82 (1974): 729–54; idem, "The Economic Value of Advertising," in Brozen, ed., *Advertising and Society*, 43–66; idem, "The Economic Consequences of Advertising," *The Journal of Business of the University of Chicago* 48 (1975): 213–41.

The Chicago school, in other words, accepts the dichotomy between persuasive and informative advertising, and many of these economists will go to great lengths to avoid coming to terms with the concept of "persuasion." See Nelson on the dubious distinction between "search" and "experience" goods. Also, see chapter 3 of this book for the discussion of rational persuasion as being dependent on a theory of free will.

30. See Robert B. Ekelund, Jr., and David S. Saurman, *Advertising and the Market Process: A Modern Economic View* (San Francisco: Pacific Research Institute for Public Policy, 1988), for a not-too-successful attempt to merge ideas from the Chicago school with those of the Austrians.

31. Friedrich A. Hayek, *Individualism and Economic Order* (South Bend, IN: Gateway Editions, 1948), 94.

32. Mises, *Human Action*, 250.

33. Ibid., 329.

34. Ibid., 355.

35. Hayek, *Individualism*, 55.

36. Israel M. Kirzner, *Competition and Entrepreneurship* (Chicago: University of Chicago Press, 1973), 29.

37. Ludwig von Mises, *Notes and Recollections*, trans. Hans F. Sennholz (South Holland, IL: Libertarian Press, 1978), 36.

38. Mises, *Human Action*, 56; cf. 350–57.

39. Ibid., 55–56, 350–52; idem, *The Ultimate Foundation of Economic Science* (1962; reprint, Kansas City: Sheed Andrews and McMeel, 1978), 101–2.

40. F. A. Hayek, *The Counter-Revolution of Science: Studies on the Abuse of Reason* (Glencoe, IL: Free Press, 1952; reprint, Indianapolis: Liberty Fund, 1979).

41. Mises, *Human Action*, 232.

42. Ibid., 257–58.

43. Cf. Joseph A. Schumpeter, *History of Economic Analysis* (New York: Oxford University Press, 1954), 888–89.

44. Ludwig von Mises, *The Theory of Money and Credit*, trans. H. E. Batson (London: Jonathan Cape, 1934; reprint, Indianapolis: Liberty Fund, 1980), 121–22.

45. Mises, *Human Action*, 217; cf. idem, *Socialism: An Economic and Sociological Analysis*, trans. J. Kahane (London: Jonathan Cape, 1936; reprint, Indianapolis: Liberty Fund, 1981), 99.

46. Mises, *Human Action*, 202.

47. These three points demonstrate the Aristotelianism of the Austrian economists; it stems directly from their strict adherence to methodological individualism, a doctrine that prevents them from either hypostatizing society, as do the German historicists, or from accepting unrealistic assumptions, as do the British and American Neoclassicists and the Chicago economists. Menger and Böhm-Bawerk are explicit about their Aristotelianism. See Carl Menger, *Investigations into the Method of the Social Sciences with Special References to Economics*, trans. Francis J. Nock (1963; reprint, New York: New York University Press, 1985); and Eugen von

Böhm-Bawerk, "The Historical vs. the Deductive Method in Political Economy," *Annals of the American Academy of Political and Social Science* 1 (1891): 244–71.

Mises, on the other hand, on the surface seems to be Kantian or neo-Kantian in epistemology. A thorough reading of his corpus, however, reveals a solid underlying Aristotelianism masked, as it were, by a thin overlay of Kantian terminology. For example, when Mises uses the term "a priori," he usually means "universal principle"—a term he uses constantly to combat the a-principled writings of his two nemeses: the German historicists and American positivists. Further, it is not uncommon for nonphilosophers uncritically to accept doctrines and terminology of philosophers, often giving the doctrines a more benevolent interpretation than they deserve. Mises certainly does not accept Kant's epistemological subjectivism, for man's mind, states Mises, does indeed "produce, out of the material provided by sensation, an undistorted representation of reality" (Mises, *Ultimate Foundation,* 18), and the laws of the universe—the laws of physics, biology, and economics—are most definitely "ontological facts" (Mises, *Human Action*, 761).

Recent scholarship has uncovered strong evidence of Aristotle's influence on all Austrians, from Menger to Mises. See Emil Kauder, "Intellectual and Political Roots of the Older Austrian School," *Zeitschrift für Nationalökonomie* 17 (Vienna, 1958): 411–25; and Barry Smith, "Austrian Economics and Austrian Philosophy," in Wolfgang Grassl and Barry Smith, eds., *Austrian Economics: Historical and Philosophical Background* (New York: New York University Press, 1986), 1–36.

48. Hayek, *Individualism,* 50–51. Cf. Ludwig von Mises, "Economic Calculation in the Socialist Commonwealth," in Friedrich A. Hayek, ed., *Collectivist Economic Planning: Critical Studies on the Possibilities of Socialism* (London: George Routledge and Sons, 1935; reprint, Clifton, NJ: Augustus M. Kelley, 1975), 102.

49. Mises, *Human Action,* 258.

50. Hayek, *Individualism,* 86–87. Cf. Eugen von Böhm-Bawerk, *Shorter Classics of Böhm-Bawerk,* trans. various (South Holland, IL: Libertarian Press, 1962), 357–58.

51. Mises, *Human Action,* 327–29.

52. Ibid., 273.

53. "The strange thing about the world in which we live is that it is a world in which $10 bills are floating around, free $10 bills! The problem is that very few of us notice these $10 bills. It is the role of the entrepreneur to notice the existence of $10 bills. An entrepreneur buys resources for $10 and he sells the product for $20. He is aware that resources available for $10 are currently being used in less than optimum fashion, that commodities for which consumers are willing to pay $20 are not being produced, and he puts these things together. He sees the $10 bill and makes the combination which other people do not see." Israel M. Kirzner, "Advertising," *The Freeman,* reprint ed. (September 1972): 5–6.

54. Kirzner, *Competition and Entrepreneurship,* 30–87.

55. Ibid., 12.

56. George Reisman, *The Government against the Economy* (Ottawa, IL: Caroline House, 1979), 1–36.

57. Kirzner, "Advertising," 6. Emphasis in original.

58. Mises, *Human Action,* 320.

59. For example, see Eugene F. Fama, "Efficient Capital Markets: A Review of the Theory and Empirical Work," *Journal of Finance* 25 (May 1970), 383–417.

60. Michael Porter, *Competitive Strategy: Techniques for Analyzing Industries and Competitors* (New York: Free Press, 1980).

61. Oscar Lange, *On the Economic Theory of Socialism,* ed. Benjamin E. Lippincott (Minneapolis: University of Minnesota Press, 1938).

Chapter 6

REFUTING THE DOCTRINE OF PURE AND PERFECT COMPETITION

Two methods exist to refute a theoretical doctrine.

One is the *reductio ad absurdum,* or demonstration that the theory, if carried to its fullest consequences, leads to false conclusions or contradictions and other absurdities. The second method is an attack on the doctrine's underlying premises, a demonstration that they do not correspond to the facts of reality, that is, that they are false; if the underlying premises of a doctrine are false, then the doctrine itself—and everything resting upon it—must collapse. The economic criticisms of advertising rest on the doctrine of pure and perfect competition; if it collapses, then so must the criticisms.

The first section of this chapter presents the *reductio* argument against the doctrine of pure and perfect competition. The next section presents the underlying premises of the doctrine—the epistemology of logical positivism—followed in the third section by a presentation of Ayn Rand's theory of concepts, which is the base from which the attack on the doctrine's underlying premises will be made. The chapter concludes with the refutation on epistemological grounds of the doctrine of pure and perfect competition. If Rand's theory successfully refutes this doctrine, we can once and for all put it to rest and release advertising from the shackles of unreality and fantasyland theory.

THE *REDUCTIO AD ABSURDUM*

Although many proponents of the doctrine of pure and perfect competition protest emphatically that it should not be taken as an exact description of reality, many of these same proponents nevertheless insist on using perfect competition as the normative standard to evaluate business practices, including marketing and advertising. George Reisman, taking the normative evaluators at their word, demonstrates in a brilliant *reductio ad absurdum* argument exactly what "pure and perfect competition" would be like if it were fully implemented.

Assumptions Are Collectivistic

Reisman, a student for many years of the Austrian economist Ludwig von Mises, rejects the concept of perfect competition outright, demonstrating that the theory's blatantly collectivistic assumptions lead ultimately to the conclusion that competition—in the sense of a rivalry among producers—must be abolished.[1]

The assumptions of the doctrine are collectivistic because "society," not the individual, is said to be the true owner of property and the only valid allocator of resources. Consult almost any economics textbook today for this hypostatization of "society" and for the elevation of "society" over the individual as the unit of analysis in economic theory.[2] The individual's right of use and disposal over his own property, say these textbooks, is limited by the needs and wants of "society." Further, contrary to what laymen and businessmen might think, prices are not payments of money that individual sellers receive from buyers in the free exchange of goods and services, but are rationing devices by which products and resources are allocated to "society's" most urgent needs and wants, by restricting demand to the limited supply that is available. And, similarly, costs are not outlays of money that individual buyers make to sellers for goods and services, but are *goods and services* that "society" must *forego* in order to obtain an *additional unit* of other goods or services.

This last means that marginal costs, rather than total or average costs, are the only relevant costs of production, because the fixed costs of existing plant and equipment are past history—"water over the dam," as textbooks put it—and of no relevance to "society" in the present. Prices, according to this theory, should be set equal to marginal costs. They can exceed marginal costs only when production is at full capacity, and then only when demand is so strong as to require a higher price than marginal costs in order to ration the limited supply of products available. When such a condition does not apply, and when the entrepreneur charges a price greater than his marginal costs—which is most of the time in the real world—the doctrine of pure and perfect competition charges the entrepreneur with monopolistic restriction of supply.

Competition Must Be Abolished

Practically speaking, this means that producers rarely can charge prices high enough to recover their ("sunk") fixed costs, which in turn means that the doctrine of pure and perfect competition charges businessmen with being monopolists for *not suffering losses*. "The ideal of contemporary economics," states Reisman,

> advanced half as an imaginary construct and half as a description of reality, with no way of distinguishing between the two—is the contradictory notion of a private-enterprise capitalist economy in which producers would act just as a socialist dictator would wish them to act, but without having to be forced to do so.[3]

> The essence of this theory of prices is the idea that every seller's goods and the use of his plant and equipment belong to "society" and should be free of charge to "society's" members unless and until a price is required to "ration" them among the excessive demands of the consumers contending for them. Prior to that point, they are held to be *free goods*, like air and sunlight; and any value they do have is held to be the result of "artificial, monopolistic restriction of supply"—of a deliberate, vicious withholding of goods from "society" by their private custodians.[4]

Competition among producers, therefore, must be abolished because the ideal of pure and perfect competition, the doctrine's state of optimal production

> is a state in which no producer is able to take any business away from another producer. If a man is producing at full capacity, he cannot meet the demand of a single additional buyer, let alone compete for that demand. And if he is not producing at full capacity and is charging a price equal to his "marginal cost," he still cannot compete for the demand of any additional buyers because he is forbidden to "differentiate" his product or to advertise it.
>
> The "pure and perfect competition" doctrine seeks to replace the competition among producers in the creation of wealth, with a *competition among consumers* in the form of a mad scramble for a fixed stock of existing wealth. It seeks a state of affairs in which no additional buyer can obtain a product without depriving some other buyer of the goods he wants—for that is what full capacity would mean. It seeks to make men competitors in consumption rather than in production.[5]

The full, practical application of this doctrine, says Reisman, would establish the kind of competition animals face in the wild: it is "a competition of animals fighting over a static quantity of prey," a competition based on the law of the jungle.[6]

To illustrate further the full, practical application of this doctrine—and its absurdity—Reisman presents a lengthy concrete example (which, unfortunately, cannot be repeated here in its entirety) of a fully implemented system of pure and perfect competition. Suffice it to say that his example consists of a "purely perfect society" of movie theaters and moviegoers in which all of the conditions of perfect competition are met, namely: prices are mathematically continuous and infinitely flexible (which means they change by tenths and hundredths of a cent each minute), all participants possess perfect and instantaneous knowledge (advertising, of course, is absent), there are many sellers and buyers (to prevent any one theater or moviegoer from influencing the market), products are homogeneous (the same movie is showing in all theaters), and the system exhibits instant mobility of resources and perfect freedom of entry and exit (that is, the theaters are actually tents, using candle power for the projectors, to ensure maximum mobility of resources). Because prices must be flexible over time, perfection "would be achieved," states Reisman, only

> if, after leaving the theater and going to a restaurant for dinner, one were not given a menu, but were seated in front of a ticker tape—and were offered a futures contract on dessert; and if afterward, on leaving the restaurant and walking back to one's apartment, one would not know whether one could afford to live there that night, or whether the rentals of penthouses had collapsed. Only then would the world be "purely perfect."[7]

"To the Left of Marxism"

Although the doctrine of pure and perfect competition, continues Reisman, was an attempt by Victorian economists to refute Marxism, and today is alleged to be a description of capitalism, in truth the doctrine is "to the left of Marxism," for "Marxism denounced capitalism merely for the existence of profits. The 'pure and perfect competition' doctrine denounces capitalism because businessmen refuse to suffer *losses* . . . which [they] would have to do if they treated their plant and equipment as costless natural resources [that is, as "sunk" costs] that acquired value only when they happened to be 'scarce.' "[8] The doctrine of pure and perfect competition denounces capitalism because it allegedly "*lacks* competition." Nothing, however, concludes Reisman, could be more absurd than a theory that flies so brazenly in the face of the facts of reality and then demands that man conform to it. "The doctrine of 'pure and perfect competition' marks the almost total severance of economic thought from reality. It is the dead end of the attempt to defend capitalism on a collectivist base."[9]

THE EPISTEMOLOGICAL ISSUE

Relying solely on a *reductio* argument as a theoretical refutation is tenuous at best, because proponents of the allegedly absurd theory can respond by simply saying, "So what?" This precisely is what Friedman does when he says "such criticism"—of the unrealistic assumptions of perfect competition—"is largely irrelevant."

The only way to refute the doctrine of pure and perfect competition—down to its root—is to challenge its underlying theory of knowledge, or epistemology. Economic thought is no stranger to epistemological debate, for its history is laced with extensive discussions of the methodological foundations of economics and the proper method of economic research. The *Methodenstreit*—or dispute over methods—between Carl Menger of the Austrian school and Gustav Schmoller of the German historical school is only the most celebrated example.[10] Because epistemology plays such a large role in the history of economic thought and in the alleged validation of perfect competition—and because the theory of perfect competition is the necessary foundation of the economic criticisms of advertising—the remainder of this chapter will focus on the *epistemological* refutation of the doctrine of pure and perfect competition.

Kant, Logical Positivism, and Friedman

The epistemological root of the doctrine of pure and perfect competition is the notion that theory somehow need not conform precisely to reality, and that assumptions, as Friedman says, can be "wildly inaccurate." I have already mentioned the influence of Plato's epistemology on the development of this doctrine, through the writings of Frank Knight and, of course, Friedman. Plato's epistemology, however, has filtered down to the present through the writings of more recent philosophers. The most influential philosophical Platonist over the past two hundred years has been Immanuel Kant. One school of thought directly influenced by Kant is the school of logical positivism. Knight, Friedman, and most of today's intellectuals of the so-called social sciences—which includes scholars in both economics and marketing—all espouse, knowingly or unknowingly, the epistemology of logical positivism.

According to Kant, reason is limited. Man's means of knowledge can never know "true" reality, because the mind is like a colored lense that distorts everything attempting to enter it. The mind, concludes Kant, does not conform to reality, as was assumed by philosophers for 2,000 years; rather, reality conforms to the mind. As a result of Kant's "Copernican revolution,"[11] science—as the study and discovery of the facts of reality, by defining universal laws of nature—was shaken from its foundations. Indeed, Kant's epistemology was the culmination of numerous post-Renaissance, philosophical assaults on the validity of scientific induction.[12]

Thus, for Kant our perception of reality is always distorted. In the late nineteenth and early twentieth centuries, philosophers and other intellectuals attempted to defend the reputation of "positive science" by reestablishing contact with reality through symbolic logic and, later, through probability theory. The Vienna Circle of the 1920s is the group of intellectuals most widely associated with this movement; "logical positivism" is the name they gave to their philosophy of science.[13]

Said the positivists: we may not be able to establish universal principles or laws, but we can establish "law-like generalizations" through the method of "successive approximations" or "gradually increasing confirmation." This method consists of extensive historical, statistical, or experimental study; such empirical generalizations as can be formulated can be shown to possess a high degree of probability. If a study predicts a hypothesized outcome, then it is said to support the hypothesis; if more studies demonstrate the same hypothesized outcome, more evidence is said to support the theory.[14]

Thus, a theory is not a set of concepts and principles that corresponds to the facts of reality; it is a hypothetical construct, or "highly informative guess," as Karl Popper puts it, that is generated for the purpose of conducting empirical tests.[15] Positivism separates the process of scientific discovery—the generation of theory—from the process of justification—the validation of theory. Because attention over the decades focused almost exclusively on testing hypotheses—that is, on validation, not on discovery—it was but a short step to conclude, as Popper did, that the generation of theory is secondary. And, as Friedman states, if assumptions are "wildly inaccurate," then so be it, because empirical tests may nevertheless confirm outcomes predicted by the theory, as allegedly has occurred with the doctrine of pure and perfect competition. Besides, according to Friedman and the positivists (and Kant), theory can never conform precisely to reality anyway.

The Mind/Body Dichotomy and Nominalism

To the layman, Friedman's comments surely must seem ludicrous, and the simplest rational answer to them is that criticism of the unrealistic assumptions of perfect competition is indeed valid; consequently, the doctrine can and should be dismissed out of hand. To intellectuals, however, steeped especially in the philosophical ideas of the past two hundred years, Friedman's comments do not seem ludicrous. The philosophical premise that Plato, Kant, the positivists, Popper, and Friedman all hold in common is the mind/body dichotomy—the unbridgeable gulf between the inner, mental world of consciousness and the outer, material world of bodily existence. It is the belief that the inner contents of man's mind can never correctly match the outer facts of the external world. What has caused this conflict to recur throughout the history of philosophy is the failure, on the part of philosophers, to define clearly the relationship between consciousness and existence and, specifically, to solve what in philosophy is called the "problem of universals."

The mind/body dichotomy arises from the refusal to acknowledge that some things in reality cannot be changed, in a metaphysical sense. The wish to walk on water or through brick walls, for example, is just one very gross form of the clash between mind and body that usually is suffered only by psychotics.

The wish for immortality, however, is embedded in the fabric of most philosophical and religious theory; this is a wish that clashes with reality and, consequently, has led men for millennia to conclude that the evil bodily, physical world somehow prevents or holds back the achievement of this wish. The wish for automatic, effortless knowledge, whether through faith, intuition, or mystical insight, is another example of this clash embedded in philosophical doctrine. The wish for automatic, effortless self-esteem and the wish for automatic, unearned income are further examples. The wish to formulate scientific knowledge about the operation of human economies without first knowing and understanding the nature of man and of his means of knowing reality, as exemplified by the advocates of the doctrine of pure and perfect competition, is still one more example.

The "problem of universals" asks the question: how do we get universal concepts in our minds from the concrete particulars that exist in the external world? We perceive individual men, but we hold in our minds the universal concept of "man." The question is, to what in individual men does the concept "man" refer? Or, where is the "manness" in men?

Traditional realism holds that universals are real and, therefore, exist intrinsically in the world external to our minds either as archetypes in another dimension of reality (Plato) or as metaphysical essences in the concretes (Aristotle). The standard objection to realism is the "I can't find it" argument, namely: reality presents us with no evidence either of another dimension or of a nugget of manness in men; consequently, the theory must be false. Nominalism, on the other hand, the dominant theory of universals today, holds that universals are entirely the subjective products of our minds and, therefore, are mere "names" we assign to groups of concretes based on their vague and shifting "family resemblances."[16]

In the modern period of the history of philosophy, post-Renaissance philosophers failed to solve the problem of universals; their failure led, in the eighteenth century, directly to Humean skepticism and Kantian subjectivism. In the contemporary period of the nineteenth and twentieth centuries—without attempting to solve the problem of universals, or considering its solution possible—logical positivists took up the banner of science. Thus, all twentieth-century philosophy of science is based on the nominalist theory of concepts. As a result, the twentieth century has seen the flowering of the philosophy of pragmatism and of various forms of subjectivism, relativism, skepticism, and nihilism.[17]

The problem of universals is the most fundamental issue in the philosophy of science, because all science—especially scientific induction—rests on the validity of a theory of concepts. Nominalism, however, is not a solution to the problem of universals; rather, it is concession of skepticism and subjectivism.

AYN RAND'S EPISTEMOLOGY

Ayn Rand's theory of concepts proposes to put an end to this trend away from science as a quest for universal, objective principles. Her epistemology rejects the mind/body dichotomy and presents a radically original theory of universals. Consequently, she provides the basis for refuting at its root the doctrine of pure and perfect competition, which in turn provides the basis for a rational theory of economics and a rational and benevolent evaluation of advertising.

Consciousness and Existence

Rand does not begin, in contrast to most past philosophers, midstream in epistemology without naming her starting point, or axiom. Her axiom is this statement: "Existence exists," which, she says, "is a way of translating into the form of a proposition, and thus into the form of an axiom, the primary fact which is existence."[18] The full statement reads: "Existence exists—and the act of grasping that statement implies two corollary axioms: that something exists which one perceives and that one exists possessing consciousness, consciousness being the faculty of perceiving that which exists."[19] As an axiom, this statement is a self-evident truth, a statement that cannot be denied without contradiction, that is, without assuming the truth of the statement in the process of attempting to deny it. From this starting point, Rand goes on to demonstrate the validity of her theory of concepts, thus solving the problem of universals and providing the basis for validating scientific induction.

Rand's axiom asserts a view of the world known as the "primacy of existence," which means that reality is real—the universe is what it is—independent of anyone's mind, wishes, fears, or thoughts; as she puts it, "Existence is Identity," or A is A.[20] Her axiom rejects the view known as the "primacy of consciousness," a form of subjectivism originated in the modern period by Descartes and called the "prior certainty of consciousness" by later philosophers; this view, present even in the writings of Plato and many pre-Socratics, holds that consciousness and its contents are known to us prior to the acquisition of any knowledge of the external world. For Rand, however, consciousness is our faculty of awareness of that which exists; or, as she puts it, "Consciousness is Identification" of reality.[21] "If nothing exists," she states, "there can be no consciousness: a consciousness with nothing to be conscious of is a contradiction in terms. A consciousness conscious of nothing but itself is a contradiction in terms: before it could identify itself as consciousness, it had to be conscious of something."[22] With this statement, she denies the validity of Descartes' cogito.[23]

The relationship between between mind and body, according to Rand, between consciousness and existence, is not one of reality creation by consciousness or of warring factions vying for supremacy in the guidance of one's life. Rather, existence—the universe or reality, which includes one's body—is what it is, regardless of what anyone may wish it to be. "Wishing won't make it so" and "Nature, to be commanded, must be obeyed" are two aphorisms—and fundamental, metaphysical facts—with which Rand agrees. Consciousness is our means of knowing what exists, what is real—and, contrary to what Plato said, our bodies are real. Thus, consciousness is not the creator or distorter of reality, as Kant concluded, but is our means of knowing what *in reality* can and cannot be created or changed.

Consciousness, according to Rand, far from being a colored lens that distorts reality, is man's *means* of knowing existence. Further, the possession of consciousness implies as a corollary that our senses are valid to perceive reality.[24] And reason, the attribute of consciousness that distinguishes man from all other animals, is the faculty that identifies and integrates the material provided by our senses; that is, reason, guided by logic and the (Aristotelian) laws of logic, is our only means of knowing the facts of reality. Finally, reason, our faculty of conceptualization that generates, directs, and controls our awareness of reality, is volitional; that is, we can make mistakes, forming concepts (or formulating propositions) that contradict the facts of reality. Thus, logic is the tool we use—by volitional choice—to ensure that the content of our minds matches or corresponds to the external facts, and the achievement of "volitional adherence to reality by the method of logic" is called objectivity.[25] The fundamental process by which man achieves objectivity is concept formation.

The Theory of Concepts

Conceptualization, according to Rand, is man's distinctive method of cognition, the method by which we organize perceptually given data and thus expand our knowledge beyond the level of perceptual concretes. Specifically, conceptualization gives man the ability to regard entities as units— that is, to regard an existent "as a separate member of a group of two or more similar members."[26] This, animals cannot do.

Concept Formation. To form a concept, according to Rand, we first isolate two or more perceptual concretes from a wider background or category; that is, we differentiate them from the background according to their similarities. Then, we integrate the concretes into a new mental unit by omitting their differences; this new mental unit is the concept, and the differences omitted are of measure or degree, not kind. Thus, abstraction, according to Rand, is essentially a process of measurement omission. Finally, the concept is symbolized by a word and identified by a definition; the concept is defined by naming the background category from which the concretes were differentiated (the genus) and by naming the fundamental characteristic(s) by which the concretes were differentiated from the background (the differentia). Thus, "a concept is a mental integration of two or more units possessing the same distinguishing characteristic(s), with their particular measurements omitted."[27]

For example, to form a basic, "first-level" concept, such as "table," we (in childhood) observe several objects in the household—one in the kitchen, one in the dining room, and one in the living room. We isolate or separate them from the other objects present in the household by noticing that they all have a certain similarity in terms of their shape. Shape is a measurable characteristic. Hence, we form the concept "table" in two steps: (1) by perceptually differentiating tables from other objects, and (2) by integrating the perceptions into a new mental unit called a "concept."

The differentiation is achieved by noticing that the measurements of the shapes of tables are *similar* when compared to the measurements of the shapes of chairs and beds. The integration is achieved by omitting the measurable differences among the individual tables—that is, the precise measurements of shape, as well as the height, area of table top, number of supports, material from which made, and so forth. The differences in this case, and in most cases, are measured only implicitly and only approximately, for example, shorter and taller, bigger and smaller. The word "table" is then assigned to the concept, and the definition—a piece of furniture consisting of a flat, level surface and supports on which other, smaller objects are placed—identifies the referents of the concept by naming the concept's genus and differentia. (The child, of course, would not formulate this precise definition until much later, if at all; it is not essential, according to Rand's theory, that we formulate explicit definitions of directly perceivable concretes. It is essential with more abstract concepts such as "man" and "freedom." The use of "table," therefore, is for illustration purposes only.)

The concept now formed is universal because it is "open-ended." It stands for and identifies all concretes (tables) of this type, past, present, and future, and it is valid because it is rooted in reality. The concept refers to *real similarities* as differentiated from a background of other concretes (chairs and beds), and it refers to a characteristic (flat, level surface with supports) that is possessed by all of the concept's units, which differ only in measure or degree. (The concept does not refer to the concretes from which it was differentiated—the chairs and beds—because these other concretes do not possess the characteristic within the measurement range in question.)

Thus, the problem of universals is solved by pointing out that the process of abstraction as measurement omission yields universals that are based on and derived from the facts of reality. The universal is neither in the concretes (the realist position) nor is it an arbitrary, subjective name that has no connection to the facts (the nominalist position). It is *objective*, because it is a product of our distinctive mode of cognition that is created through strict adherence to the *object* of cognition, the factual concretes. Objective concepts, in other words, refer to facts in the world—real similarities—as processed by our means of cognition.

The Role of Measurement. The essential original discovery in Rand's theory of concepts is that concept formation is a mathematical process. Measurement is the identification of a "quantitative relationship established by means of a standard that serves as a unit."[28] Once a standard is established, additional units may be counted; the standard that serves as the unit, however, must be appropriate to the attribute being measured; indeed, the standard itself must be a concrete instance of the attribute being measured. Entities, for example, are measured by their attributes, and we measure persons by such attributes as height and weight. Height is measured in inches (the inch being a concrete instance of length, or height), not pounds, and weight is measured in pounds (the pound being a concrete instance of weight), not inches.

The purpose of measurement (and conceptualization) is to expand the range of man's consciousness beyond the directly perceivable. We cannot, for example, directly perceive a distance of ten thousand miles, but we can *conceive* it. By establishing the inch or foot as a directly perceivable and specific length, we can measure distance. By relating the inch to the foot, the foot to the mile, and one mile to ten thousand, we can grasp the distance of ten thousand miles conceptually. Measurement makes an unlimited range of knowledge available to us by reference to a directly perceivable concrete. "The process of measurement is a process of integrating an unlimited scale of knowledge to man's limited perceptual experience—a process of making the universe knowable by bringing it within the range of man's consciousness, by establishing its relationship to man."[29] This, also, is precisely what conceptualization achieves.

For Rand, conceptualization and measurement are *two forms of the same process*. One, concept formation, uses measurement implicitly; the other, numerical measurement, uses it explicitly. Thus, the role of measurement in concept formation is that we implicitly identify a quantitative relationship among concretes. This is achieved by identifying a characteristic of the concretes that is commensurable, that is, a characteristic that can be measured by using the same standard unit. (The requirement of commensurability, please note, means that concepts cannot be formed arbitrarily; the facts of reality dictate whether or not two concretes possess commensurable characteristics. Note also that we do not have to know numerically how to measure a concrete to form a concept of it. Our concepts of the color spectrum were formed long before the method of measuring color was discovered.)

Thus, "shape" is a commensurable characteristic of the concept "table"; that is, all tables possess a similar shape (along with other commensurable characteristics), differing only in their specific measurements. Because shape is the characteristic by which we distinguish tables from other types of furniture, the shape that pertains to tables—flat, level surface with supports—is retained in the formation of the concept and the particular measurements of shape and all other measurements of tables (height, area of tabletop, number of legs, and so forth) are omitted.

Rand designates a commensurable characteristic a "conceptual common denominator," or CCD for short, and defines it as "the characteristic(s) reducible to a unit of measurement, by means of which man differentiates two or more existents from other existents possessing it."[30] The distinguishing characteristic (or DC) of a concept represents a range of measurements within the CCD. Thus, the CCD of "furniture" is shape, but the DC of "table" is the particular kind of shape—flat, level surface with supports—that falls within the range of shapes possible for all types of furniture.

In forming concepts, measurement omission does not mean that measurements do not exist. "It means that *measurements exist, but are not specified*. That measurements *must* exist is an essential part of the process. The principle is: the relevant measurements must exist in *some* quantity, but may exist in *any* quantity."[31] Thus, Rand refers to concept formation as the "algebra of cognition," because a concept is like the variable in an algebraic equation: it must be given some numerical value, but it may be given any. In this way, too, as with the algebraic variable, a concept does not specify the number of concretes subsumed under it; it represents all such concretes, past, present, and future.

Thus, as Rand's intellectual heir, Leonard Peikoff, puts it in his book on the philosophy of Objectivism:

> Mathematics is the substance of thought writ large, as the West has been told from Pythagoras to Bertrand Russell; it does provide a unique window into human nature. What the window reveals, however, is not the barren constructs of rationalistic tradition, but man's method of extrapolating from observed data to the total of the universe.
>
> What the window of mathematics reveals is not the mechanics of deduction, but of *induction*. Such is Ayn Rand's unprecedented and pregnant identification in the field of epistemology.[32]

ATTACKING PERFECT COMPETITION'S UNDERLYING PREMISES

Rand's epistemology denies the mind/body dichotomy by showing that consciousness, guided by reason and logic, is our means of knowing the facts of reality. Her theory of concepts solves the problem of universals by showing that, although universal concepts are products of our minds, they are created by strictly adhering to the objects of reality. Measurement omission provides the universal; reality provides the concept's content. Thus, the source of the doctrine of pure and perfect competition—its view that assumptions need have no connection to reality—disappears.

Further, several implications of Rand's theory of concepts also prove fatal for the epistemology of logical positivism and the theory of perfect competition. One implication is that science and numerical measurement are not identical. Another implication is that theoretical research in the human sciences must be approached differently than in the physical sciences. A third is that statistics must play a different role in such sciences as economics and marketing than it has throughout much of the twentieth century. And a final implication, sympathizing with the layman's skepticism about perfect competition, shows two schools of economic theory to be highly irrelevant to economics and marketing.[33]

Science Is Not (Numerical) Measurement

The development of any science necessarily requires the formation of concepts and, by extension, propositions (which are combinations of concepts), some of which are laws and principles. Consequently, the first implication of Rand's theory of concepts is that theory formation requires the conceptual process of implicit measurement, or rather, of measurement omission.

Now the use of explicit, numerical measurement was and is an invaluable tool in the development of the physical sciences—numerical measurement does give us more information about the facts of reality than we obtain through qualitative concept formation—but note that even those principles of physics and chemistry that are stated as algebraic equations also omit the measurements of the specific concretes that led to the discovery of the equations. Concepts of measurement, after all, are concepts, and their specific measurements are omitted in the process of forming the concept of measurement, or equation, in question. In a sense, we can say that science is primarily measurement *omission;* it involves *implicit* measurement, not explicit, numerical measurement. This point in itself should cast doubt on the assertion that the goal of theoretical research in the so-called social sciences, such as economics and marketing, is the quantification of propositions.

The tendency to equate science with measurement ("it's not science unless it can be quantified") is at least as old as Pythagoras. Rand's theory of concepts cuts this whole approach to science off at its roots, because measurement omission is what gives us the universality of our concepts and, by extension, of our laws and principles. The assertion by the positivists that all laws are probabilistic does not differ from the claim skeptics make that certainty is impossible; both statements are self-contradictions, because the former is a claim to universality and the latter to certainty. The conclusion one must draw from this "self-excepting" fallacy[34] (which is a species of Ayn Rand's "stolen concept" fallacy[35]) is that both universality and certainty are possible; the challenge is to formulate a theory that correctly corresponds to the facts of reality, not to abandon knowledge or water it down with "law-like generalizations."

What the explicit, numerical measurements provide us are the differences among individual concretes. Or, to put it in the terminology of the psychological sciences: science is *not* numerical measurement; rather, numerical measurement is *the essence of individual differences*. For example, the laws of motion are generalizations that apply to all types of bodies at rest or in motion, past, present, or future. However, the measurements of motion that the planets in our solar system make are unique to our solar system, as are the measurements of motion that certain atoms make in a given molecule unique to that molecule. Specific measurements are a unique point within the range of measurements that constitutes the concept in question.

Thus, the goal of the mathematical economists to make economics "more scientific" by quantifying perfect competition was fundamentally misguided.

No Quantitative Laws in Human Science

Applied to the human sciences—that is, the humanities or so-called social sciences, which include economics and marketing[36]—numerical measurement represents something more specific. It represents a unique, *historical* point in time that is unrepeatable. It is unrepeatable because the human faculty of volition gives rise to man-made facts that could have been otherwise. The faculty of volition itself—free will—is a metaphysical fact that stands at the very base of all human sciences.[37]

Rand denies the validity of the distinction—prominent throughout the history of philosophy and almost universally accepted today—between "necessary" and "contingent" facts; she points out that the proper distinction is between the metaphysical and the man-made. Man-made facts, according to Rand, are those "that depend upon the exercise of human volition." They are teleological (purposeful) causes and effects that "could have been otherwise"—in the sense that the United States did not *have to* consist of fifty states or that consumers did not *have to* buy brand "X." Metaphysical facts, however, are facts that are "inherent in the identities of that which exists."[38] They are deterministic causes and effects that "could *not* have been otherwise"—in the sense that water at sea level pressure *has to* boil at 212°F or that price controls imposed on an economy *have to* lead to shortages.

Indeed, when man identifies the laws of nature—the laws and principles that constitute a theory—what he discovers are metaphysical facts. When he identifies man-made facts, however, he discovers the causes and effects of historical events.[39]

Thus, the laws and principles constituting the human sciences must always take into account the most basic metaphysical fact of the field: human free will. As a result, the laws and principles of the human sciences will *not* be quantitative, algebraic equations, because man is not a mechanistic robot, as the positivists seem to think he is. Man's specific actions over time do not exhibit the constant relations that exist in the motions of inanimate matter.[40]

The motions of inanimate matter are *mechanistically* determined by the nature of matter; consequently, matter and its motions can be identified and precisely predicted by algebraic equations. The actions of man, however, are *teleologically* determined by his nature as a being of volitional consciousness; consequently, human choices and actions cannot be identified or precisely predicted by algebraic equations. There are constant relations in human actions—these are the metaphysical facts of human actions that the human sciences must discover; they just are not quantitative. Hence, the laws and principles of the human sciences are *qualitative* statements of relationships among variables.

To illustrate further, the psychologist Kurt Lewin claimed that human "behavior" can be explained by multiplying "person" variables by "environmental" variables: $B = P \times E$.[41] This formula, however, is not only false, because it omits volition entirely, but it simplifies nothing and adds nothing to our knowledge of human psychology. Studies that attempt to verify (or falsify) the theory only complicate matters and even obfuscate the problems of defining a science of psychology. And adding a variable to cover volition ($B = P \times E$, given the constraint of V) will not preserve the quantitative integrity of the equation. The power of choice in human beings is precisely what causes the replication of so-called empirical studies of human behavior to fail. The difference between the physical and human sciences is fundamental, and the idea that the human sciences should be modeled on the physical sciences patently contradicts the facts of reality.

This does not mean, however, that numerical measurements should not be made or used in the human sciences; it means only that algebraic equations are not part of the theoretical arsenal. Numerical measurements can be made and equations formulated for such concepts as "attitude" and "demand," but the measurements and formulas do not have the theoretical status of their counterparts in the physical sciences. In the human sciences, such measurements and formulas are always unique, historical data, and any attempt to make scientific predictions on the basis of them is doomed to failure because of the human faculty of volition. Further, numerical measurements of such concepts of consciousness as "attitude" and "intelligence" that are made today via self-report questionnaires are only *grossly approximate,* because no concrete instance of the attribute being measured (no concrete instance of "attitude" or "intelligence") has been identified to serve as the standard of measure.[42] The self-report method of measuring the intensity of concepts of consciousness is the equivalent of measuring temperature—before the invention of the thermometer—by asking survey respondents to check a box on a five-point scale to indicate how hot they think it is.

Such is the absurdity of the perfect competition economists—and marketing intellectuals—who attempt to define their field without reference to man's distinctive nature.[43]

The Role of Statistics in Economics and Marketing

Man-made facts are facts that could have been otherwise; they form the subject matter of the science of *human* history, a human science, which studies past events as caused by man's choices and actions. Metaphysical facts are facts that could not have been otherwise; they form the subject matter of the theoretical sciences, both physical and human, and of *natural* history.[44]

One metaphysical fact of the human sciences is that man possesses free will, but man's actions, nevertheless, tend to be similar to what they were in the past. "People are consistent" is a principle of psychology. Thus, *if* we know the choices other men have made in the past, we can make predictions, within a range, about what they will do in the future. Consequently, numerical measurement in the human sciences, as a tool of history, can be helpful in making predictions about the *specific* actions men will take in the future—but, again, please note, the predictions are *not theoretical* predictions; they are extrapolations from historical data. Theoretical prediction in the human sciences takes the form of a general, *qualitative* principle, such as: men will tend to act in the future similarly to the way they did in the past, or: quantity demanded varies inversely with price.[45]

Thus, numerical measurement is used in the human sciences, but only in situations in which we do not or cannot have complete knowledge of the causal factors involved, and the equations derived from the data are historical concretes, not theoretical universals. Consider, for example, the quantification of the law of demand. Historical data can be collected and an equation can be derived from the data, say, $Q = 2000 - 2.5P$, where "Q" stands for "quantity demanded" and "P" for "price." Any prediction, however, of the quantity demanded tomorrow based on this formula is *inherently* approximate, because volition is involved in what constitutes both demand and supply and in the formation of prices; in other words, prices, both relative and absolute, are a function of the choices—the value judgments—of consumers and producers, not of mathematical models. The data of the market, as the Austrian economists have propounded as an integral part of their theory for a hundred years, are constantly changing.[46]

Consider market research, the kind of data-collection activity and measurement making that marketing practitioners perform. Market research data is often quantitative, but it also is *historical* data. It is numerical measurement of the "state of the market," the identification of what the competition and customers are doing at one point in time (or several recent points). On the basis of this historical data, but guided by the principles or theory of the human sciences, including psychology, economics, and marketing, marketing managers then extrapolate—that is, forecast—what the future state of the market might be. On the basis of these forecasts, managers make decisions and take actions.

The one branch of mathematics that market researchers find most useful—the one that collects and interprets numerical facts about groups and, on the basis of a sample taken from one segment, measures how accurate our projections are about all members of the group—is statistics.

Statistics is a branch of mathematics and, as such, is a method of measurement. Statistical inference, which is *not* the same as induction,[47] is used only in contexts in which we do not know—or there do not exist—universal laws that could explain the causal relations of the variables. Thus, the meteorologist makes an expected frequency forecast based on historical data (the data of *natural* history) because he does not have sufficient information concerning the relevant variables with which to formulate universal laws. Similarly, the medical researcher makes an expected frequency prediction about the survival rate of a particular operation because he also does not have sufficient information concerning the relevant variables with which to formulate universal laws. Both the meteorologist and the medical researcher, however, could, in principle, someday know the universal laws that describe the cause and effect relationships of phenomena within their respective domains.[48]

The human scientist, on the other hand, including the quantitative, perfect competition economist and market researcher, will never discover universal laws that explain deterministically every concrete act of human beings. The market researcher uses historical data, taken from a study of consumer behavior at a given point in time or over a period of time, in order to make expected frequency forecasts about consumer purchase behavior in the relatively near future. This historical data and the accompanying forecasts are extremely helpful to the marketing manager, who must make decisions on the basis of what he expects consumers will do in this relatively near future.[49] The historical data has little value to anyone else. Some of it may be interesting from a historical perspective, and therefore it may be appropriate to present the data at an economic or marketing history conference or in an economic or marketing history journal, but most of this historical data does not belong in academic journals, pretending as much of it does today to be theoretical research. This last, it is not.[50]

Perfect Competition Is Totally Irrelevant

It should be apparent from the above discussion that Rand's epistemology precludes—rules out in advance—the typical logical positivist, logical empiricist, or Popperian approach to theory formation: namely, formulating quantitative hypotheses that may or may not be based on facts and testing them through the collection of statistical data.

Objectivity, the root concept of Rand's philosophy, means the strict adherence to facts by means of logic.[51] If a theory claims objectivity, according to Rand, it must be founded on facts. This is the essential answer to Friedman's statement that criticism of the unrealistic assumptions of perfect competition is "largely irrelevant." The fundamental distinction between the physical and human sciences puts the lie to claims that such human sciences as economics and marketing should emulate the methods of the physical sciences. There is, of course, nothing wrong with many of the methods used today in the physical sciences; they simply are inappropriate for the sciences of man. Thus, the whole apparatus of the doctrine of pure and perfect competition—from its false assumption of homogeneous products to its goal of seeking quantitative exactness through algebraic equations—is irrelevant to economic and marketing science.

Indeed, the criticism of the doctrine of pure and perfect competition—namely, that it does not adhere to the facts of reality—renders highly irrelevant the thought of two schools of economic thought: the Neoclassical and Chicago schools.

NOTES

1. George Reisman, "Platonic Competition," *The Objectivist* (August 1968): 8–16, and (September 1968): 7–11. A fuller treatment of this "Platonic competition" can be fund in Reisman's forthcoming book, *Capitalism: A Treatise on Economics*.

2. The past ten to fifteen years have seen free-market economic theory, primarily from the Chicago school of economists, regain respectability. The inclusion of free-market ideas in today's textbooks seems to be accompanied by a subtle trend toward the de-hypostatization of "society." For example, compare any textbook from the 1950s or 1960s with one from the 1980s or today. Such a trend is evident across the many editions of Paul Samuelson's *Economics*.

3. Reisman, "Platonic Competition" (August 1968), 9–10.

4. Ibid., 11. Emphasis in original.

5. Ibid. (September 1968), 10.

6. Ibid.

7. Ibid. (August 1968), 16.

8. Ibid. (September 1968), 7. Emphasis in original. Cf.: "Actually, requiring

P = MC or *marginal-cost pricing* is the ideal target for economic efficiency. But
...setting P = MC while AC is still falling *will involve the firm in a chronic loss."*
Paul A. Samuelson and William D. Nordhaus, *Economics*, 12th ed. (New York:
McGraw-Hill, 1985), 526. Emphasis in original.

9. Reisman, "Platonic Competition" (September 1968), 7. For another critique
of perfect competition—from the Austrian perspective—see the microeconomics
textbook by Milton M. Shapiro, *Foundations of the Market-Price System* (1974;
reprint, Lanham, MD: University Press of America, 1985), 319–72.

10. Samuel Bostaph, "The Methodological Debate between Carl Menger and
the German Historicists," *Atlantic Economic Journal* 6 (September 1978): 3–16.

11. "Kant's new hypothesis was a reversal of the old, rejected hypothesis (corresponding to the Copernican shift from a geocentric to a heliocentric system). It
was originally assumed that the mind must agree with its objects; however, this
assumption proved not only hopelessly inadequate to account for universal truths
but a caricature of the nature of scientific thought. Thus, Kant adopted the hypothesis that the mind's objects must agree with the mind." W. T. Jones, *A History
of Western Philosophy*, 2d ed., rev. (New York: Harcourt Brace Jovanovich, 1975),
4:19. The "old, rejected hypothesis," essentially, was the theory of intrinsicism;
Kant's new hypothesis was a proposal for abject subjectivism.

12. Both the Continental rationalists and the British empiricists—from Descartes
to Hume—were unable to validate the newly discovered and practiced scientific
method. David Hume, denying the existence of a "necessary connection" in observed causal relations, concluded "that the pretensions of the natural sciences to
demonstrative certainty are utterly without basis. . . . Inductive inference is not a
way of reaching rationally justified conclusions; it is a leap in the dark." Ibid.,
3:320–21.

Kant accepted Hume's conclusion but not his old-fashioned skepticism. Inductive
inference, agrees Kant, is not a valid means of knowing the facts of reality, but it
is a valid means of knowing the "phenomena" of consciousness, because necessary
connections do exist—*in our minds*, in *everyone's* minds. Necessary connections—
actually, causality—compose one of the categories contributed by our minds to the
acquisition of knowledge. According to Kant, however, this "knowledge" of causal
relations that we have in our minds cannot be claimed to correspond to the facts
of reality. Such correspondence, says Kant, we can never know. Thus, Kant is
fundamentally still a skeptic and fundamentally also a subjectivist. It is the alleged
universality of Kant's categories—the universality of his subjectivism—that makes
him a more "modern" skeptic than Hume, a "complacent skeptic," as Leonard
Peikoff describes him.

13. In the marketing literature, see Shelby Hunt, *Modern Marketing Theory:
Critical Issues in the Philosophy of Marketing Science* (Cincinnati: South-Western
Publishing, 1991), 208–304, for an excellent summary of the historical roots and
development of logical positivism (and its later form, logical empiricism). Also,
see Jones, *Western Philosophy*, 5:219–49.

14. Through this method, states Rudolph Carnap, we cannot establish or verify
a universal law, "but we can test it by testing its single instances, i.e. the particular
sentences which we derive from the law and from other sentences established
previously. If in the continued series of such testing experiments no negative instance is found but the number of positive instances increases then our confidence

in the law will grow step by step. Thus, instead of verification, we may speak here of gradually increasing *confirmation* of the law." Rudolph Carnap, *Testability and Meaning* (New Haven, CT: Graduate Philosophy Club, Yale University, 1950), 425. Emphasis in original.

15. According to Popper, a theory is generated for the specific purpose of attempting to *falsify* it. Whatever propositions remain unfalsified, as the result of empirical tests, are supported; those falsified are discarded. Theories, states Popper, are "highly informative guesses about the world which although not verifiable (i.e., capable of being shown to be true) can be submitted to severe critical tests." Karl Popper, *Conjectures and Refutations: The Growth of Scientific Knowledge* (London: Routledge and Kegan Paul, 1963), 115. Elsewhere, Popper states: "Our science is not knowledge (*episteme*): it can never claim to have attained truth, or even a substitute for it, such as probability. . . . *We do not know: we can only guess.*" Sir Karl Popper, *The Logic of Scientific Discovery,* rev. ed. (New York: Harper and Row, 1968), 278. Emphasis in original.

16. Realism is the fundamental form of intrinsicism, as identified by Ayn Rand. Nominalism is the fundamental form of subjectivism.

17. In the marketing literature, see Hunt, *Modern Marketing Theory,* 305–93, for a summary of these philosophies. Also, see Jones, *Western Philosophy,* 5:250–399.

18. Ayn Rand, *Introduction to Objectivist Epistemology,* expanded 2nd ed., ed. Harry Binswanger and Leonard Peikoff (New York: New American Library, 1990), 3. For a more detailed, systematic presentation of Rand's epistemology, see the first five chapters of Leonard Peikoff, *Objectivism: The Philosophy of Ayn Rand* (New York: Penguin Books, 1991).

19. Ayn Rand, *For the New Intellectual* (New York: New American Library, 1961), 124.

20. Ibid., 125. Rand credits Aristotle with originating the "primacy of existence" view of the world.

21. Ibid.

22. Ibid., 124.

23. *Cogito ergo sum,* or "I think, therefore I am." Descartes' method was to doubt—completely arbitrarily—every known belief until he could find a metaphysical absolute that, according to him, could not be doubted. This "Cartesian doubt" led to his conclusion that only the self, or consciousness, can be known to exist with certainty prior to the knowledge of anything else, especially the external world. See Jones, *Western Philosophy,* 3:162–65. "I am, therefore I'll think" is a statement Rand says is more in line with her epistemology.

24. Rand denies the dichotomy between primary and secondary sense qualities, which gives rise to the representationalist theory of perception and thus gives further aid to the "primacy of consciousness" doctrine; the proper distinction, says Rand, is between man's unique *form* of perception and the *object* of perception, because "everything we perceive is perceived *by some means,*" that is, we perceive both color and length through our eyes—color and length both being the *forms* in which we perceive the *objects* of reality. The forms of perception, in other words, vary from species to species, but the objects of perception remain the same—because A is A. Rand, *Objectivist Epistemology,* 281. Emphasis added.

25. Peikoff, *Objectivism,* 116–17.

26. Rand, *Objectivist Epistemology*, 6.

27. Ibid., 13.

28. Ibid., 7.

29. Ibid., 8.

30. Ibid., 15.

31. Ibid., 12. Emphasis in original.

32. Peikoff, *Objectivism*, 90–91. Emphasis in original.

33. The development of these implications is entirely mine. Rand did not apply her epistemology to any of the special sciences.

34. Maurice Mandelbaum, "Some Instances of the Self-Excepting Fallacy," *Psychologische Beiträge* 6 (1962), 383–86.

35. Harry Binswanger, ed., *The Ayn Rand Lexicon: Objectivism from A to Z* (New York: New American Library, 1986), 478–79.

36. Economics is a fundamental human science, derivative from psychology; marketing is an applied human science, derivative from psychology and economics. Psychology is more fundamental than economics because it primarily studies the motivation and behavior of individuals and, only secondarily, their relationships with one another. Economics, on the other hand, primarily studies man's motivation and behavior—to produce and consume—in a social context.

Psychology, unfortunately, is not a well-developed science and consequently has had little influence on economics, although the early Austrian economists were criticized for being "too psychological," which, according to their critics, meant "too subjective." While the Austrian economists do exhibit tendencies to subjectivism, they nevertheless, I submit, were headed in the right direction to integrate psychology with economics. See chapter 7 for my argument that market value be viewed ultimately as psychological, rather than subjective.

37. Ayn Rand, "The Metaphysical Versus the Man-Made," in *Philosophy: Who Needs It* (New York: Dobbs-Merrill, 1982), 28–41.

38. Leonard Peikoff, "Analytic-Synthetic Dichotomy," in Rand, *Objectivist Epistemology*, 110–11.

39. Cf. Hayden V. White, "Windelband, Wilhelm," in Paul Edwards, ed., *The Encyclopedia of Philosophy* (New York: Macmillan and the Free Press, 1967), 8:320–22, for a discussion of Windelband's distinction between nomothetic and idiographic sciences. See Ludwig von Mises, *Theory and History: An Interpretation of Social and Economic Evolution* (New Rochelle, NY: Arlington House, 1969), for a discussion of his distinction between theory and history. The root of these two distinctions in Rand's distinction between the metaphysical and the man-made.

40. Cf. Ludwig von Mises, *Human Action: A Treatise on Economics*, 3d rev. ed. (Chicago: Henry Regnery, 1966), 55–56.

41. Kurt Lewin, *Field Theory in Social Science: Selected Theoretical Papers* (New York: Harper and Brothers, 1951), 239.

42. On concepts of consciousness, see Rand, *Objectivist Epistemology*, 29–39.

43. Cf. Ayn Rand, "What Is Capitalism?," in *Capitalism: The Unknown Ideal* (New York: New American Library, 1966), 11–16.

44. I do not mean to imply here that there are only two fundamental categories of science. It has been said that there are three fundamental sciences: physics, biology, and psychology, or physical science, life science, and human science.

(Philosophy is not a separate science; it is the science of all sciences, the foundation of them all.) I agree with this three-way distinction.

Another way to describe the division is: (1) the sciences of inanimate matter; (2) the sciences of the life forms that possess a vegetative function of life or, in addition, the conscious function of sensation, or, still further, the conscious function of perception; and (3) the sciences of the life form that possesses, in addition to the vegetative functions and the conscious functions of sensation and perception, a volitional, conceptual consciousness. Note that the sciences are cumulative in the sense that principles of physics and chemistry and of the vegetative actions of life are used in the life science of human medicine in such specialties as biomedical engineering, molecular medicine, and cardiology. Cf. Harry Binswanger, *The Biological Basis of Teleological Concepts* (Los Angeles: Ayn Rand Institute Press, 1990), 4–16.

45. Explanation and prediction today are said to be the two goals of a valid theory. Explanation, however, implies prediction; therefore, this is really only one goal. The two alleged goals omit any reference to normative "how to," or value goals. This, of course, is consistent with logical positivism, which holds that science must be "value-free" and, therefore, strictly descriptive.

Rand, on the other hand, holds that a theory is "a set of abstract principles purporting to be either a correct description of reality or a set of guidelines for man's actions." Thus, the two purposes of theory, according to Rand, are explanation and guidance. Theories can be either descriptive or prescriptive—most probably are both, as are marketing and advertising, because the descriptive principles easily convert to guidelines for man's choices and actions. Ayn Rand, "Philosophical Detection," in *Philosophy: Who Needs It,* 14–27.

46. See Mises, *Human Action,* 350–57. Econometrics, to the extent that it is based on sound principles, is not economic theory; it is business forecasting. Most econometric forecasting, however, has a bad track record for predicting future business conditions, because it is based on unsound "macroeconomic" theory.

47. Scientific induction is the process by which universal facts, such as "*all* men possess the capacity to reason," are discovered. The process involves a generalization from several particular facts—for example, the observed men A, B, C, and D each possess a rational capacity—to a universal conclusion—all men by nature possess the same capacity. Statistical inference, in contrast, is the process by which a particular fact about some members of a group is inferred to apply to the group as a whole. For example, the particular finding that 45 percent of a sample group prefers a large box of cereal is inferred, within a margin of error, to apply to the market as a whole. Statistical inference is not generalization but the process of drawing a *particular* conclusion about a group based on a *particular* finding taken from a sample.

48. Statistical prediction presupposes a causal context. Thus, the meteorologist and medical researcher both operate within a vast context of previously established universal conclusions. Where their causal knowledge falls short, then and only then must they resort to probability theory. As new laws are discovered, however, the need for statistical prediction disappears—or should disappear! Logical positivism today, unfortunately, has turned virtually every scientist into a statistician.

49. Note that we all use this technique in our daily lives: husbands make expected

frequency predictions, based on historical data, of what their wives will do tomorrow, and vice versa.

I say "expected frequency" because I am identifying frequency of occurrence based on a past relative frequency as the essence of probability. For example, the historical, relative frequency with which consumers purchased a large box of cereal was 45 percent; therefore, the expected frequency forecast—that is, the extrapolation of historical data into the future—is that consumers, other things equal, will continue to purchase the large box 45 percent of the time.

50. Much of what passes today for theoretical research in the human sciences, especially in economics and marketing, to the extent that it is valid at all, merely verifies the obvious and belabors the trivial.

51. Rand, *Objectivist Epistemology*, 80–81, 211–15, 301–4.

Chapter 7

THE ALLEGED MONOPOLY POWER OF ADVERTISING

Advertising is a tool of monopoly power. This, in essence, is the economic criticism of advertising.

According to the argument, advertising allegedly erects barriers to market entry by differentiating one brand from another and thereby creating brand loyalty for the advertised brand. The brand loyalty, in turn, makes it difficult for competitors to enter the market and, at the same time, enables the advertiser to increase prices. Advertisers can increase prices because the consumers' sensitivity to changes in price—that is, the product's price elasticity of demand—has been reduced by the advertising-created loyalty. The increased price, in turn, leads to reduced output. Thus, advertising allegedly is a tool of monopoly power by erecting barriers to entry, increasing prices, and reducing the overall output of the economy.

In the voluminous literature that criticizes advertising, there is essentially only this one economic criticism, but there are two separate lines of argument within it: the charge that advertising erects barriers to market entry; and the charge that it increases prices. The first two sections of the chapter discuss in turn the "barriers-to-entry" and "increases prices" arguments. They are followed by a section on the underlying theme of these two lines of argument—namely, that advertising does not create value. The chapter concludes by discussing the correct meaning of monopoly power.

Given the previous discussion of the doctrine of pure and perfect competition, the arguments that advertising is a tool of monopoly power should readily fall by the wayside.

ADVERTISING ALLEGEDLY ERECTS BARRIERS TO MARKET ENTRY

The barriers-to-entry argument, it should be noted, is not different in principle from one more well-known argument that accuses the steel and automobile industries of lacking freedom of competition, because of the barriers the market leaders have allegedly established. The barrier that prevents other firms from competing with the established steel and automobile companies is the large amount of capital required to invest in plant and equipment just to open for business. Many companies do not have the capital and cannot obtain it from investors. Consequently, there exists a barrier to market entry.

Advertising allegedly creates the same kind of barrier. A competitor, the critics say, must spend large amounts of money on advertising equal to or, more likely, greater than the market leaders in order to enter the market. Potential competitors often cannot obtain the money; hence, a barrier to market entry exists—a "market failure," as it is called, has occurred—and freedom of competition supposedly is denied by the operations of a free-market economy.

Equivocation on "Barrier"

The argument, however, equivocates on the meaning of "barrier."[1] Specifically, it fails to distinguish between two kinds of obstacles, or barriers, to the achievement of human goals: those imposed by government-initiated coercion and those imposed voluntarily. A government-imposed barrier is a law that forbids or compels some form of association or activity, independently of the mutual consent of the individuals involved; the threat of physical force stands behind the law and thus compels the association or activity. A voluntarily imposed barrier, on the other hand, is the refusal of one individual to cooperate with another; the party who sought and is denied cooperation is free to go elsewhere in search of a partner in whatever activity he was seeking.

An example of a government-imposed barrier is the monopoly the United States Postal Service holds on the delivery of first-class mail. Many entrepreneurs over the years, including teenagers, have been ready, willing, and able—capital in hand—to enter the market; all, however, have been ruthlessly stopped or put out of business by the police power of the government. An example of a voluntarily imposed barrier, which in ordinary speech is usually not called a barrier, would be the refusal of a bank to grant me a loan because it did not judge me sufficiently qualified. I am free to seek a loan elsewhere—from other banks, from venture capital firms, or from friends and relatives.

The alleged barrier to entry that the economic critics are describing is of the latter type—a voluntarily imposed "barrier." A company that cannot obtain the capital required to enter a market and compete with such brands as Bayer aspirin is, in fact, a company that is *failing to compete*. And the investors, in effect, are saying to the Bayer challenger, "We are not convinced that you have a sufficiently good product on which to risk our money." Bayer, it turns out, is the master competitor; the challengers are merely less competent "me-tooers" who are trying to get a handout from the government in the form of an antitrust judgment. The challenger's freedom of competition has not been violated by Bayer; the challenger is still free to seek help elsewhere, if he can find it.

Collectivized Rights

The equivocation ultimately rests on the notion of collectivized rights and collectivized freedom—namely, that certain groups have the "right" to be provided the material means by which to satisfy their desires.[2] If the means—such as food, a job, or capital with which to advertise—are not provided, then the group's (collectivized) "freedom" has been violated. Freedom, however, is the absence of the initiation of physical force by others (especially the government). And rights, which define one's freedom of action in a social context, apply only to individuals; rights apply to groups, as in a corporation or partnership, only insofar as the rights derive from those of each individual member.

A right, most emphatically, is not the material means by which some men seek—at the expense of others—to have their desires satisfied. Such a "right" must be satisfied at the expense of others because that is the only way "collectivized rights" can be implemented. If food, a job, or capital with which to advertise is demanded as a "right," then someone else must provide these items. If they are not provided voluntarily, then they are provided at the point of a gun. The notion of collectivized rights reduces to the doctrine that some men have "rights," while others do not.

According to Ayn Rand, "a right does not include the material implementation of that right by other men; it includes only the freedom to *earn that implementation by one's own effort*."[3] As stated in the Declaration of Independence, each man has the right to *pursue* his own happiness; it does not state that the government or anyone else must make him happy. Thus, each individual in a free society has the right to pursue food, the right to pursue a job, or the right to pursue capital with which to advertise. As long as force is not used against the company seeking to challenge Bayer aspirin's market leadership—and it is not—then the challenger's freedom has not been violated.

Clearly, this charge against advertising—and Bayer aspirin—is the case of a less competent business seeking an unearned advantage at the expense of a more competent business; antitrust cases based on this criticism of advertising is an example of what Rand calls "the penalizing of ability for being ability."[4]

Advertising Is a Means of Entry

Contrary to what the critics assert, advertising is a means of market entry, not a barrier.

Advertising is salesmanship via the mass media. If an entrepreneur introduces a genuinely better product than the competition—that is, one that better meets the universal needs or optional wants of the consumer, and/ or one that is priced lower—he will secure a foothold in the market simply by advertising the product's superior features and benefits. A market challenger does not have to advertise on prime-time television, as both laymen and economists seem to think. Inexpensive local newspaper or radio advertising, or even direct mail, often provides the key to success for such upstart companies.[5] If a challenging company delivers what it promises in its advertising, almost immediately it will begin to reap one of its most cherished values: repeat customers. More importantly, it will begin to acquire something even more valuable: referral customers, favorable word-of-mouth communication being one of the most powerful factors in the successful marketing of any product.

Indeed, business success does not require advertising at all; the Hershey Corporation did not do any media advertising until 1970! This fact, however, should not be taken to mean that advertising is superfluous or that "the product will sell itself." Communication—which, in marketing, means salesmanship of some kind—is necessary.[6] Hershey has always had a large sales force pushing its products through the distribution system. In the store, the product's package is the "silent salesman."

The point here is, assuming a free market, an entrepreneur who practices sound marketing, offering a product that is truly better than the competition, will gain entry into the market and eventually grow large enough to challenge the market leaders. If necessary, he also will be able to raise the capital required to support his efforts. In contrast, if he is trying to market one more imitation, or worse, an exact copy, of the competition's product, then he deservingly will be doomed to mediocrity and, eventually, to bankruptcy.

The Product Creates Loyalty

Contrary also to what the critics assert, advertising creates *dis*loyalty in consumers, not brand loyalty. The product creates the loyalty.[7] Why?

Consumers are curious and like to try new products. One ad announcing a new product that has better features and benefits than the competition is sufficient to generate high trial—if for no other reason than the curiosity to see what the new product is like. If consumers like what they tried this one time, they will buy again. Advertising is what has taken business away from the established brands; the new product has created a new base of loyal users. "Nobody," states Ludwig von Mises, "believes that any kind of advertising would have succeeded in making the candlemakers hold the field against the electric bulb, the horsedrivers against the motorcars, the goose quill against the steel pen and later against the fountain pen. But whoever admits this implies that the quality of the commodity advertised is instrumental in bringing about the success of an advertising campaign."[8]

ADVERTISING ALLEGEDLY INCREASES PRICES

The second version of the economic criticism of advertising states that advertising increases prices, because persuasive advertising differentiates commodity products, such as aspirin, and reduces the consumer's sensitivity to changes in price, thereby allowing the advertised brand to command a price premium over what otherwise would occur under perfect competition. The price premium, consequently, leads to reduced output and social waste. The discrepancy in price between national brands and private brands, say the critics, illustrates this alleged truth.

First, this argument rests on a false dichotomy between production costs and selling costs. Second, the example of national versus private brands ignores the historical relationship between the two.

Production Costs vs. Selling Costs

The distinction between production costs and selling costs holds that selling costs are expenditures incurred by businesses to stimulate the product's demand and thereby create a market for it, whereas production costs are expenditures incurred to make or fabricate the product and transport it to the consumer. Selling costs allegedly affect only the product's demand. Production costs affect only its supply. Advertising, of course, is a selling cost.

According to the doctrine of pure and perfect competition, however, consumers have perfect information. Consequently, advertising or other forms of selling are not needed to stimulate demand. Without advertising and the other selling costs, the critics say, the price of the product would be lower. Thus, advertising must necessarily—and wastefully—raise the price of the product.

In chapter 3, I argued that all advertising is at once informative and persuasive. Similarly, I maintain here that all costs incurred by a business are at once production costs and selling costs, because there is no way to distinguish between the two.

To illustrate the point, Mises gives the following example: Two restaurants are identical in every respect, including the meals they offer. The only difference is that one has not swept the floor in six weeks; the other sweeps the floor every night. Asks Mises: how do you account for the second restaurant's cost of sweeping the floor every night? Production cost or selling cost? Sweeping the floor does not alter the food but it may encourage more customers to patronize the second restaurant rather than the first; thus, one might call sweeping the floor a selling cost. But do patrons of restaurants buy only the food? No, they buy atmosphere and ambience, not to mention clean surroundings and clean, healthy food. They buy a total package that is more than the obvious physical part of the core product (that is, they buy features *and benefits*). Whatever gets spent to change the total package of the product is as much production cost as the money paid for the salary of the cook or for the ingredients that go into the meals.[9]

The addition of a new factory, to give another example, is as much selling cost as it is production cost, for the new factory makes it possible to increase the firm's sales and profits. Advertising, alternatively, can be viewed as a production cost—the production of consumer awareness. And for some products, especially fragrances and beverages, advertising is extremely important in creating—that is, in producing—the benefits the consumer buys, such as a certain image or style of living. Mises states:

> The costs incurred by advertising are, from the point of view of the advertiser, a part of the total bill of production costs. A businessman expends money for advertising if and as far as he expects that the increase in sales resulting will increase the total net proceeds. In this regard there is no difference between the costs of advertising and all other costs of production. . . . All costs of production are expended with the intention of increasing demand.[10]

The accountant may distinguish production costs from selling costs in order to maintain an accurate historical record of the company's expenditures. However, any attempt in economics to distinguish production costs from selling costs confuses economic theory with accounting practice.

If advertising, then, is a factor of production indistinguishable in essential terms from any other factor of production, there is no reason why advertising—as opposed to, say, research and development, or the hiring of an additional janitor—should be singled out as a source of waste or as a cause of increased prices. The critics of advertising, no doubt, would get no pleasure out of condemning R&D expenditures—or the expenditure to hire an additional janitor—as a "waste of resources" or cause of increased prices.[11] No proper economic distinction between production costs and selling costs can be maintained; there is only one kind of cost that goes into the producer's asking price: the *full cost* of making and delivering the product.

National Brands vs. Private Brands

What about the beleaguered Bayer aspirin and its relationship to private store brands? It is true that national brands are priced higher than private brands—about 20 percent on average.[12] In historical perspective, however, national brands are introduced first. National brand marketers are the innovators. They develop a unique product that is highly valued by consumers. They create the market by advertising heavily and by setting up an extensive, national distribution system. Millions of dollars frequently are spent just in establishing the market.

Later—sometimes decades later—after the innovative product has been imitated or modified by other national branders, the market matures. In a mature market, several national brands compete with one another within the same product category, each trying to fulfill essentially the same universal, human need. The retailer, with respect to this one product category, however, finds himself in an unenviable position. He stocks, for example, not just Bayer aspirin, but also Excedrin and Anacin analgesic products. But so does his competitor across the street and his three other competitors who are located within a five-minute drive of his store. The retailer needs a way to differentiate his store from his competition. How does he do it?

The retailer goes to a local private brand producer (or maybe he produces it himself, or maybe he even goes to a national brand manufacturer) and signs a contract for the production of an analgesic product on which he can put his own name. That is, he buys a private brand that he can put on the shelf next to the national brands in order to give his store a competitive advantage. To ensure that he has an advantage over the national brands, the retailer prices the product well below the prices of the national brands. He can readily do this because the product is usually produced locally and he does not have to advertise it. Consumers already know what analgesic products are because the national brand marketers have told them through their advertising.[13]

Private brands thus, in effect, cash in on or "freeload" off the effort and expense of the national brands.[14] Private brands are almost entirely dependent on national brands. Were there no national brands, there more than likely would be no private brands. (In the few historical instances in which there existed only private brands, the market created national brands.[15]) To make a fair comparison of prices between national brands and private brands, researchers—in addition to making an adjustment for inflation over time, which almost never is done in such studies—should subtract a large portion of the national brand's past marketing expenditures and add it to the private brand; the amount subtracted should be sufficient to equalize the efforts of both brands independently of one another, that is, sufficient to enable the private-brand marketer to achieve a market as large as he now achieves but without relying on the previous efforts of the national branders. If such adjustments were made, differences in price would disappear.

Advertising Lowers Real Prices over Time

The dead end of this criticism is that advertising in truth lowers prices. The decline in the *nominal* price of many products during our recent inflationary times, in spite of the millions of dollars spent on advertising, should have silenced this criticism. The dramatic decline in *real* prices, however, over the past two hundred years, and corresponding rise in standard of living—in spite of the tremendous growth in advertising spending—makes this charge even more ludicrous.

Advertising creates a larger market than otherwise would occur because it reaches many more people at one time than is possible using only personal selling. This larger market leads to economies of scale across the board—in distribution, in transportation, and in manufacturing—and the lowered costs are passed along in the form of lower prices. In addition, heavy advertising stimulates price cutting at the retail level, where retailers competing for the same customers gradually reduce their margins in order to stimulate turnover.[16]

The only relevant issue in this criticism of advertising is the effect of advertising expenditures on *real prices over time*. The question is: Has the emergence of modern advertising in a free-market economy led to increased real prices? Clearly, real prices have declined. And, needless to say, the *real* prices of such heavily advertised products as Bayer aspirin also have declined.[17]

This charge against advertising, however, is just an application of the more general charge that laissez-faire capitalism lacks price competition. The source of the charge is the doctrine of pure and perfect competition. Quoting Reisman:

> Actual price competition is an omnipresent phenomenon in a capitalist economy. But it is completely unlike the kind of pricing envisioned by the doctrine of "pure and perfect competition." . . .
>
> Price competition is not the self-sacrificial chiseling of prices to "marginal cost" or their day by day, minute by minute adjustment to the requirements of "rationing scarce capacity." It is the setting of prices—perhaps only once a year—by the most efficient, lowest-cost producers, motivated by their own self-interest. The extent of the price competition varies in direct proportion to the size and the economic potency of these producers. It is firms like Ford, General Motors and A & P—not a microscopic-sized wheat farmer or sharecropper—that are responsible for price competition. The price competition of the giant Ford Motor Company reduced the price of automobiles from a level at which they could be only rich men's toys to a level at which a low-paid laborer could afford to own a car. The price competition of General

Motors was so intense that firms like Kaiser and Studebaker could not meet it. The price competition of A & P was so successful that the supporters of "pure and perfect competition" have never stopped complaining about all the two-by-four grocery stores that had to go out of business.[18]

Price leaders in a given market have the lowest costs relative to the competition. Thus, price leaders set their prices at a level that earns them a higher rate of return than their higher cost followers, who must match the leaders' prices or lose market share. Efficiency, earned in a free market through technological innovation, ultimately drives real prices down. Advertising, to be sure, is not the only, or even the major, cause of declining real prices. Nevertheless, it is one factor of production that contributes to the drive for efficiency.

There is historical irony in the charge that advertising increases prices. In the 1920s, the use of color printing—on labels, in magazine advertisements, in packaging—was said to cause increased prices. In the 1950s, the large-scale adoption of air conditioning by retail stores was cited as a cause of increased prices. The critics have long since abandoned color printing and air conditioning as causes of higher prices, apparently because they have acknowledged that real prices have not been affected by these two innovations. It will be a long time, I am afraid, however, before advertising is exonerated from unjust accusations.

ADVERTISING CREATES VALUE

The economic criticism holds that advertising adds no value to products but nevertheless differentiates them sufficiently to enable marketers to protect their markets against potential competitors.

The core of this issue is the assumption of product homogeneity—an assumption central to the doctrine of pure and perfect competition. According to contemporary economics, perfect competition is achieved only when products in a given market are identical, like grains of wheat in a silo. Product differentiation, however, disturbs the perfection of the competitive marketplace. Specifically, advertising makes competition less than perfect by adding a pseudo-value to the homogeneous products, solely for the purpose of differentiating them to induce brand loyalty and command a price premium.

Differentiation Is the Norm

As a characteristic of competition, the assumption of product homogeneity is a difficult one to take seriously, for product *heterogeneity* surely is, or should be, a self-evident fact of life. Indeed, the assumption of product homogeneity violates the law of identity, which states that A is

A, or a thing is itself; to exist, according to the law, is to be something specific, to possess an identity. To be something specific, however, means to be different from something else. Competition—as laymen and businessmen understand it—thrives on product differentiation and stagnates in markets of homogeneity. Product differentiation—heterogeneity—whether created physically in the factory or psychologically in media advertising, is an essential requirement of real-world competition.

Some categories of products—such as consumer convenience goods (supermarket products)—may appear to an outside observer to be homogeneous, but to consumers they do not; the soap and detergent markets, as well as the canned goods and frozen foods markets, are highly segmented, which means product differentiation is the norm. Product differentiation is the norm because marketers, when they develop new and different products, simply are trying to meet the consumers' diverse tastes and preferences.[19] When the doctrine of pure and perfect competition upholds product homogeneity as an essential characteristic of competition, it assumes away the diversity of consumer tastes and preferences.

And critics ignore consumer tastes when they expect businesses to compete on the basis of product homogeneity. The barriers-to-entry argument assumes that it is good if a competitor who markets *the identical* product as the competition can gain entry into the market. The very sensible reason why such challengers cannot acquire capital with which to enter such a market is that *they have nothing to offer*—that is, they have nothing *better* than what the competition now offers to convince investors they are worth the risk. "Better," here, means *differentiated* in a more valuable way toward meeting the needs and wants of the market. Similarly, the "increases prices" argument, which denigrates differentiation for leading to higher prices, would demand that technological innovation and progress grind to a halt, because innovation is precisely what *causes* differentiation (and, often, higher *nominal* prices, but lower *real* prices).

It is worth noting in this connection that Bayer aspirin's dominant market share in the analgesic market did not begin to erode until products made from *different* ingredients—first acetaminophen, then ibuprofen—began to appear. At that time, consumers decided they wanted to try something other than Bayer aspirin. Differentiation through innovation—not cheap imitation—is the lifeblood of competition.

Market Value Is Psychological Value

A product, further, is not just its physical and chemical properties, as the doctrine of pure and perfect competition would have us believe; it is a bundle of features *and benefits* created to meet the needs and wants of consumers. In origin the needs may be physical, such as the needs for food and shelter, but in man the rational animal our psychological needs—and desires—more frequently outweigh the physical ones. Consequently, the product benefits that consumers value most highly are the psychological ones. States Leonard Peikoff:

> All animal needs and pleasures are transfigured in the context of the rational animal. This is apparent even in regard to such simple needs as food and shelter. Human beings, precisely to the extent that they have attained human stature, gain comparatively little enjoyment from the mere sensation of satisfying these needs. Their pleasure comes ultimately from the accompanying emotions. It comes from the constellation of conceptually formulated values that define the needs' *human* satisfaction. Thus the joys of haute cuisine with special friends amid crystal and tapestries in a fine restaurant, or of beef stew and a glass of wine with a loving wife in one's own dining room, as against the act, equally nutritious and shielded from the elements though it may be, of chewing a piece of meat in a vacant cave somewhere. The principle is that a pleasure which was once purely biological becomes, in the life of a conceptual being, largely spiritual.[20]

Thus, the purchase and use of products is primarily a psychological experience.

Different consumers, however, experience different emotions in the use of the same product. For example, one consumer, a woodworking hobbyist, buys a cordless electric drill for the convenience of not having to worry about a cord when puttering around in his shop. The physical benefit of the drill, and initial reason for purchasing it, is convenience, but a closer inspection of the hobbyist's emotions might reveal as well an enhanced sense of pride resulting from the use of the drill to make a new bookcase. A second consumer, a do-it-yourself novice, feels insecure about handiwork. He examines the cordless drill in a store and, after deciding that this one appears least intimidating of all the others available, buys it to perform some job around the house. The benefit, or end result of product use, for this consumer might be a sense of accomplishment in successfully using an electric drill for the first time. Still a third consumer might be a carpenter who buys the cordless drill for convenience—but also for the recognition he enjoys from his fellow carpenters for valuing and using state-of-the-art tools. The differences in emotional experience among these three consumers result from the different "constellations of conceptually formulated values" that each holds—values about themselves, about the tasks for which they are buying the product, and about the product itself.

However, the emotions that consumers experience as a result of product use are not subjective. First of all, as products of consciousness, the emotions do exist. Therefore, they are as objective in a metaphysical sense as the physical features of the product that call forth the emotional experience. What connects a physical product to an emotional experience is the consumer's evaluation of the product. And the evaluations—as products of consciousness—also do exist. Therefore, they too are metaphysically objective.[21]

Epistemologically, product evaluation results from the volitional efforts of a rational consciousness to relate the product to himself in terms of its beneficial or harmful consequences—at one particular time and in the context of his own life. Such an evaluation—and therefore the product's market value—is neither intrinsic (in the product), nor subjective (created by the consumer's emotions cut off from reality). The evaluation—and therefore the product's market value—is *objective*. This evaluation (or rather, the sum of these value judgments) is precisely what Rand calls "socially objective value."[22]

Now, in addition, it is a metaphysical fact that products can evoke a range of emotions in consumers, but there exists an objective limit to the range, determined by the universal needs and rationally optional wants (or tastes) of the consumer for whom the product is intended; these needs and wants in turn determine the objective limit to the different evaluations that consumers can make of the product. The range of rational evaluations (and corresponding emotions) that consumers in the market actually hold (and feel) toward a particular product is the product's market value; in this sense, market value can be said to be *psychological* value.[23] And all products have it, regardless of how physical or tangible they may appear to be.

Thus, from the perspective of consumers, products have psychological value. From the perspective of marketers, who in the conduct of market research must identify and analyze their product's attributes, psychological value is more commonly known as a product's psychological benefits. The difference between physical features and physical benefits, on the one hand, and psychological benefits, on the other, is that psychological benefits— that is, psychological values—are more difficult to identify and measure. And there are more of them—that is, the range of psychological benefits is wider than that of either physical features or physical benefits.

It is this range of possible evaluations that a consumer can make of a product, along with the corresponding emotional reactions, that successful marketers must be aware of and manage. If the marketer chooses not to be aware of and manage the market value of his product, the market will form an opinion—called a brand image—anyway. This evaluation may or may not coincide with the marketer's own judgment.[24] A major means (in addition to personal selling) by which marketers manage consumer evaluations and emotions is through advertising. Over time, a company that successfully satisfies its customers—say, by delivering a quality product when and as it promises—acquires goodwill and a favorable reputation.[25]

Thus, two brands of aspirin that are physically identical to the last molecule may be perceived and experienced by consumers so differently that one brand—the one heavily advertised—commands a substantial price premium. The price premium results from the psychological value created by the advertising—namely, that the advertised brand is superior to, and to be strongly desired over, the one not advertised. This psychological value is created by the various kinds of information communicated in the advertising, such as the results—both physical and psychological—that can be expected from product use, the nature of the product's ingredients, and the advertiser's promise to stand behind the product, which thus evokes in the consumer a feeling of confidence and trustworthiness. The price premium, in other words, results from the image or goodwill created by the advertising.

The advertised brand, therefore, in comparison to the one not advertised, is in fact a different—not an identical—product. It differs precisely to the extent to which its advertising-created image or goodwill differentiates it from the non-advertised brand. Advertising can and does differentiate so-called commodity products, but this differentiation is not the result of pseudo, non-existent, or subjective value. It is the result of agency-, rather than factory-, created *psychological value.* In the end, such a product costs more to produce but offers greater value to the consumer, who, it must be noted, gladly—and voluntarily—pays the higher price.

Indeed, since advertising is "just salesmanship," goodwill created by the advertising of an allegedly homogeneous product differs not a whit from the goodwill created by the salesman of such a product (or any other representative of the marketer's firm, for that matter). All goodwill—regardless of how intangible or psychological it may be—is economically valuable.[26]

THE MEANING OF MONOPOLY POWER

Another issue underlying the economic criticism of advertising is that inelastic demand is a sign of monopoly power. Both the Neoclassical and Chicago schools of economists hold this view; the Austrian school rejects it.

Inelastic Demand Does Not Indicate Monopoly

The Neoclassical school of economists asserts that advertising causes inelastic demand, through brand differentiation and brand loyalty; inelastic demand is a sign of monopoly power because inelasticity is precisely what enables the marketer to increase total revenue by increasing product price.[27] The Chicago school asserts the opposite, stating that advertising reduces inelasticity of demand (that is, makes demand more elastic) by increasing consumer sensitivity to price changes. Both hold that inelasticity is a sign of monopoly power. According to the Austrian economists, both schools are wrong, because any measurement of elasticity is nothing more than a unique historical fact that applies to only one time and one place; such measurements have little or no bearing on the theory of monopoly.[28]

The reason for this is that elasticity, at its root, is the consumer's intensity of desire for a particular product. Consumer intensities of desire, however, change—monthly, daily, hourly; therefore, elasticities are constantly changing. The changing value judgments of market participants are what create the ever-changing relations of market exchange ratios, or prices. A highly intense desire for a certain product, such that an increase in the product's price fails to reduce its demand by very much, does not mean that the marketer of the product holds monopoly power. It means only that consumers intensely desire this product. And because substitutes exist for all products, and consumers at any time may choose to go without a particular product, such entrepreneurs cannot continue to raise their prices indefinitely in the absence of a government-granted privilege.

This last is true even for an entrepreneur who is sole owner of the resources necessary to manufacture an inelastically demanded product. (Entrepreneurs who hold patents and copyrights are merely exercising their property rights, not monopoly power.[29]) This also is true of entrepreneurs who hold their methods of manufacturing as "trade secrets," and, for that matter, of anyone who has the foresight, intelligence, and initiative to see (and seize) profit-making opportunities long before anyone else. Demand for the products of any of these entrepreneurs may be inelastic, but the marketers of the products earn entrepreneurial, not monopoly, profits; morally, they deserve all the entrepreneurial profits they can produce.

Nor Do High Profits or Industry Concentration Indicate Monopoly Power

Accompanying the issue of inelastic demand, especially in the minds of government regulators, are the issues of high profits and industry concentration as alleged indicators of monopoly power. Advertising, again, is seen to be a contributor to the establishment of these two types of monopoly power.

Competition in a free-market economy leads to lower prices and better products. It does not, however, necessarily lead to low profits, and advertising may or may not be a cause of high profits. What is certain about the consequences of an ever-changing, competitive market is that profits above the average rate—that is, entrepreneurial profits—are earned by those entrepreneurs who perceive profit-making opportunities ahead of anyone else and take advantage of them. High profits are a consequence and reward of successful entrepreneurship, which means that high profits are a consequence of competition, not of monopoly. They are the incentive by which human progress is achieved—through innovation, lower prices relative to wages, and better products. High profits are irrelevant to the issue of monopoly.

So too is the issue of industry concentration irrelevant to the issue of monopoly power. The number of firms in a given industry is a function of many factors, not least of which is the participants' innovative and entrepreneurial competence at continually anticipating the needs and wants of consumers and doing so ahead of others. If four firms happen to hold, say, 80 percent of a particular market (the so-called four-firm concentration ratio), or even if one firm, such as Alcoa Aluminum from 1910 to 1937, is the sole producer of a given product, these firms, according to Austrian economic theory, would not be guilty of oligopoly or monopoly. Such firms are constantly facing competition—from outside their industries and from within; to maintain their market leadership positions over many years is a feat deserving praise, not antitrust judgments.[30]

Economic Monopoly vs. Political Monopoly

If inelastic demand, high profits, and industry concentration do not indicate monopoly power, then just what is monopoly? In the history of economic thought, two different concepts have developed.[31] Seldom, unfortunately, have they been carefully defined or kept separate in discussions of monopoly.

The economic concept holds that a monopoly is a single seller in a given market. It holds that if there exists only one drugstore in town—the local town being the "relevant market"—then that one store is a monopoly. The concept holds that if Alcoa Aluminum is the sole producer of primary aluminum, then Alcoa is (or was, from 1910 to 1937) a monopoly. This concept is the one most widely accepted today—by laymen, by both the Neoclassical and Chicago schools of economists, and by virtually all government policymakers.

The Austrian economists, themselves not always clear on which concept they espouse, tend toward the acceptance of the political concept, which defines monopoly in its original, political sense as a government-granted privilege—"original," because this meaning of the concept predates the classical economists; "political," because monopoly is exclusively a government policy. In essence, monopoly is the initiation of physical force by the government—in the form of licenses, franchises, tariffs, price and wage controls, exchange rates, and so forth—to reserve and protect a specific market for the exclusive enjoyment of a specific individual or group. Political monopoly is a barrier to market entry erected by the government and enforced by the police power of the state.[32]

This last must be the only valid meaning of monopoly because, as Reisman points out,[33] the economic concept leads ultimately to a contradiction. On the one hand, according to the theory of monopolistic competition, everyone is a monopolist—that is, everyone, because of product differentiation, is a single seller in a given market in some sense.[34] On the other hand, no one is a monopolist, because every entrepreneur competes with every other entrepreneur for the same consumer dollar. Competition takes place economy-wide, not just on a brand or company level.[35] A single drugstore in a given town faces competition from all the drugstores in nearby towns; Alcoa Aluminum faced considerable competition from non-aluminum materials. Competition exists on many levels: brand vs. brand, product form vs. product form, company vs. company, industry vs. industry, and last, but not least, as I have mentioned before, product vs. the consumer's choice to go without.

It is notorious in antitrust cases that the lawyers for the Justice Department and Federal Trade Commission argue for the *narrowest* market they can find, which, if sufficiently narrow, could turn every businessman in the country into a monopolist. It is just as notorious that the lawyers for the defendants in such cases argue for the *broadest* market they can find, which, if successful, will acquit their clients of monopolization charges.

The mischief the economic concept of monopoly has caused is exactly analogous to that caused by the confusion, covered in my earlier discussion of production costs vs. selling costs, between economic theory and accounting practice. The marketing practitioner, to be sure, must define his markets. Markets, however, change over time, because consumers' needs and wants change, thereby creating newer, different markets. It is not uncommon for a marketer to think he is competing in one particular market, only to discover later—and sometimes too late—that he actually is competing in an entirely different market.[36]

Defining the "relevant market" is not an easy task, even for the entrepreneurs who are competing in it. It is impossible for an outside observer, such as an economic theorist or government policymaker, looking down on the economy, as it were, as if he were God, to define the "relevant markets" and thus decide who is and who is not a monopolist. This confuses economic theory with marketing practice. The only way to determine who is and who is not a monopolist is to look for entrepreneurs who enjoy a government-granted privilege or other protection. These "political entrepreneurs" clearly hold monopoly power; "market entrepreneurs," on the other hand, ones who build their business empires entirely free of government favors or protection, are the true free-market competitors.[37]

A concept as malleable as the economic concept of monopoly—such that everyone and no one at the same time can be said to be a monopolist—is one that should be discarded as invalid.[38] In the context of economics, the political concept of a government-granted privilege is the only valid concept of monopoly power. States Reisman, "Only the government can violate the freedom of competition, the freedom of entry, or any other freedom."[39] Only the government can erect barriers to market entry, cause prices to increase above what they would be in a free market, and, therefore, reduce the total quantity and quality of goods available in the economy. Only the government, through its coercive powers, can inflict the harm that critics unjustly attribute to advertising.

The government—not private businesses operating in a free market—is the culprit that creates monopolistic practices.

NOTES

1. George Reisman, *The Government against the Economy* (Ottawa, IL: Caroline House, 1979), 97–98. My analysis here is based on Reisman's.

2. Ayn Rand, "Man's Rights" and "Collectivized Rights," in *The Virtue of Selfishness: A New Concept of Egoism* (New York: New American Library, 1964), 92–106.

3. Rand, "Mans' Rights," 96–97. Emphasis added.

4. Ayn Rand, "America's Persecuted Minority: Big Business," in *Capitalism: The Unknown Ideal* (New York: New American Library, 1966), 57.

5. How many examples just from recent times must be given to critics to demonstrate the fast rise of small companies to become, if not market leaders in their own right, then at least major players in multibillion-dollar markets? Apple Computer, one such company that comes to mind, in 1975 consisted of two men working out of their garage; by 1984, they were large enough to run cocky advertisements baiting "big brother" IBM.

6. The principle guiding management decision making is: choose the method of promotion—advertising or personal selling—that is most efficient in dollars per contact for the information that must be communicated. For industrial products, which require the communication of much technical information, personal selling is the preferred method, but for consumer goods, which require the communication of less information, advertising is more efficient. Both industrial and consumer marketers, however, usually use both, but at different stages of the selling process. The difference between the two kinds of marketing is one of emphasis.

7. Yale Brozen, "Is Advertising a Barrier to Entry?," in *Advertising and Society* (New York: New York University Press, 1974), 79–109.

8. Ludwig von Mises, *Human Action: A Treatise on Economics,* 3d rev. ed. (Chicago: Henry Regnery, 1966), 321.

9. The example is given in Israel Kirzner, "Advertising," *The Freeman,* reprint ed. (September 1972), 3–4.

10. Mises, *Human Action,* 322. Cf. Carl Menger, *Principles of Economics,* trans. James Dingwall and Bert F. Hoselitz (1950; reprint, New York: New York University Press, 1981), 189–90, 242.

11. The issue of waste applies only to particular entrepreneurs who take specific actions. Entrepreneurs who spend millions of dollars on advertising and fail to increase their net proceeds have wasted only *their* resources—no one else's, least of all "society's."

12. See Neil H. Borden, *The Economic Effects of Advertising* (Chicago: Richard D. Irwin, 1942), 39–41, 599–602.

13. Ibid., 605–6.

14. I do not mean to imply that there is anything at all unethical about the actions of retailers or of private-brand marketers. I use the strong language solely to drive home the differences between national brands and private brands.

15. Borden, *Economic Effects of Advertising,* 41–46.

16. Ibid., 880–82; Robert L. Steiner, "Does Advertising Lower Consumer Prices?," *Journal of Marketing* (October 1973), 19–26.

17. I challenge the reader to conduct an "empirical" test of the economic effects of advertising on the pricing of Bayer aspirin. The July 1938 issue of *American Druggist* magazine reports that a bottle of Bayer aspirin at that time cost 59 cents (set and controlled under the price maintenance laws of the time). This was a bottle of 100 5-grain tablets, 325 mg. each. My challenge to you is to obtain a comparable price of Bayer, in whatever year you are reading this, and deflate it to 1938 dollars, using the Consumer Price Index or the hourly earnings of a manufacturing worker or any other method of adjusting for the increase in the quantity of money in the economic system since 1938. And to make the comparison unfair to Bayer, obtain your price from a supermarket—drugstore prices are usually lower. I guarantee that you will find the *real* price of Bayer aspirin to have declined—despite the billions of dollars spent on advertising. And not only that, I think you will find that Bayer is cheaper in real terms despite the fact that the product today is a *better* one than it was in 1938, because Bayer aspirin today, for the most part, is sold as a *micro-coated* tablet or caplet, which further makes the comparison to Bayer unfair.

18. George Reisman, "Platonic Competition," *The Objectivist* 7 (September 1968), 8–9.

19. "Differentiation by the seller is an adaptation to differences in taste and requirements among consumers. Demand is radically heterogeneous or diversified and quite independent of the actions of the seller." Wroe Alderson, *Marketing Behavior and Executive Action: A Functionalist Approach to Marketing Theory* (Richard D. Irwin, 1957; reprint, New York: Arno Press, 1978), 102. Unfortunately, Alderson goes on to accept approvingly the normative implications of Edward Chamberlin's theory of monopolistic competition.

20. Leonard Peikoff, *Objectivism: The Philosophy of Ayn Rand* (New York: Penguin Books, 1991), 344–45. Emphasis in original. The context of this statement is the philosophic meaning of sex, but the principle also obviously applies to economic consumption.

21. In the context of psychology, these emotions and evaluations can be called subjective, in the sense that they are "in the head," that is, in the subject. But confusion between these two contexts—the metaphysical and the psychological—has wrought havoc in the minds of both economists and laymen.

22. Ayn Rand, "What Is Capitalism?," in *Capitalism,* 24–25. Cf. my discussion of product quality in chapter 4. It is possible to imagine a "socially *subjective* value," although "pathological value," perhaps, would be more descriptive. For example, a consumer who uses an electric drill to torture animals for sadistic pleasure is one whose values and emotions are certainly cut off from reality.

23. Or "psychic profit," as Mises puts it. "Profit and loss," he continues, "in this original sense are psychic phenomena. . . . We cannot even think of a state of affairs in which people act without the intention of attaining psychic profit and in which their actions result neither in psychic profit nor in psychic loss." Mises, *Human Action,* 289–90. Austrian economists, including, unfortunately, Mises, call

this "subjective value." "Psychological value," I submit, provides the most accurate description of the facts.

24. Marketers create products that they judge to possess some degree of "philosophically objective value" (to use Ayn Rand's terms). A brand image represents the market's evaluation of the product, or its "socially objective value." The challenge of marketing is to persuade the market of the product's philosophical value— that is, to bring into agreement the product's social and philosophical values. Some marketers, however, because of their intrinsicism (and "engineer's fallacy"), hold inflated views of their product's philosophical value; this causes, among other problems, disappointment and resentment when the market does not agree with the marketer.

25. Is goodwill subjective? Is reputation subjective? Absolutely not! Later Austrian economists, however, who have accepted without question the more irrational elements of the earlier Austrians' confusion over the nature of value, have concluded that reputation is indeed subjective and, therefore, that the law of defamation is invalid.

26. Cf. Eugen von Böhm-Bawerk, *Shorter Classics of Böhm-Bawerk*, trans. various (South Holland, IL: Libertarian Press, 1962), 119–27, and Mises, *Human Action*, 379–83.

27. According to the law of demand, as price goes up, quantity demanded goes down, and as price goes down, quantity demanded goes up. *Inelastic* demand means that as price goes up, quantity demanded goes down *only a little*, thus resulting in an increase in total revenue; as price goes down, quantity demanded goes up *only a little*, resulting in a decrease in total revenue. *Elastic* demand exhibits the opposite effects: an increase in total revenue resulting from a price decrease and a quantity demanded that "stretches" a lot, and vice versa. Salt is a typical example of an inelastically demanded product; home mortgages are an example of an elastically demanded product.

28. Mises, *Human Action*, 55–56. Elasticity is usually measured by dividing the percentage change in the quantity of a product demanded by the percentage change in the product's price.

29. Ayn Rand, "Patents and Copyrights," in *Capitalism*, 130–34.

30. Dominick T. Armentano, *Antitrust and Monopoly: Anatomy of a Policy Failure* (New York: John Wiley and Sons, 1982).

31. My discussion of the two concepts of monopoly relies heavily on the lengthy and thorough discussion in George Reisman's forthcoming book, *Capitalism: A Treatise on Economics*.

32. Cf. Böhm-Bawerk, *Shorter Classics*, 155–56; Mises, *Human Action*, 361; Reisman, *Government against the Economy*, 74–76, 95–98; and Yale Brozen, *Is Government the Source of Monopoly? and Other Essays* (San Francisco: Cato Institute, 1980), 1–21.

33. Reisman, *Capitalism*.

34. This point is not controversial among contemporary economists. See Edward Hastings Chamberlin, *The Theory of Monopolistic Competition: A Re-Orientation of the Theory of Value*, 8th ed. (Cambridge, MA: Harvard University Press, 1962), 8–9.

35. Cf. Milton M. Shapiro, *Foundations of the Market-Price System* (1974; reprint, Lanham, MD: University Press of America, 1985), 327–29.

36. Supermarkets today are competing not just among themselves, as the economic concept of monopoly would have us think, but also against a rather formidable competitor, fast-food restaurants, which actually indicates the consumer's preference to eat out, rather than at home.

37. The terms "political entrepreneur" and "market entrepreneur" are from Burton W. Folsom, Jr., *Entrepreneurs vs. the State: A New Look at the Rise of Big Business in America, 1840–1920* (Reston, VA: Young America's Foundation, 1987). These terms—and Folsom's book—eloquently capture the essence of the difference between a political monopolist and the so-called economic monopolist. These terms also illustrate and concretize the distinction made eminently clear by Rand between political power and economic power. Rand, "America's Persecuted Minority," 46–48.

38. On invalid concepts, see Ayn Rand, *Introduction to Objectivist Epistemology,* expanded 2d ed., ed. Harry Binswanger and Leonard Peikoff (New York: New American Library, 1990), 65.

39. Reisman, *Government against the Economy,* 98.

Chapter 8

THE BENEVOLENCE OF ADVERTISING

Advertising is just salesmanship.

It is not a drooling ogre, waiting to feed on the helpless consumer. Nor is it a vaudevillian's hook that has the power to yank consumers out of their socks (and wallets) to force-feed them unwanted products. Nor is it a vaudeville show, as many people, including some advertisers, seem to want it to be.

Advertising is just salesmanship, the product and expression of laissez-faire capitalism. Unfortunately, this is precisely why the critics hate advertising; namely, that it is the means by which millions of self-interested individuals become aware of the self-interested, productive achievements of millions of other individuals. Advertising is the means by which millions of men learn how to enhance their tastes and increase their standard of living above the ordinary, humdrum existence of their forebears. It is the means by which the masses—including the "proletariate," the "bourgeoisie," *und* the "intelligentsia"—are given the opportunity to live far beyond the wildest fantasies of the rich nobility of earlier years. Advertising, indeed, is the intellectual conduit by which everyone can seek the good life.

Daniel Boorstin calls advertising the symbol of American "voluntariness." "It is an educational device to provide opportunities for freedom of choice." In societies in which there is no such opportunity, states Boorstin, there also is no need to advertise. Advertising's presence, he says, is a "clue to the increasing opportunities for choice."[1] These opportunities, which originate as political and economic freedom from government-initiated coercion, manifest themselves to consumers as the many new products the entrepreneurs offer for sale.

It was through newspaper advertisements in 1652 that English consumers were first introduced to coffee. In 1657 they were similarly introduced to chocolate and in 1658 to tea. Indeed, advertising, as Boorstin points out, played a critical role in the founding and settling of the United States:

> Advertising, of course, has been part of the mainstream of American civilization, although you might not know it if you read the most respectable history books on the subject. It has been one of the enticements to the settlement of this new world; it has been a producer of the peopling of the United States; and in its modern form, in its worldwide reach, it has been one of our most characteristic products.[2]

Boorstin sees advertising "perhaps even as a prototype of American epistemology . . . a touchstone of the sociology of knowledge, of the ways in which Americans have learned about all sorts of things."[3]

If advertising is as valuable as Boorstin maintains, and as I have argued throughout this book, then when will it begin to gain the respect it deserves? Not, I am afraid, until egoism and capitalism are no longer defiled as unquestioned evils, and thus are allowed to gain the respect that they deserve. Not until intellectuals of all types acknowledge that man, as an integrated being of mind and body, possesses not only the capacity to reason, but also a consciousness that is *volitional*. Not until an objective theory of concepts—the foundation of objectivity and scientific induction—becomes internalized on a wide scale. And not until the objectivity of values and the existence of rational options become accepted and understood.

To borrow a phrase from Ayn Rand, I ask you to "check your premises"—to introspect and examine the ideas on which your value appraisal of advertising rests. If you do this conscientiously, I think you will find that your negative evaluations stem from the anti-reason, anti-man, anti-life, *authoritarian* world view that permeates our culture. It is this world view that paints such a satanic, malevolent picture of advertising. It is this world view that also paints such a satanic, malevolent picture of capitalism.

If, on the other hand, you examine these ideas in light of Ayn Rand's pro-reason, pro-man, pro-this-earth philosophy of Objectivism, and in light of the pro-individualist laissez-faire economics of Ludwig von Mises—that is, in light of a truly *liberal* world view—I think you will begin to look at advertising differently and begin to react to it differently. You will begin to see that advertising and capitalism both are life-giving and benevolent institutions. You will begin to see that capitalism is the social system that provides man with continuous economic progress. And you will begin to see that advertising is the beacon that guides man to the fruits of this progress.

Nothing, as far as I am concerned, could be more benevolent than advertising, beacon of the free society.

NOTES

1. Daniel J. Boorstin, "The Good News of Advertising," *Advertising Age*, November 13, 1980, 20. The recent lifting of the American Bar Association's ban on advertising by attorneys has brought "opportunities for choice" in legal aid to many more people, especially the middle classes. Prior to this change in attitude toward advertising, legal help was available primarily to the wealthy, who could afford the monopoly prices lawyers were (and still are) able to charge because of their government-granted privileges, and to the poor, who received legal aid from lawyers who were paid for their time under other government-granted privileges. The middle classes simply went without legal services.

Studies of attitudes toward advertising by professionals provide revealing insight into the motivation of some of these professionals. One study of dentists showed that the majority of older, established dentists opposed advertising, while the majority of younger, unestablished dentists—the ones who most needed some means of finding new customers—not surprisingly favored advertising. So much for principled thought among licensed professionals—not that they are more pragmatic than any other segment of our society.

2. Daniel J. Boorstin, "Advertising and American Civilization," in Yale Brozen, ed., *Advertising and Society* (New York: New York University Press, 1974), 11.

3. Ibid., 13.

SELECT BIBLIOGRAPHY

Albion, Mark S. *Advertising's Hidden Effects*. Boston: Auburn House, 1983.

Albion, Mark S., and Paul W. Farris. *The Advertising Controversy*. Boston: Auburn House, 1981.

Alderson, Wroe. *Marketing Behavior and Executive Action: A Functionalist Approach to Marketing Theory*. New York: Arno Press, 1978.

Armentano, Dominick T. *Antitrust and Monopoly: Anatomy of a Policy Failure*. New York: John Wiley and Sons, 1982.

Backman, Jules. *Advertising and Competition*. New York: New York University Press, 1967.

Bartels, Robert. *The History of Marketing Thought*. 3d ed. Columbus, OH: Publishing Horizons, 1988.

Binswanger, Harry, ed. *The Ayn Rand Lexicon: Objectivism from A to Z*. New York: New American Library, 1986.

———. *The Biological Basis of Teleological Concepts*. Los Angeles: Ayn Rand Institute Press, 1990.

Böhm-Bawerk, Eugen von. "The Historical vs. the Deductive Method in Political Economy." *Annals of the American Academy of Political and Social Science* 1 (1891).

———. *Capital and Interest*. Three volumes in one. Trans. George D. Huncke and Hans F. Sennholz. South Holland, IL: Libertarian Press, 1959.

———. *Shorter Classics of Böhm-Bawerk*. Trans. various. South Holland, IL: Libertarian Press, 1962.

Borden, Neil H. *The Economic Effects of Advertising*. Chicago: Richard D. Irwin, 1942.

———. *Advertising In Our Economy*. Chicago: Richard D. Irwin, 1945.

Bostaph, Samuel. "The Methodological Debate Between Carl Menger and the German Historicists." *Atlantic Economic Journal* 6 (September 1978).

Brozen, Yale, ed. *Advertising and Society*. New York: New York University Press, 1974.

Caples, John. *Tested Advertising Methods*. 4th ed. Englewood Cliffs, NJ: Prentice-Hall, 1982.

Ekelund, Robert B., Jr., and David S. Saurman. *Advertising and the Market Process: A Modern Economic View*. San Francisco: Pacific Research Institute for Public Policy, 1988.

Fox, Stephen. *The Mirror Makers: A History of American Advertising and Its Creators*. New York: William Morrow, 1984.

Grassl, Wolfgang, and Barry Smith, eds. *Austrian Economics: Historical and Philosophical Background*. New York: New York University Press, 1986.

Hayek, F. A. *Individualism and Economic Order*. South Bend, IN: Gateway Editions, 1948.

———. ed., *Capitalism and the Historians*. Chicago: University of Chicago Press, 1954.

———. "The *Non Sequitur* of the 'Dependence Effect.'" *Southern Economic Journal* (April 1961).

———. *The Counter-Revolution of Science: Studies on the Abuse of Reason*. Indianapolis: Liberty Fund, 1979.

Hazlitt, Henry. *Economics in One Lesson*. New York: Harper and Brothers, 1946.

Hopkins, Claude. *Scientific Advertising*. Chicago: Crain Books, 1966.

Hovland, Roxanne, and Gary B. Wilcox. *Advertising in Society*. Lincolnwood, IL: NTC Business Books, 1989.

Hunt, Shelby. *Modern Marketing Theory: Critical Issues in the Philosophy of Marketing Science*. Cincinnati: South-Western Publishing, 1991.

Kauder, Emil. "Intellectual and Political Roots of the Older Austrian School." *Zeitschrift für Nationalökonomie* 17 (Vienna, 1958).

Kirkpatrick, Jerry. "Theory and History in Marketing." In Ronald F. Bush and Shelby D. Hunt, eds., *Marketing Theory: Philosophy of Science Perspectives*. Chicago: American Marketing Association, 1982. Reprint, *Managerial and Decision Economics* 4 (March 1983).

———. "Theory and History in Marketing: Reply." *Managerial and Decision Economics* 6 (September 1985).

———. "A Philosophic Defense of Advertising." *Journal of Advertising* 15 (June 1986).

Kirzner, Israel M. "Advertising." *The Freeman* (September 1972).

———. *Competition and Entrepreneurship*. Chicago: University of Chicago Press, 1973.

Menger, Carl. *Principles of Economics*. Trans. James Dingwall and Bert F. Hoselitz. New York: New York University Press, 1981.

———. *Investigations into the Method of the Social Sciences with Special References to Economics*. Trans. Francis J. Nock. New York: New York University Press, 1985.

Mises, Ludwig von. *Bureaucracy*. New Haven, CT: Yale University Press, 1944.

———. *Planned Chaos*. Irvington-On-Hudson, NY: Foundation for Economic Education, 1947.

———. *Human Action: A Treatise on Economics*. 3d rev. ed. Chicago: Henry Regnery, 1966.

———. *Theory and History: An Interpretation of Social and Economic Evolution*. New Rochelle, NY: Arlington House, 1969.

————. "Economic Calculation in the Socialist Commonwealth." In F. A. Hayek, ed., *Collectivist Economic Planning: Critical Studies on the Possibilities of Socialism*. Clifton, NJ: Augustus M. Kelley, 1975.

————. *Notes and Recollections*. Trans. Hans F. Sennholz. South Holland, IL: Libertarian Press, 1978.

————. *The Ultimate Foundation of Economic Science*. Kansas City: Sheed Andrews and McMeel, 1978.

————. *The Theory of Money and Credit*. Trans. H. E. Batson. Indianapolis: Liberty Fund, 1980.

————. *Socialism: An Economic and Sociological Analysis*. Trans. J. Kahane. Indianapolis: Liberty Fund, 1981.

————. *Liberalism in the Classical Tradition*. Trans. Ralph Raico. San Francisco: Cobden Press, 1985.

Ogilvy, David. *Confessions of An Advertising Man*. New York: Atheneum, 1980.

————. *Ogilvy on Advertising*. New York: Crown Publishers, 1983.

————. *The Unpublished David Ogilvy*. Ed. Joel Raphaelson. New York: Crown Publishers, 1986.

O'Toole, John. *The Trouble with Advertising: A View from the Inside*. New York: Times Books, 1985.

Packer, Edith. "The Psychological Requirements of a Free Society." *The Objectivist Forum* 5 (February 1984).

————. "Understanding the Subconscious." *The Objectivist Forum* 6 (February and April 1985).

————. "The Art of Introspection." *The Objectivist Forum* 6 (December 1985) and 7 (February 1986).

Peikoff, Leonard. *The Ominous Parallels: The End of Freedom in America*. New York: New American Library, 1982.

————. *Objectivism: The Philosophy of Ayn Rand*. New York: Penguin Books, 1991.

Pollay, Richard W., ed. and comp. *Information Sources in Advertising History*. Westport, CT: Greenwood Press, 1979.

Presbrey, Frank. *The History and Development of Advertising*. New York: Greenwood Press, 1968.

Rand, Ayn. *Atlas Shrugged*. New York: Random House, 1957.

————. *For the New Intellectual*. New York: New American Library, 1961.

————. *The Virtue of Selfishness: A New Concept of Egoism*. New York: New American Library, 1964.

————. *Capitalism: The Unknown Ideal*. New York: New American Library, 1966.

————. *The Romantic Manifesto: A Philosophy of Literature*. New York: New American Library, 1971.

————. *Philosophy: Who Needs It*. New York: Bobbs-Merrill, 1982.

————. *Introduction to Objectivist Epistemology*. Expanded 2nd ed., ed. Harry Binswanger and Leonard Peikoff. New York: New American Library, 1990.

Reeves, Rosser. *Reality in Advertising*. New York: Alfred A. Knopf, 1968.

Reisman, George. "The Revolt Against Affluence: Galbraith's Neo-Feudalism." *Human Events*. (February 3, 1961.)

————. "Platonic Competition." *The Objectivist* (August and September 1968).

———. "The Myth of Planned Obsolescence." *Il Politico*. University of Pavia, 38 (1973).

———. *The Government against the Economy*. Ottawa, IL: Caroline House, 1979.

———. "Classical Economics Versus the Exploitation Theory." In Kurt R. Leube and Albert H. Zlabinger, eds., *The Political Economy of Freedom: Essays in Honor of F. A. Hayek*. Munich: Philosophia Verlag, 1985.

———. "The Toxicity of Environmentalism." *The Freeman* 42 (September 1992).

———. *Capitalism: A Treatise on Economics*. Forthcoming.

Ridpath, John. "The Philosophical Origins of Antitrust." *The Objectivist Forum* 1 (June 1980).

Rotzoll, Kim B., James E. Haefner, and Charles H. Sandage. *Advertising in Contemporary Society: Perspectives Toward Understanding*. Cincinnati: South-Western Publishing, 1990.

Seiden, Hank S. *Advertising Pure and Simple*. Chicago: American Marketing Association, 1976.

Shapiro, Milton M. *Foundations of the Market-Price System*. Lanham, MD: University Press of America, 1985.

Thompson, Howard A., ed. *The Great Writings in Marketing*. Tulsa: Petroleum Publishing, 1976.

Tosdal, Harry R. *Selling In Our Economy*. Homewood, IL: Richard D. Irwin, 1957.

Tuerck, David G., ed. *Issues in Advertising: The Economics of Persuasion*. Washington, DC: American Enterprise Institute for Public Policy Research, 1978.

Wieser, Friedrich von. *Natural Value*. Trans. Christian A. Malloch. New York: Augustus M. Kelley, 1989.

INDEX

About the Author

JERRY KIRKPATRICK is Professor of Marketing at California State Polytechnic University, Pomona. His publications have appeared in the *Journal of Advertising*, *Marketing Theory: Philosophy of Science Perspectives*, *Managerial and Decision Economics*, *Developments in Marketing Science, Vol. IX*, and *The Mid-Atlantic Journal of Business*. In addition, he has contributed an essay to *Business Ethics and Common Sense*, Robert W. McGee, ed. (Quorum Books, 1992).